THE POPULAR
OXFORD
ATLAS
OF THE WORLD

PEERAGE BOOKS

Contents

First published in Great Britain in 1981 by
Octopus Books Limited under the title
The Oxford Atlas

This revised edition published in 1986 by
Peerage Books
59 Grosvenor Street
London W1

© 1981 Oxford University Press
© 1986 Revised material Oxford University Press

Reprinted 1986

ISBN 1 85052 062 3

Printed in Hong Kong

World Facts and Figures

GEOGRAPHICAL

The Earth

	km	miles
Diameter at Equator	12,757	(7,927)
Diameter at poles	12,714	(7,900)
Circumference at Equator	40,076	(24,902)
Circumference at poles	40,008	(24,860)

The Continents: Area

	km²	sq miles
Asia	44,518,000	17,188,000
Africa	30,319,000	11,706,000
North America	24,386,000	9,415,000
South America	17,834,000	6,886,000
Europe	9,933,000	3,835,000
Oceania	8,942,000	3,453,000

Oceans and Seas: Area

	km²	sq miles
Pacific	165,246,300	63,801,600
Atlantic	82,463,800	31,839,300
Indian	73,442,700	28,356,300
Arctic	14,090,100	5,440,200
Caribbean	2,754,100	1,063,350
Mediterranean	2,581,600	996,750

Largest Islands

	km²	sq mile
Greenland	2,175,600	840,00
New Guinea	821,000	317,00
Borneo (Malaysia/Indonesia)	743,300	287,00
Madagascar	590,500	228,00
Baffin (Canada)	476,600	184,00
Sumatra (Indonesia)	474,000	183,00
Honshū (Japan)	230,500	89,00
Great Britain	225,300	87,00
Ellesmere (Canada)	212,600	82,10
Victoria (Canada)	212,100	81,90
Sulawesi (Celebes; Indonesia)	189,100	73,00
South Island (New Zealand)	150,500	58,10
Java (Indonesia)	128,500	49,60
North Island (New Zealand)	114,700	44,30
Cuba	114,500	44,20
Newfoundland (Canada)	110,600	42,70
Luzon (Philippines)	110,100	42,50
Iceland	103,100	39,80
Mindanao (Philippines)	96,900	37,40
Ireland	84,400	32,60

Longest Rivers

	km	mile
Nile (Africa)	6,700	4,16
Amazon (S. America)	6,280	3,90
Mississippi/Missouri (U.S.A.)	6,050	3,76
Ob/Irtysh (U.S.S.R.)	5,570	3,46
Yangtze (China)	5,430	3,37
Hwang (China)	4,620	2,87

POPULATION (1980 ESTIMATES)

The World

	4,415,000,000

The Continents
To nearest million

Asia (less U.S.S.R.)	2,557,000,000
Africa	469,000,000
North America	368,000,000
South America	246,000,000
Europe	483,000,000
Oceania	22,000,000

Most Populous Countries
To nearest million

China	956,000,00
India	775,000,00
U.S.S.R.	266,000,00
U.S.A.	222,000,00
Indonesia	151,000,00
Brazil	126,000,00
Japan	116,000,00
Bangladesh	88,000,00
Pakistan	82,000,00
Nigeria	77,000,00
Mexico	70,000,00
West Germany	61,000,00
Italy	58,000,00
United Kingdom	55,000,00

	m	ft
aïre (Africa)	4,380	2,720
mur (U.S.S.R./China)	4,350	2,700
ena (U.S.S.R.)	4,280	2,660
ackenzie (Canada)	4,250	2,640
ekong (Asia)	4,185	2,600
iger (Africa)	4,185	2,600
araná (Argentina)	4,150	2,580
enisey (U.S.S.R.)	3,880	2,410
urray/Darling (Australia)	3,720	2,310
olga (U.S.S.R.)	3,685	2,290
adeira (Brazil)	3,380	2,100
ukon (N. America)	3,220	2,000
urús (Brazil)	3,140	1,950
t Lawrence (N. America)	3,060	1,900
io Grande (U.S.A./Mexico)	3,045	1,890
yr Dar'ya (U.S.S.R.)	2,915	1,810
rahmaputra/Tsangpo (India/Tibet)	2,900	1,800
dus (Pakistan/India)	2,900	1,800
ão Francisco (Brazil)	2,900	1,800
anube (Europe)	2,820	1,750
uphrates (W. Asia)	2,755	1,710
ocantins (Brazil)	2,690	1,670

Highest Mountains

sia

	m	ft
verest (Tibet/Nepal)	8,848	29,028
2 (Godwin Austen; Pakistan)	8,611	28,251
angchenjunga (India)	8,585	28,146
akalu (Tibet/Nepal)	8,470	27,788
haulāgiri (Nepal)	8,172	26,811

	m	ft
Nanga Parbat (Pakistan)	8,126	26,660
Annapurna (Nepal)	8,078	26,502
Nanda Devi (India)	7,817	25,646
Kamet (India)	7,756	25,446
Namcha Barwa (China)	7,756	25,446
Ulagh Muztagh (China)	7,723	25,338
North America		
McKinley (Alaska)	6,187	20,298
Logan (Yukon)	6,050	19,850
Orizaba (Mexico)	5,700	18,701
St Elias (Alaska/Yukon)	5,489	18,008
Popocatépetl (Mexico)	5,452	17,887
Ixtacihuatl (Mexico)	5,286	17,342
South America		
Aconcagua (Argentina)	7,035	23,080
Ancohuma (Bolivia)	7,014	23,012
Ojos del Salado (Argentina/Chile)	6,870	22,539
Pissis (Argentina)	6,780	22,244
Huascarán (Peru)	6,768	22,204
Tocorpuri (Bolivia/Chile)	6,754	22,160
Africa		
Uhuru (Kilimanjaro: Tanzania)	5,895	19,340
Kenya (Kenya)	5,199	17,058
Ruwenzori (Zaïre/Uganda)	5,118	16,791
Dashan (Ethiopia)	4,620	15,157
Meru (Tanzania)	4,565	14,977
Elgon (Uganda)	4,321	14,178
Europe		
El'brus (U.S.S.R.)	5,633	18,481
Dykh Tau (U.S.S.R.)	5,198	17,054
Kazbek (U.S.S.R.)	5,047	16,558
Mont Blanc (France)	4,810	15,781
Monte Rosa (Dufourspitze; Switzerland)	4,634	15,203
Matterhorn (Switzerland)	4,478	14,691

rance	53,000,000
ietnam	52,000,000
hilippines	51,000,000
hailand	47,000,000
urkey	45,000,000
gypt	42,000,000

Most Populous Cities
he largest urban agglomerations, to nearest 100,000

ew York/NE New Jersey (U.S.A.)	20,400,000
okyo/Yokohama (Japan)	20,000,000
exico City (Mexico)	15,000,000

São Paulo (Brazil)	13,500,000
Shanghai (China)	13,400,000
Los Angeles/Long Beach (U.S.A.)	11,700,000
Peking (China)	10,700,000
Rio de Janeiro (Brazil)	10,700,000
London (England)	10,200,000
Buenos Aires (Argentina)	10,100,000
Paris (France)	9,900,000
Osaka/Kobe (Japan)	9,500,000
Rhine/Ruhr (W. Germany)	9,300,000
Calcutta (India)	8,800,000
Seoul (South Korea)	8,500,000
Bombay (India)	8,300,000
Chicago/NW Indiana (U.S.A.)	8,300,000
Moscow (U.S.S.R.)	7,800,000
Cairo (Egypt)	7,500,000
Jakarta (Indonesia)	7,300,000

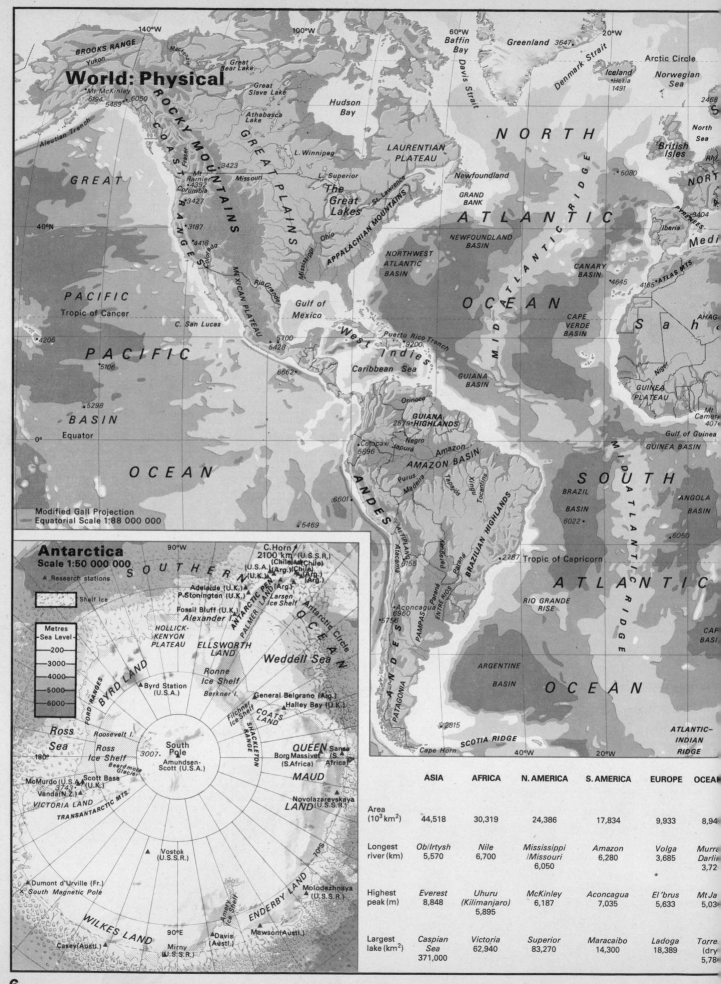

World: Physical

Modified Gall Projection
Equatorial Scale 1:88 000 000

Antarctica
Scale 1:50 000 000
▲ Research stations
Shelf Ice

	ASIA	AFRICA	N. AMERICA	S. AMERICA	EUROPE	OCEAN...
Area (10³ km²)	44,518	30,319	24,386	17,834	9,933	8,94...
Longest river (km)	Ob/Irtysh 5,570	Nile 6,700	Mississippi /Missouri 6,050	Amazon 6,280	Volga 3,685	Murra... Darlin... 3,72...
Highest peak (m)	Everest 8,848	Uhuru (Kilimanjaro) 5,895	McKinley 6,187	Aconcagua 7,035	El 'brus 5,633	Mt Ja... 5,03...
Largest lake (km²)	Caspian Sea 371,000	Victoria 62,940	Superior 83,270	Maracaibo 14,300	Ladoga 18,389	Torre... (dry 5,78...

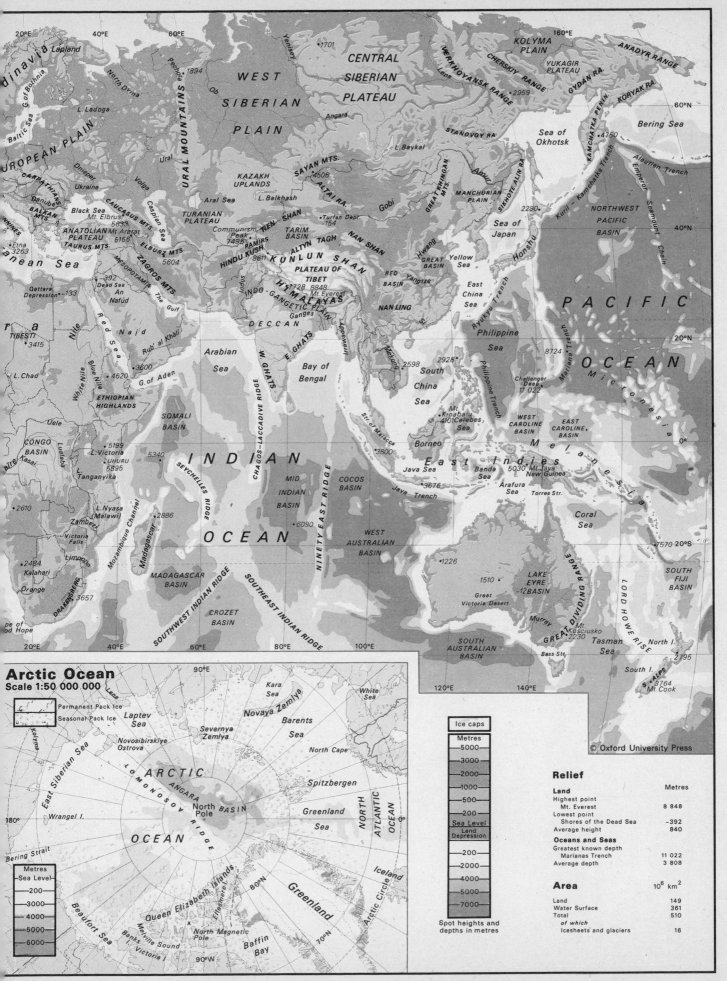

Arctic Ocean
Scale 1:50 000 000

Permanent Pack Ice
Seasonal Pack Ice

Ice caps

Metres
5000
3000
2000
1000
500
200
Sea Level
Land
Depression
200
2000
4000
5000
7000

Spot heights and
depths in metres

Metres
Sea Level
200
3000
4000
5000
6000

© Oxford University Press

Relief

	Metres
Land	
Highest point	
Mt. Everest	8 848
Lowest point	
Shores of the Dead Sea	−392
Average height	840
Oceans and Seas	
Greatest known depth	
Marianas Trench	11 022
Average depth	3 808

Area	10^6 km^2
Land	149
Water Surface	361
Total	510
of which	
Icesheets and glaciers	16

7

Europe: Physical

Precipitation figures on graphs in 10mm except for annual totals.

ATHENS Alt. 107m — 396mm Annual
BASEL Alt. 316m — 818mm Annual
BERLIN Alt. 35m — 564mm Annual
BUCHAREST Alt. 84m — 589mm Annual
CLERMONT-FERRAND Alt. 387m — 645mm Annual
HAMBURG Alt. 20m — 734mm Annual
KIEV Alt. 180m — 539mm Annual
LILLE Alt. 28m — 656mm Annual

ALGIERS Alt. 61m — 696mm Annual
BARCELONA Alt. 7m — 538mm Annual
BERGEN Alt. 18m — 2056mm Annual
BORDEAUX Alt. 12m — 782mm Annual
BUDAPEST Alt. 130m — 635mm Annual
COLOGNE Alt. 56m — 696mm Annual
ISTANBUL Alt. 9m — 734mm Annual
LENINGRAD Alt. 9m — 477mm Annual

© Oxford University Press

Conical Orthomorphic Projection

Europe: Physical
Scale 1:19 000 000
0 200 400 600 km

Maximum extent of Glaciation

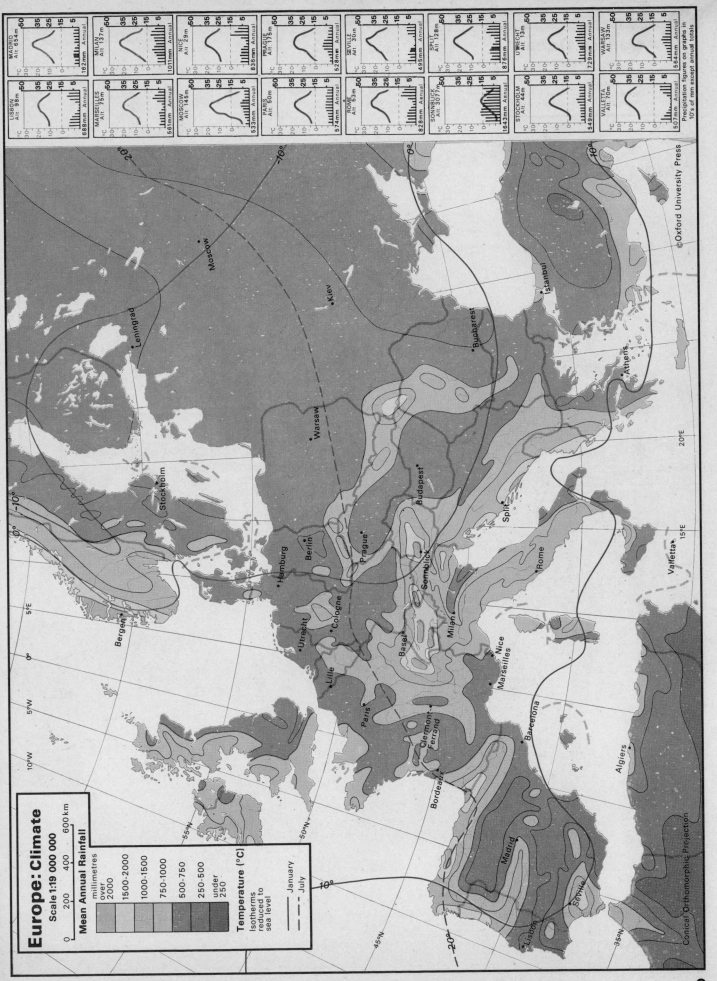

Europe: Climate

Scale 1:19 000 000

0   200   400   600 km

Mean Annual Rainfall

millimetres

over 2000
1500-2000
1000-1500
750-1000
500-750
250-500
under 250

Temperature (°C)

Isotherms reduced to sea level

January
July

Precipitation figures on graphs in 10's of mm except annual totals

MADRID Alt 654m · 162mm Annual
MILAN Alt 137m · 1011mm Annual
NICE Alt 29m · 836mm Annual
PRAGUE Alt 175m · 528mm Annual
SEVILLE Alt 30m · 495mm Annual
SPLIT Alt 128m · 876mm Annual
UTRECHT Alt 13m · 729mm Annual
WARSAW Alt 133m · 564mm Annual
LISBON Alt 98m · 688mm Annual
MARSEILLES Alt 75m · 561mm Annual
MOSCOW Alt 145m · 533mm Annual
PARIS Alt 50m · 574mm Annual
ROME Alt 63m · 828mm Annual
SONNBLICK Alt 3077m · 1643mm Annual
STOCKHOLM Alt 44m · 549mm Annual
VALLETTA Alt 70m · 507mm Annual

© Oxford University Press

Conical Orthomorphic Projection

2   1   A B C D E F G H J K L M N O P

Atlantic Ocean

Scale 1:63 000 000

0   500   1000   1500   2000 km

Ocean Currents   → Warm currents   --→ Cold currents

GREENLAND

Davis Strait

Denmark Strait

ICELAND

Norwegian Sea

Arctic Circle

Min. Aug.–Sept.

Norwegian Current

FINLAND

NORWAY SWEDEN

U. S. S. R.

Baltic Sea

Feb.–March

Labrador Current

Limit of pack ice max.

Labrador Basin

Reykjanes Ridge

Faerøe Is.

Rockall Plateau

North Sea

UNITED KINGDOM

IRISH REP.

London

NETH.

W. E. GERMANY

Berlin

POLAND

CZECH.

CANADA

Great Lakes

Chicago

Ottawa

Montreal

St. Lawrence

UNITED STATES

Washington

Limit of floating ice-maximum

North Atlantic Drift

West European Basin

•5050

FRANCE

Paris

SWITZ.

AUS.

HUNG.

ROMANIA

BELG.

YUGO-SLAVIA

BULGARIA

Black Sea

ITALY

GREECE

TURKEY

Istanbul

40°N

Mississippi

New York

Gulf Stream

30°N

Nova Scotia Basin

N O R T H

Newfoundland Basin

Peake Deep •5944

PORTUGAL SPAIN

Lisbon

M e d i t e r r a n e a n   S e a

TUNISIA

Gulf of Mexico

Bermuda

Sargasso Sea

North American Basin

Azores

MOROCCO

ALGERIA

LIBYA

THE BAHAMAS

6095•

Tropic of Cancer

•6995

A T L A N T I C

Madeira

Canary Basin

30°N

Yucatan Basin

CUBA

HAITI

DOMINICAN REP.

Puerto Rico Trench

North Equatorial Current

M i d - A t l a n t i c   R i d g e

Cape Verde

Canary Islands

Canary Current

WESTERN SAHARA

MAURITANIA

MALI

NIGER

Metres
5000
3000
2000
1000
500
300
200
100
Sea level
Land depression
200
3000
4000
5000
6000

JAMAICA

PUERTO RICO (U.S.A.)

Leeward Is.

Cape Verde Basin

Dakar

SENEGAL

THE GAMBIA

Caribbean Sea

DOMINICA

ST. LUCIA

Guiana Basin

Venezuelan Basin

CAPE VERDE ISLANDS

GUINEA BISSAU

GUINEA

BURKINA

NIGERIA

Spot heights in metres

COSTA RICA

PANAMA

Panama

GRENADA

TRINIDAD AND TOBAGO

Caracas

VENEZUELA

Windward Is.

SIERRA LEONE

LIBERIA

IVORY COAST

GHANA

TOGO

BENIN

Lagos

COLOMBIA

Bogotá

GUYANA

SURINAME

FR. GUIANA

O C E A N

Equatorial Counter Current

Guinea Current

Bioko

Principe

EQ. GUINEA

CAMEROON

ECUADOR

Equator

Amazon

St. Paul Rocks

Guinea Basin

São Tomé

GABON

CONGO

PERU

Lima

10°S

Humboldt Current

BRAZIL

Recife

Rocas I.

Fernando de Noronha

S O U T H

Brazil

South Equatorial Current

Ascension I.

Zaire

10°S

ANGOLA

La Paz

BOLIVIA

Brazil Current

Brazil Basin

•6022

St. Helena

Angola Basin

•2255

•6050

Peru Basin

PARAGUAY

Trinidad

Martin Vaz

Tropic of Capricorn

A T L A N T I C

20°S

NAMIBIA

Nasca Ridge

San Felix I.

Rio de Janeiro

São Paulo

Asunción

REP. OF SOUTH AFRICA

A n d e s

C e n t r a l

ARGENTINA

Paraná

URUGUAY

Rio Grande Rise

O C E A N

Tristan da Cunha

Cape Basin

Walvis Ridge

Benguela Current

Cape Town

30°S

SOUTH

Juan Fernandez Is.

Santiago

Buenos Aires

Montevideo

Argentine Basin

Gough I.

Cape Rise

Agulhas Current

C h i l e   R i s e

Chile Basin

P e r u   –   C h i l e   T r e n c h

Falkland Current

West Wind Drift

•6212

Limit of floating ice – maximum

West Wind Drift

40°S

Agulhas Plateau

PACIFIC

South East Pacific Basin

Tierra del Fuego

Falkland Is.

West Scotia Basin

Scotia Sea

South Georgia

East Scotia Basin

Limit of pack ice max. Aug.–Sept.

Bouvet I.

Atlantic – Indian Ridge

50°S

OCEAN

South Orkney

South Sandwich Is.

SOUTHERN OCEAN

Minimum Feb.–March

Modified Zenithal Equidistant Projection

© Oxford University Press

13   14

Grid References (column headers)
A   B   C   D

Row 1
Dun Laoghaire, Enniskerry, Greystones, Vartry Res., Wicklow, Wicklow Hd.
Holyhead, Holy I., Valley, Benllech, Anglesey, Beaumaris, Conwy, Llandudno, Colwyn Bay, Prestatyn, Rhyl, Rhuddlan, Holywell, Neston, Runcorn, Wilmslow, Alderley
Llangefni, Menai Bridge, Bethesda, Bangor, Llanfairfechan, Abergele, Elwy, Clwyd, Corinah's Quay, Flint, Hawarden, Northwich, Knutsford, Macclesfield, Middlewich, CHESHIRE, Chester
Caernarfon, Caernarfon Bay, 1062, GLYDER FAWR 999, 942, Betws-y-Coed, Llanrwst, Denbigh, Ruthin, Mold, Buckley, Winsford, Sandbach, Dane, Crewe, Nantwich, Alsager, Kidsgrove, Biddu
SNOWDON 1085, Blaenau Ffestiniog, Alwen Res., Cerrig, Mossel, Wrexham, Whitchurch, Market Drayton, Eccleshall, Newcastle-under-Lyme, Stoke-on-Trent, STAFF

Row 2
Cahore Pt.
YR EIFL 754, Nefyn, Lleyn Peninsula, Porthmadog, GWYNEDD, 782, Bala, Corwen, Dee, Llangollen, Overton, Ellesmere, Oswestry, Wem, Prees, Hodnet, Telford, Dawley, THE WREKIN 407, Canno
Aberdaron, Abersoch, Criccieth, Pwllheli, Tremadog Bay, Harlech, SNOWDONIA N.P., 720 RHINOG FAWR, 734, CLWYD, MOEL FFERNA 630, FOEL WEN 690, Bala Lake, Berwyn, Llanfyllin, Welshpool, Much Wenlock, Church Stretton, Bridgnorth, Wolverhampton, W. Brom, Dudley
Bardsey I., Barmouth, Barmouth Bay, 893 CADER IDRIS, Dolgellau, Dysynni, Tanat, Vyrnwy, Vyrnwy, Montgomery, Newtown, Bishop's Castle, Clun Forest, Wenlock Edge, BROWN CLEE HILL 540, Stourbridge, Halesowe, Kidderminster
C a r d i g a n, Tywyn, Machynlleth, Rhiw, MOELFRE 468, Llanidloes 528, Clun, Cleobury Mortimer, Ludlow, Bewdley, Stourport-on-Severn, Bromsgro
Aberdyfi, Borth, Nant-y-moch Res., PLYNLIMON 752, RHYDDHYWEL 585, Radnor 660 Forest, 547 BEACON HILL, Knighton, Tenbury Wells, Droitwich, Worcester
B a y, Aberystwyth, Rheidol, Llyn Clywedog Res., POWYS, Rhayader, Presteigne, Leominster, Bromyard, HEREFORD AND WORCESTER, Great Malv

Row 3 / 2-3 area
Devil's Bridge, Aberaeron, New Quay, Aeron, 484, Claerwen Res., DRYGARN FAWR 641, Llandrindod Wells, Arrow, Lugg, Pershore
Cardigan, Teifi, Tregaron, Lampeter, 415 MYNYDD PENCARREG, Builth Wells, Mynydd Eppynt, Llanwrtyd Wells, Irfon, Wye, Frome, Upton upon Severn, Ledbury, Tewkesbury
Strumble Hd., Dinas Hd., Newcastle Emlyn, MYNYDD BACH 361, Llandovery, Brecon, 811, Black Mts., Ross-on-Wye, Newent, Severn, Cheltenham
Fishguard, PEMBROKESHIRE COAST N.P., Mynydd Preseli 536, 335 MOELFRE, DYFED, Cothi, Llandeilo, Tywi, Mynydd du 802, Fforest Fawr, BRECON BEACONS N.P., 886 Brecon Beacons, Usk, Abergavenny, Monmouth, Mitcheldean, DEAN NAT FOREST, Newnham, Gloucester, Stonehouse, Stroud
St. David's Hd., St. David's, Ramsey I., St. Brides Bay, Haverfordwest, Tai, Crwn, Carmarthen, Ammanford, Merthyr Tydfil, Aberdare, Rhymni, Tredegar, Ebbw Vale, Aberillery, Pontypool, Coleford, Lydney, Nailsworth, Dursley
Skomer I., Milford Haven, Neyland, Narberth, Kidwelly, Pontardulais, Llanelli, W. GLAMORGAN, Mountain Ash, Rhondda, MID GLAMORGAN, Gelligaer, Abercarn, GWENT, Cwmbran, Chepstow, Thornbury, Yate, Maimesh
Skokholm I., St. Ann's Hd., Pembroke Dock, Pembroke, Tenby, Carmarthen Bay, Burry Port, Swansea, Neath, Maesteg, Port Talbot, Pontypridd, Caerphilly, Newport, Caerleon, Llanwern, Chipping Sodbury, Mangotsfield, Chippen
St. Govan's Hd., Caldey I., Worms Hd., Gower, Swansea Bay, The Mumbles, Margam, GLAMORGAN, Llantrisant, Bridgend, Porthcawl, Cardiff, S. GLAMORGAN, Penarth, Avonmouth, Portishead, Severn, Patchway, M4, AVON, Bristol, Kingswood, Corsham, Keynsham
Mumbles Hd., Barry, Bristol Channel, Clevedon, Weston-super-Mare, Bath, Bradford-on-Avon, Melksha

Channel Islands inset
a — Casquet Banks, Burhou, C. de la Hague, Alderney, Nez de Jobourg, b
i — FRANCE, 49°30'N
St. Peter Port, Herm, Jéthou, Sark
ii — Guernsey, Channel Islands, Les Écréhou, Passage de la Déroute
Grosnez Pt., Jersey, St. Peters, St. Aubin, St. Helier, 2°W
Same scale, Noirmont Pt.
iii — c, 6°W, d Penzance
50°N, Cape Cornwall, Land's End, Gwennap Hd.
iv — Bryher, St. Martin's, Tresco Isles of Scilly, St. Mary's, Hugh Town, St. Agnes, Same scale

Scale / Legend
Metres
2000
1000
500
300
200
100
Sea level
Land depression
Spot heights in metres

South West England
Lundy I., Bull Pt., Ilfracombe, Morte Pt., Lynton, Foreland Pt., Lynmouth, Minehead, Watchet, Brean Down, Burnham-on-Sea, Bridgwater Bay, Brue, Cheddar, 325, Mendip Hills, Wells, Chew Valley Lake, Midsomer Norton, Wellington
Baggy Pt., Braunton, Combe Martin, DUNKERY BEACON 560, EXMOOR N.P., Exmoor Forest, Wiveliscombe, Quantocks, Shepton Mallet, Glastonbury, Westt
Barnstaple or Bideford Bay, Westward Ho!, Clovelly, Barnstaple, Yeo, South Molton, Dulverton, Milverton, Taunton, SOMERSET, Street, Bridgwater, Bruton, Mere, Warminster
Hartland Pt., Hartland, Bideford, Great Torrington, Chulmleigh, Little Dart, Bampton, Wellington, Blackdown Culm Hills, Uffculme, Ilminster, Crewkerne, Somerton, Ilchester, Yeovil, Wincanton, Castle Cary, Sherborne, Shaftes
Sharpnose Pts., Taw, Torridge, Tiverton, Exe, Cullompton, Chard, Axminster, Beaminster, Blackmoor V, North Dorset Downs, Stour, Foru
Bude Bay, Bude, Stratton, Holsworthy, Hatherleigh, Credition, Honiton, Ottery, Axe, Yarty, Crediton, DORSET
Dizzard Pt., Boscastle, Ottery, Carey, Okehampton, Thrushel, 619 YES TOR, Moretonhampstead, St. Mary, Lyme Regis, Bridport, Dorchester, Wareham
Tintagel Hd., Tintagel, Launceston, DEVON, Dartmoor, Chudleigh, Topsham, Exeter, Sidmouth, Seaton, South Dorset Downs, Weymouth
Pentire Pt., Trevose Hd., Port Isaac, BROWN WILLY 420, Lydford, Inny, DARTMOOR N.P., Bovey Tracey, Exmouth, Budleigh Salterton, Lyme Bay, Chesil Beach, Isle
Padstow, Bodmin Moor, Tavistock, 539 GREAT MIS TOR, Forest, Newton Abbot, Dawlish, Teignmouth, Bill of Portland, Isle of Portland, St. Albar
Wadebridge, St. Columb Major, Bodmin, Callington, Lostwithiel, Ashburton, Buckfastleigh, Babbacombe Bay, Hope's Nose, Portland
Newquay, CORNWALL, Fowey, Liskeard, Saltash, Plym, Buckfastleigh, Torbay, Paignton, Berry Hd., Brixham
Kelsey Hd., 312, St. Austell, Par, Looe, Torpoint, Plymouth, Devonport, Ivybridge, Dartmouth
St. Agnes Hd., St. Agnes, Truro, Fal, St. Austell Bay, Rame Hd., Bigbury Bay, Kingsbridge, Start Bay, Start, Start Pt.
Gurnard's Hd., St. Ives, Redruth, Camborne, Mevagissey, Eddystone Rocks, Salcombe, Bolt Hd., Prawle Pt.
Hayle, St. Mawes, Penryn, Helston, Matazion, Zone Pt., Falmouth Bay
St. Just, Penzance, Mousehole, Mount's Bay, 112, Manacle Pt.
Land's End, Black Hd., Lizard, Lizard Pt., ENGLISH CHANNEL
5°W, 4°W, 3°W

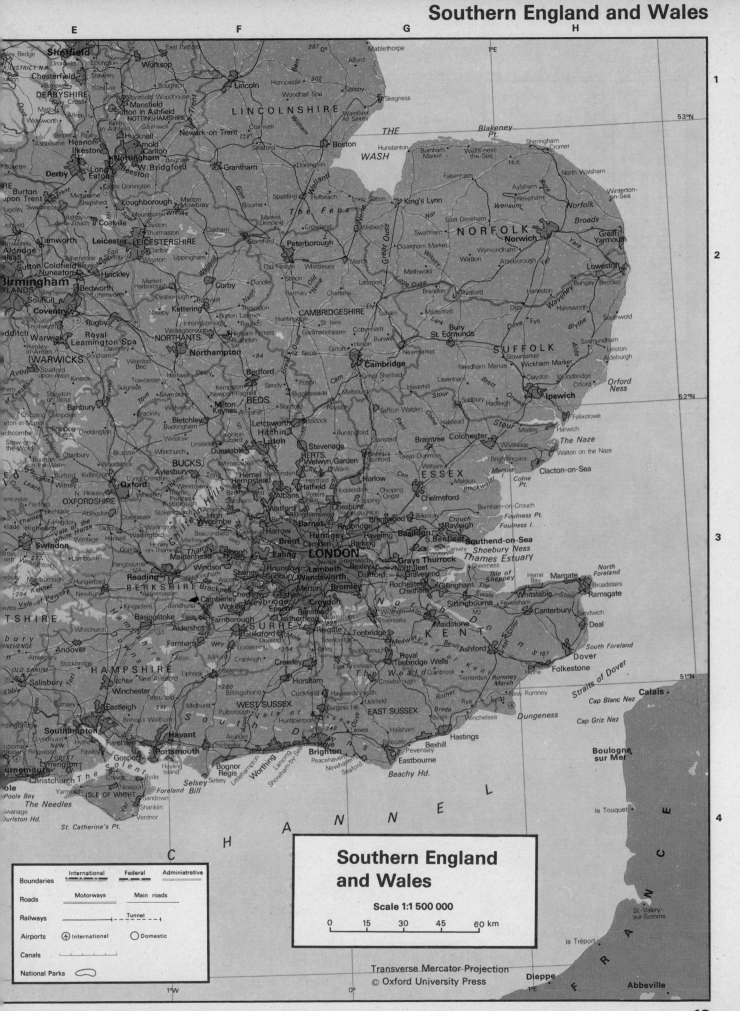

**Southern England
and Wales**

Scale 1:1 500 000

0   15   30   45   60 km

Transverse Mercator Projection
© Oxford University Press

Boundaries — International | Federal | Administrative
Roads — Motorways | Main roads
Railways — Tunnel
Airports — ⊕ International | ◯ Domestic
Canals
National Parks

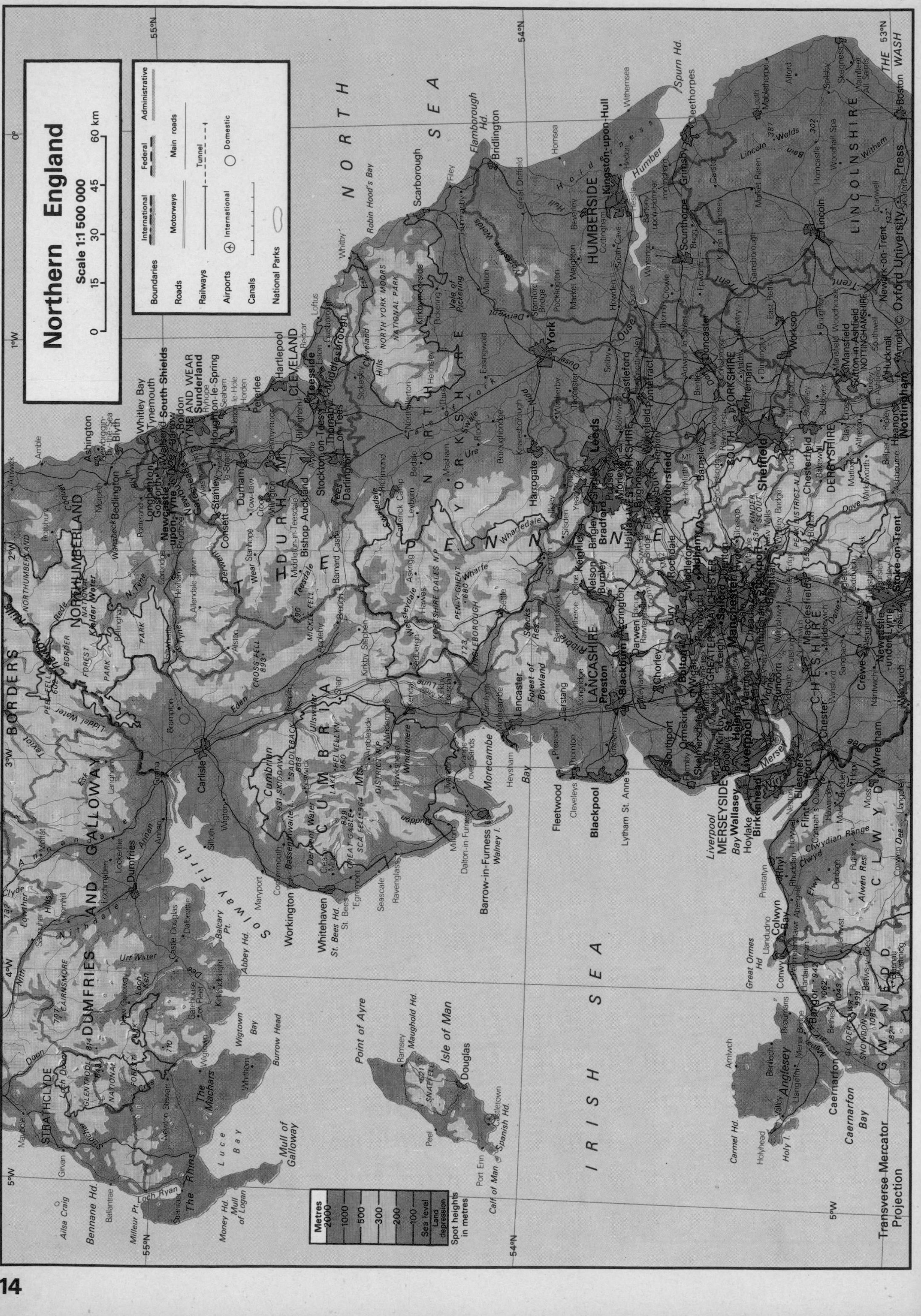

Northern England

Northern England

Scale 1:1 500 000

0 15 30 45 60 km

Boundaries
International
Federal
Administrative

Roads
Motorways
Main roads
Tunnel

Railways
Tunnel

Airports
✈ International
○ Domestic

Canals

National Parks

Metres
2000
1000
500
300
200
100
Sea level
Land depression

Spot heights in metres

Transverse Mercator Projection

© Oxford University Press

14

NORTH SEA
IRISH SEA

STRATHCLYDE
DUMFRIES AND GALLOWAY
BORDERS
NORTHUMBERLAND
CUMBRIA
DURHAM
TYNE AND WEAR
CLEVELAND
NORTH YORKSHIRE
WEST YORKSHIRE
SOUTH YORKSHIRE
HUMBERSIDE
LINCOLNSHIRE
LANCASHIRE
GREATER MANCHESTER
MERSEYSIDE
CHESHIRE
DERBYSHIRE
NOTTINGHAMSHIRE
CLWYD
GWYNEDD

THE PENNINES
LAKE DISTRICT N.P.
YORKSHIRE DALES N.P.
NORTH YORK MOORS NATIONAL PARK
PEAK DISTRICT N.P.

Isle of Man
Anglesey

Newcastle upon Tyne
Sunderland
South Shields
Tynemouth
Whitley Bay
Blyth
Ashington
Morpeth
Alnwick
Durham
Hartlepool
Middlesbrough
Stockton-on-Tees
Darlington
Bishop Auckland
Carlisle
Workington
Whitehaven
Barrow-in-Furness
Lancaster
Morecambe
Fleetwood
Blackpool
Lytham St Anne's
Preston
Blackburn
Burnley
Bolton
Wigan
Liverpool
Birkenhead
Wallasey
Southport
Manchester
Stockport
Warrington
Crewe
Chester
Wrexham
Sheffield
Rotherham
Doncaster
Barnsley
Huddersfield
Halifax
Bradford
Leeds
Wakefield
Harrogate
York
Scarborough
Whitby
Bridlington
Kingston-upon-Hull
Grimsby
Cleethorpes
Scunthorpe
Lincoln
Gainsborough
Mansfield
Nottingham
Newark-on-Trent
Stoke-on-Trent
Macclesfield
Caernarfon
Bangor
Holyhead

Solway Firth
Morecambe Bay
The Wash
Humber
Spurn Hd.
Flamborough Hd.
Robin Hood's Bay
Mull of Galloway
Point of Ayre

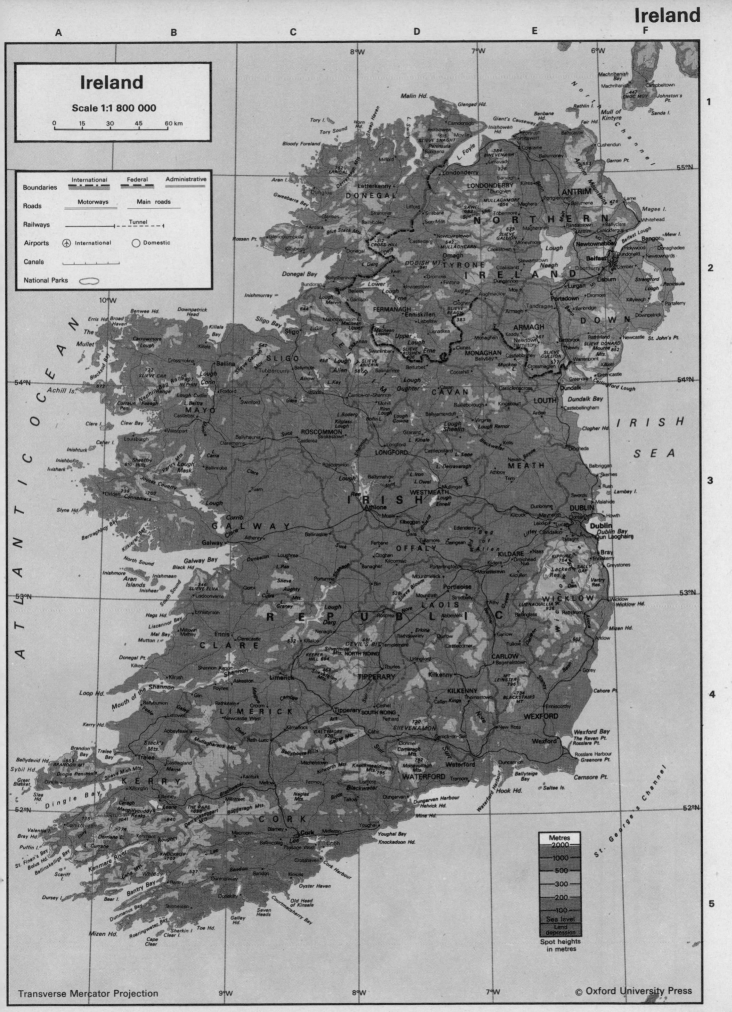

Ireland

Scale 1:1 800 000

0 15 30 45 60 km

Boundaries — International — Federal — Administrative
Roads — Motorways — Main roads
Railways — Tunnel
Airports — International — Domestic
Canals
National Parks

Transverse Mercator Projection

Metres
2000
1000
500
300
200
100
Sea level
Land
depression
Spot heights
in metres

© Oxford University Press

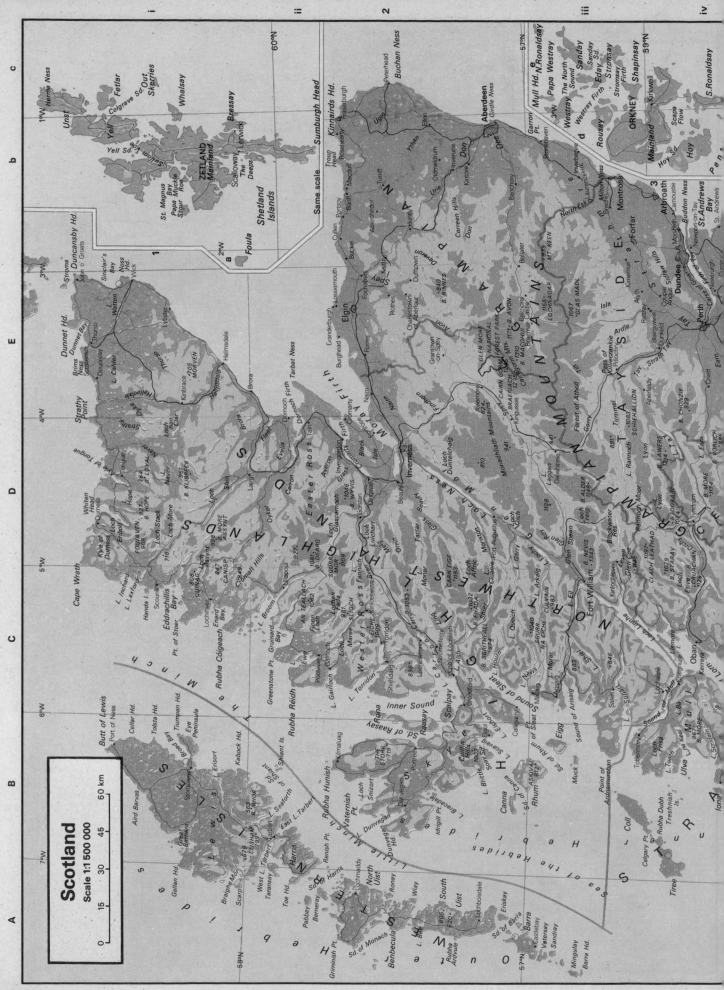

Scotland
Scale 1:1 500 000

0 15 30 45 60 km

16

Transverse Mercator Projection
© Oxford University Press

Scandinavia and Iceland

Scale 1:6 250 000

```
0    50   100  150  200 km
```

Boundaries International ——— (in sea) ——— (disputed) ———
Internal ———

Roads Motorways ——— Other roads ——— Tracks ———

Railways ———

Airports International ⊕ Domestic ○

Canals ———

Seasonal rivers, lakes

Salt pan

Marshes

Icecaps

Sand desert limits:

National Parks, etc.

Metres
```
5000
3000
2000
1000
500
300
200
100
Sea level
Land depression
```
Spot heights in metres

Map labels

BARENTS SEA

ARCTIC OCEAN

WHITE SEA

GULF OF BOTHNIA

U. S. S. R.

FINLAND

R. S. F. S. R.

ICELAND

Greenland Sea

Faxa Bay

Breidha Fjörd

Reykjavik · Kopavogur · Hafnarfjördhur · Keflavik

Akureyri

Vatnajökull 2000

SNAEFELL 1833

Arctic Circle

North Cape

Barents Sea

Kola Pen.

Severomorsk · Murmansk

Monchegorsk

Kirovsk · Apatity

Kandalaksha

Rovaniemi

Kemi

Oulu · Oulu

Luleå

Kiruna

Gällivare

Tromsø

Bodø

Mo i Rana

Östersund

Trondheim

Sundsvall

Härnösand

Umeå

Skellefteå

Arctic Circle

200 m oceandeep

NORWAY

SWEDEN

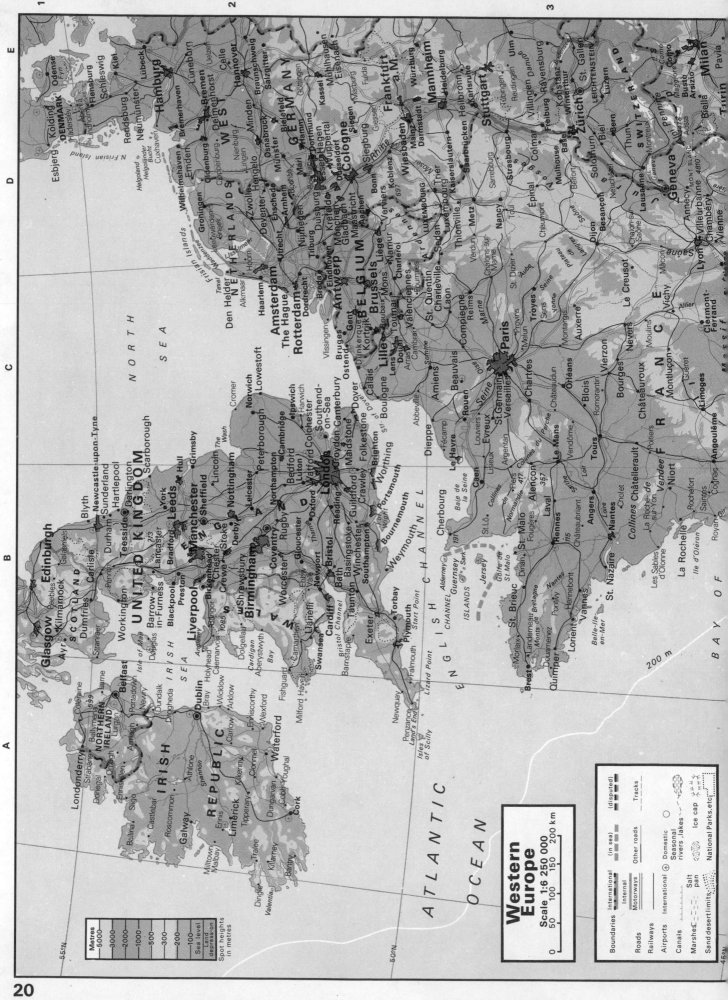

Western Europe

Scale 1:6 250 000

0   50   100   150   200 km

Boundaries International ────────
            Internal ────────
            (in sea) ────────
            (disputed) ────────

Roads   Motorways ────────
        Other roads ────────
        Tracks ────────

Railways ────────

Airports International ⊕
          Domestic ⊕

Canals ────────

Marshes ≡≡≡≡   Seasonal rivers, lakes ◯
Salt pan   Ice cap
Sand desert limits   National Parks, etc.

Metres
5000
3000
2000
1000
500
300
200
100
Sea level
Land
depression
Spot heights
in metres

20

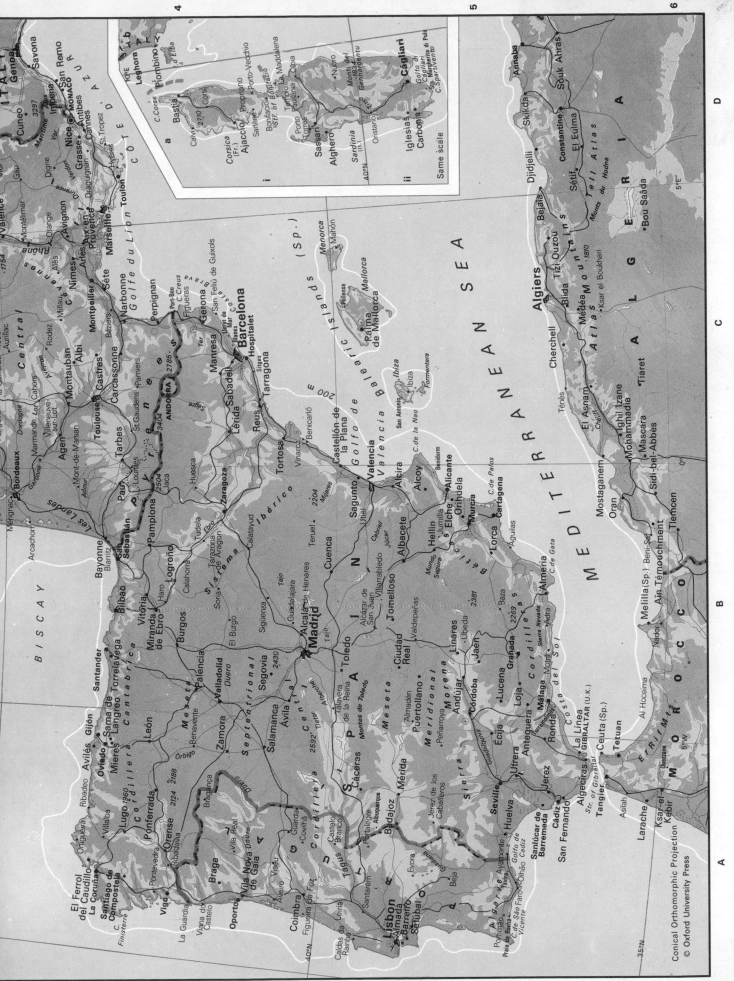

Conical Orthomorphic Projection

© Oxford University Press

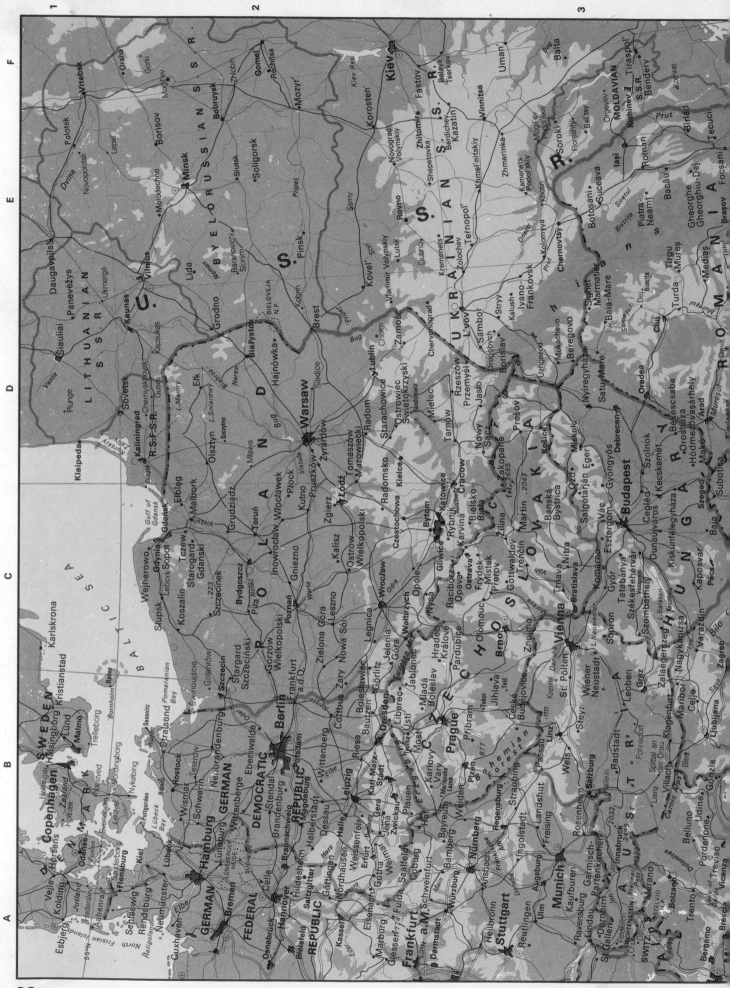

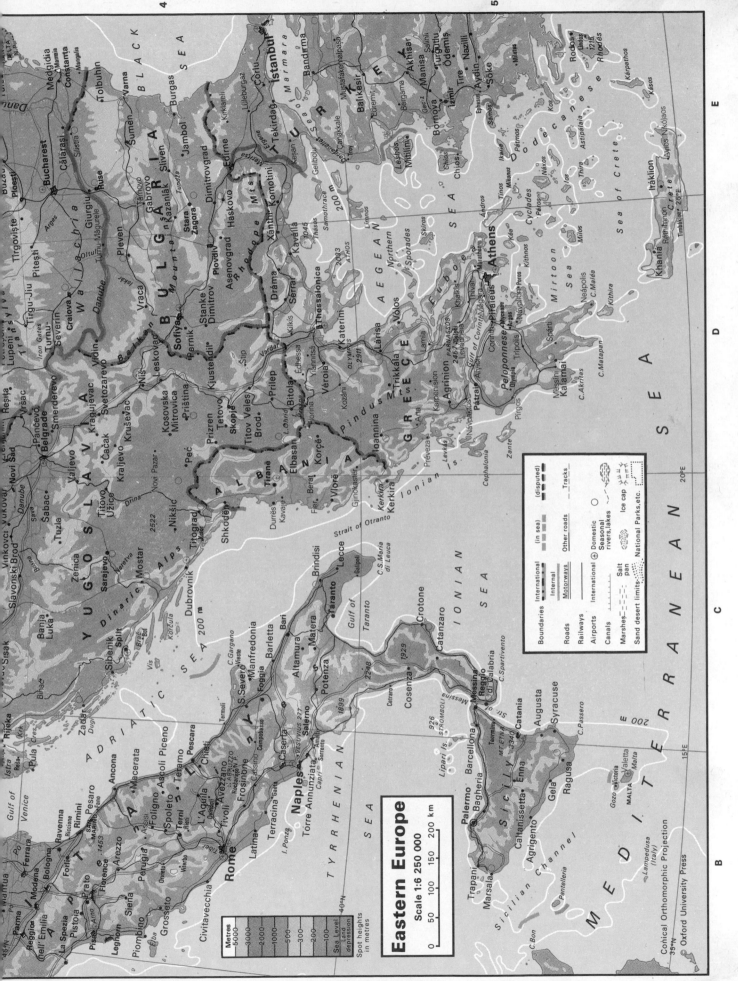

Eastern Europe

Scale 1:6 250 000

Metres
5000
3000
2000
1000
500
300
200
Sea Level
Land
depression

Spot heights
in metres

0 50 100 150 200 km

Conical Orthomorphic Projection

© Oxford University Press

Boundaries
International
Internal
(disputed)

Roads
Motorways
Other roads
Tracks

Railways

Airports ⊕ International ○ Domestic

Canals

Marshes

Salt pan

Seasonal
rivers, lakes

Ice cap

Sand desert limits

National Parks, etc.

(in sea)

23

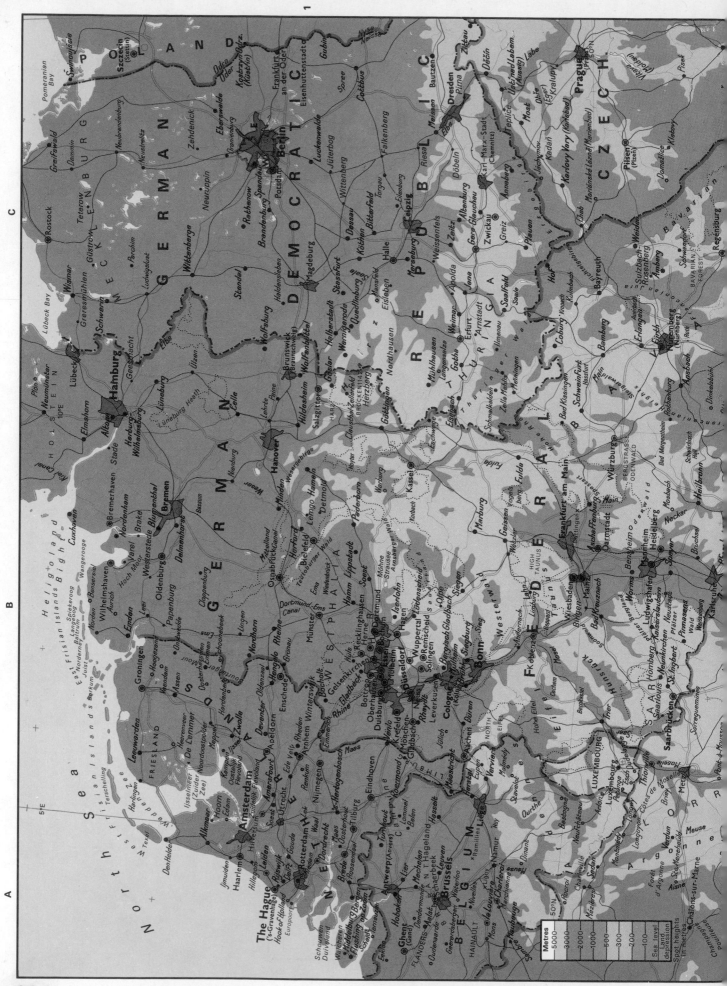

North Sea

POLAND

Pomeranian Bay
Swinoujście
Szczecin (Stettin)
Greifswald
Rostock
Stralsund
Wismar
Odra Oder
Kostrzyn Odz. (Küstrin)
Frankfurt an der Oder
Eberswalde
Neubrandenburg
Zehdenick
MECKLENBURG
Tetarow
Güstrow
Neuruppin
Brandenburg
Rathenow
Spandau Berlin Spree
Potsdam
Fürstenwalde
Eisenhüttenstadt
Gubin
Cottbus
Nysa Neisse

GERMAN DEMOCRATIC REPUBLIC

Lübeck Bay
Plön
Neumünster
HOLSTEIN
Lübeck
Elmshorn
Altona Hamburg
Harburg Wilhelmsburg
Geesthacht
Wittenberge
Stendal
Luckenwalde
Jüterbog
Wittenberg
Dessau
Torgau
Falkenberg

CZECH.
Prague (Praha)
Bautzen
Dresden Pirna
Děčín
Zittau
Ústí nad Labem (Aussig)
Teplice
Mělník
Kadaň
Karlovy Vary (Karlsbad)
Plzeň (Pilsen)

Heligoland Bight
East Frisian Islands
Cuxhaven
Bremerhaven
Bremen
Oldenburg

GERMANY
WESTPHALIA
Münster
Dortmund
Essen Düsseldorf
Cologne
Bonn

Amsterdam
Rotterdam
The Hague ('s-Gravenhage)
NETHERLANDS

BELGIUM
Brussels
Ghent (Gand)
Antwerp (Anvers)

LUXEMBOURG

FRANCE
SAAR
Saarbrücken
Metz

Frankfurt am Main
Wiesbaden
Mainz
Würzburg
Nürnberg (Nuremberg)
Regensburg
BAVARIA

Metres	
5000	
3000	
2000	
1000	
500	
300	
200	
100	
Sea level	
Land depression	

Spot heights in metres

24

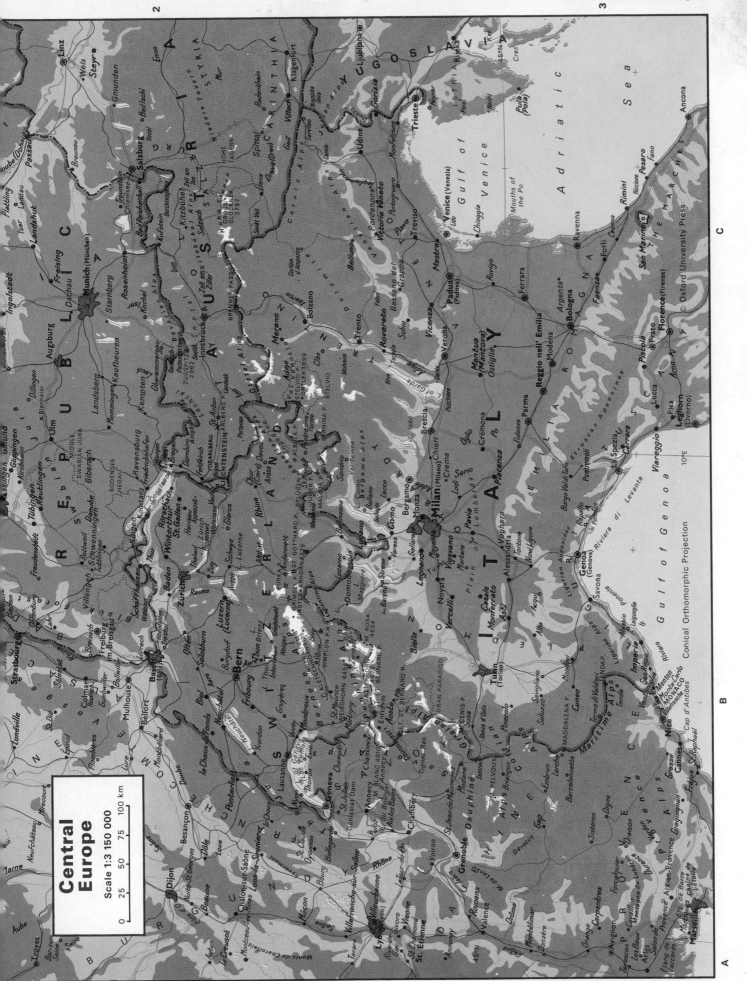

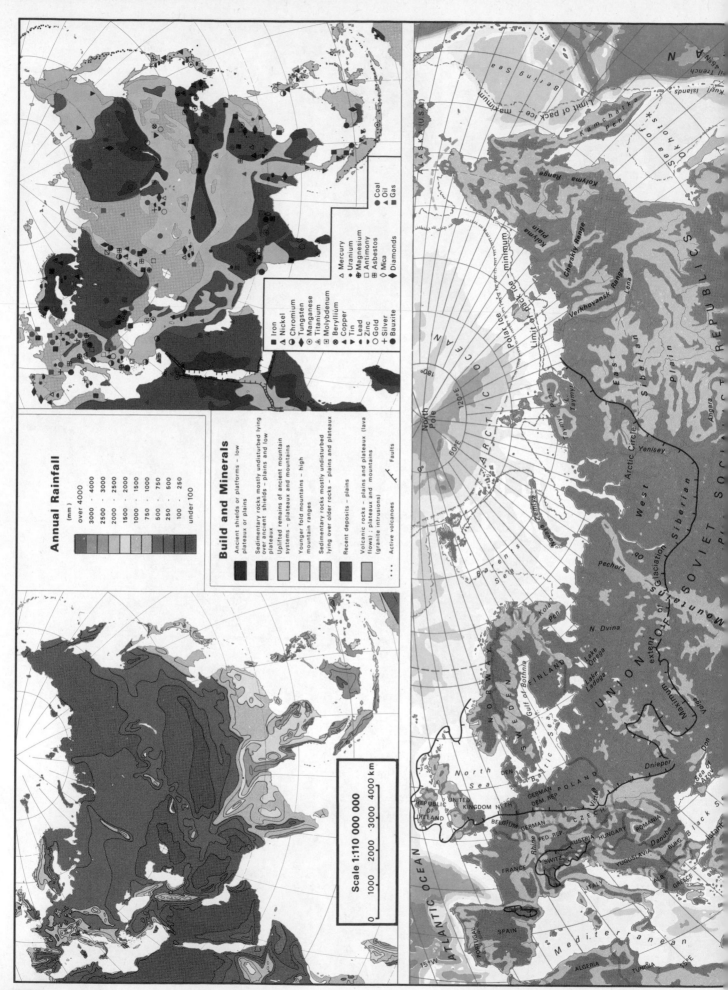

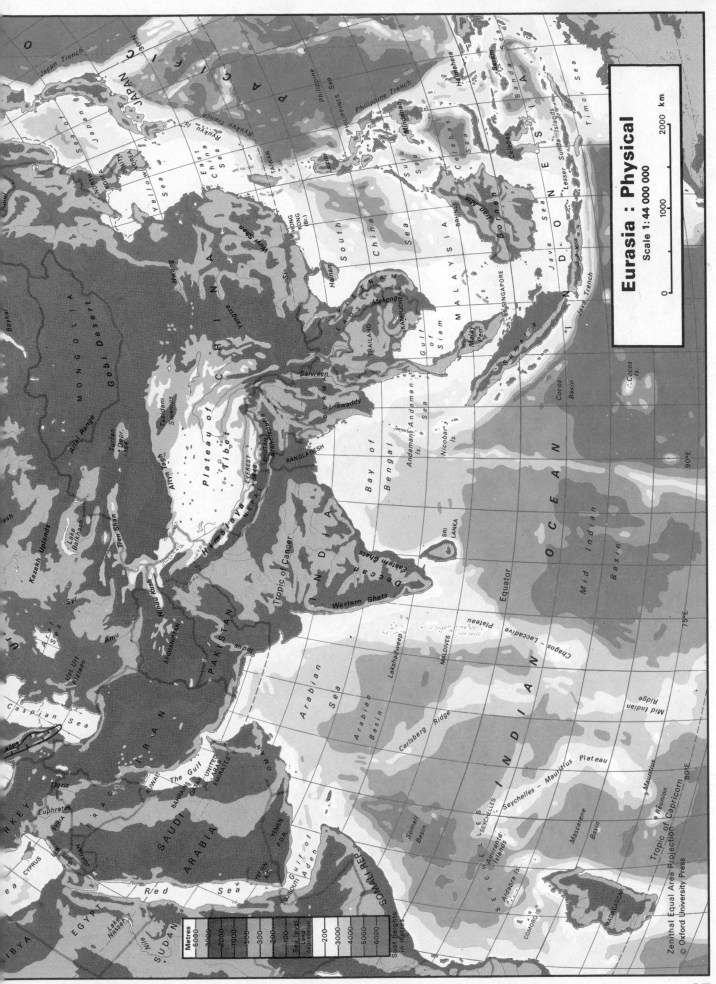

Eurasia : Physical

Scale 1:44 000 000

km

2000

1000

0

© Oxford University Press

Zenithal Equal Area Projection

Metres
5000
3000
2000
1000
500
300
200
100
Sea level
Land depression
200
3000
4000
5000
6000

Spot heights in metres

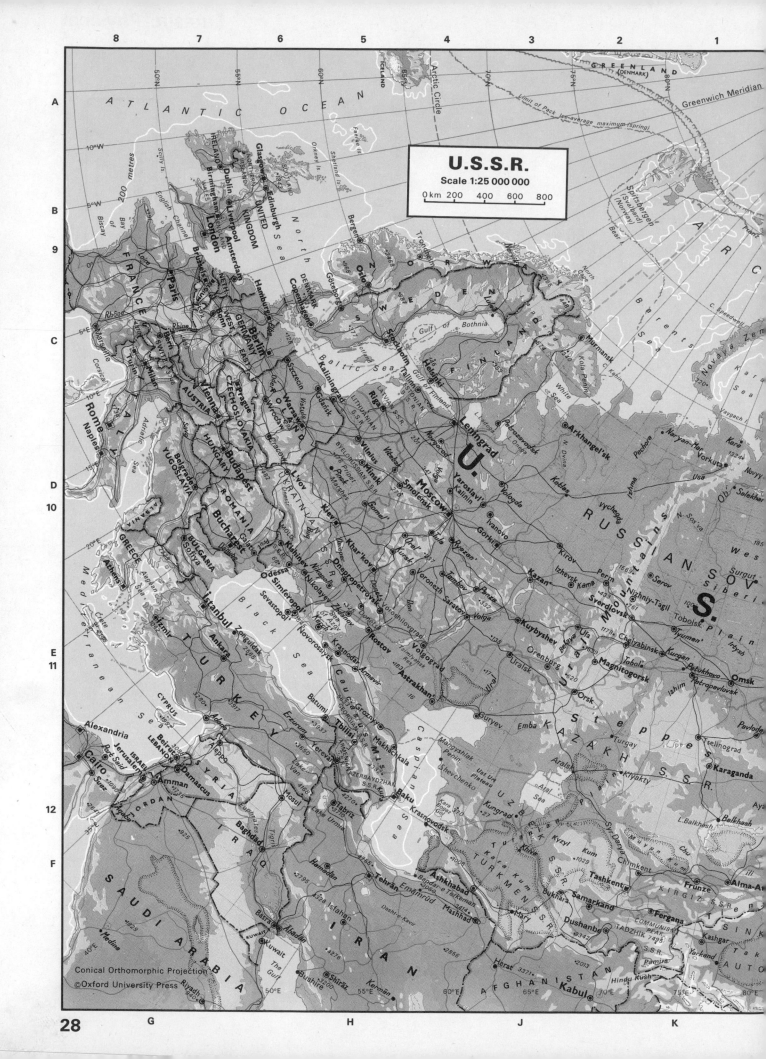

North
Pole

60° E

100° E

Metres
5000
3000
2000
1000
500
300
200
100
Sea level
Land
depression

Spot heights
in metres

Boundaries — International — (in sea) — (disputed)
— Internal
Roads — Motorways — Other roads — Tracks
Railways
Airports — International ✈ — Domestic ○
Canals
Marshes — Salt Pan — Ice Cap
Sand desert limits — National Parks etc.
Seasonal
rivers, lakes

ALASKA

W

Bering
Strait

Chukchi
Sea

Nome

Bering
Sea

V

International Date Line

East Siberian Sea

Novosibirskiye
Ostrova

Laptev
Sea

C. Chelyuskin

Severnaya
Zemlya
Wiese I.
(Vize)
Bol'shevik I.

ICE OCEAN

U

Kazachiye

Anadyr

Kamchatka
Bay

Kronotskiy
Bay

Petropavlovsk-
Kamchatskiy

7
T

Taymyr
Penin.
L. Taymyr
Nordvik

Khatanga

Tiksi

Verkhoyansk
Range

Cherskiy Range

Magdan

Okhotsk

Gyda
Penin.

Karaul
Dudinka
Norilsk
Putoran
Mts.
Igarka

Central
Siberian
Plateau

Lena

Sangar

Yakutsk

Sea of Okhotsk

Sakhalin

Sakhalin
Bay

Aleksandrovsk-Sakhalinskiy

S
8

Tarko-Sale

Lower Tunguska

Vilyuy

Elgyay

Olekminsk

Buyaga

Aldan

Neryungri

Nikolayevsk-
na-Amur

Yuzhno
Sakhalinsk

Yenisey

Stony Tunguska

Vitim

Lena

Vitim

Komsomolsk-
na-Amur

Soviet Harbour

Khabarovsk

FEDERATIVE SOCIALIST REPUBLIC
S. R.

Ob

Yeniseysk

Angara

Chuna

Ust-Kut

Zhigalovo

Tynda

Never

Tygda

Zeya

Mogocha

Amur

Chekunda

Blagoveshchensk

Bureya
Birobidzhan

Sikhote Alin Range

Uanka

9
R

Tomsk
Krasnoyarsk
Tayshet
Bratsk

Cheremkhovo
Irkutsk
Usolye

Zhigalovo

Lake Baykal

Chita
Ulan-Ude

Bukachacha

Nerchinsk
Sretensk
Sharlovaya Gora

Shilchan

Nünkiang

Tsitsihar

Harbin

Ussuri

Kholmsk

Partizansk

Sapporo
Muroran
Hakodate
Aomori

novosibirsk
Kemerovo
Prokop'yevsk
Novokuznetsk
Shelym

Abakan
Minusinsk

Kyzyl

Ulan-Ude

Aksha

Hulun

Erenesab

Mukankiang
Kirin

Vladivostok

Sea of Japan

Honshu

10

ipalatinsk
Leninogorsk

Ulan Gom
Selenga
Bulagan

Uliastay

Altai Range

Hovd

Ulan Bator

Choibalsan

Tamsag Bulag

Uldza

Ulanhoto

Great Khingan Mts.

Changchun

Mukden
Anshan

NORTH
KOREA
Pyongyang
Nampo

SOUTH
KOREA

Seoul

Kyoto
Kobe

Q

MONGOLIA

Sayn Shanda

Gobi Desert

Inner Mongolia

Chengteh
(Jehol)

Yingkow

Lü-ta

Yentai

Pusan
Hiroshima
Shimonoseki
Kitakyushu

11

Wulumuchi (Urumchi)
Turfan depr.
Hami (Qomul)

Ala Shan

Changkiakow
(Kalgan)
Huhehot
Paotow

Peking
(Peiping)
Tientsin

Po Hai
(G. of
Chihli)

Tsingtao

Yellow
Sea

Nagasaki

UIGHUR
REGION

Ansi

Yinchwan
(Ningsia)

Shihkiachwang

Tsinan

East
China
Sea

Ryuku Is.

12

Tagh
Altyn
Tsaidam
Swamps

Sining
Lanchow
(Kaolan)

Hwang

Taiyuan

Anyang

Loyang Hwang

Suchow
(Tungshan)

Nanking Shanghai

CHINA

85° E
90° E
100° E
110° E
115° E
120° E

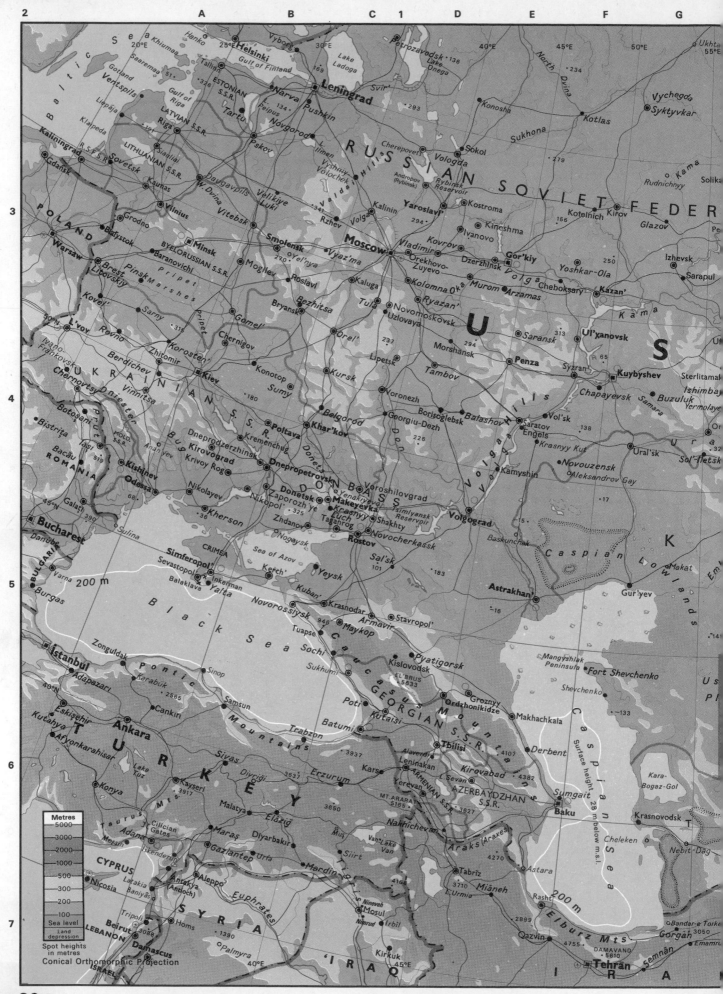

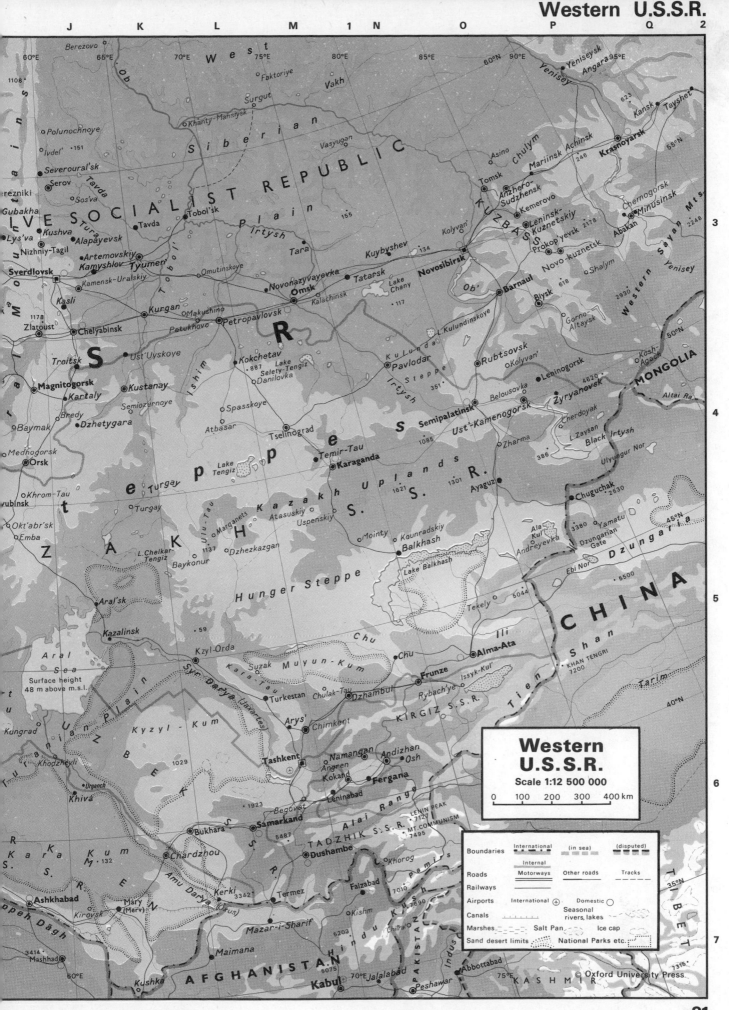

West

Siberian

SOCIALIST REPUBLIC

Plain

S   S   R

S

S   t   e   p   p   e   s

Z   A   K   H   S.   S.   R.

Kazakh Uplands

Hunger Steppe

Lake Balkhash

CHINA

MONGOLIA

Tien Shan

KIRGIZ S.S.R.

Kyzyl - Kum

Kara Kum

Turan Plain

UZBEK S.S.R.

TADZHIK S.S.R.

Pamirs

AFGHANISTAN

PAKISTAN

KASHMIR

Hindu Kush

Surface height
48 m above m.s.l.

Aral
Sea

Western U.S.S.R.

Scale 1:12 500 000

0   100   200   300   400 km

Boundaries	International	(in sea)	(disputed)
	Internal		
Roads	Motorways	Other roads	Tracks
Railways			
Airports	International ⊕	Domestic ○	
Canals		Seasonal rivers, lakes	
Marshes		Salt Pan	Ice cap
Sand desert limits		National Parks etc.	

© Oxford University Press

3

4

5

6

7

31

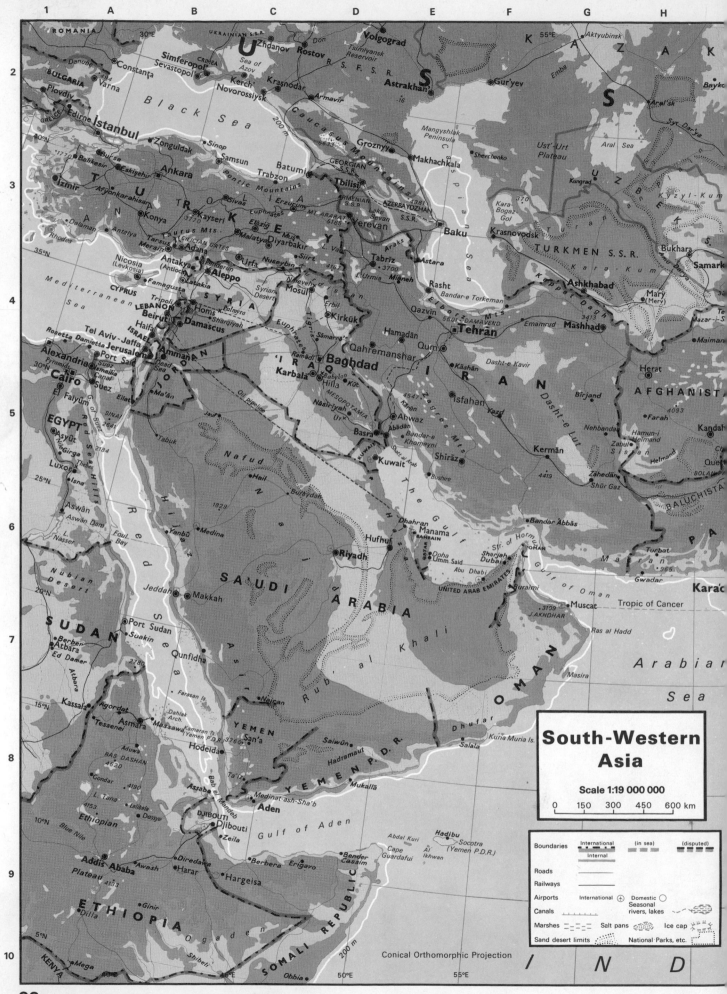

South-Western Asia

Scale 1:19 000 000

0   150   300   450   600 km

Boundaries	International	(in sea)	(disputed)
	Internal		
Roads			
Railways			
Airports	International ⊕	Domestic ○	
Canals		Seasonal rivers, lakes	
Marshes	Salt pans	Ice cap	
Sand desert limits	National Parks, etc.		

Conical Orthomorphic Projection

S.S.R.

Kazakh Uplands

Mointy
Kounradskiy
Balkhash
Andreyevka
Ayaguz
L.Zaysan
Ulyunger Nor

MONGOLIA
Altai Range
4226
Gobi Desert
2847

Chu
Lake Balkhash
Ebi Nor
Dzungaria
Wulumuchi (Urumchi)
Hami (Oomul)
158
154
Tulufan
Paotow
Yin Shan
Ordos Plateau
40°N

R

Chimkent
Tashkent
Frunze
Rybach'ye
Issyk-Kul
Alma-Ata
KIRGIZ S.S.R.
Bagrach Kol
Ansi pa
Kiuchuan
Nan Shan
Ala Shan
Yin-Chuan
Lanchow
35°N

Andizhan
Osh
Fergana
7200 KHAN TENGRI
Tarim
6346
Sining (Koko Nor)
Tsing Hai
Great Wall
Tsinling Shan

Kokand
ushanbe
1495 COMMUNISM PEAK
TADZHIK S.S.R.
Sufu (Kashgar)
SINKIANG – UIGHUR
AUTONOMOUS REGION
Takla Makan
Amne Machen Shan
Tsaidam Swamps
Wei

Faizabad
Pamirs
Soche (Yarkand)
Hotien (Khotan)
Altyn Tagh
Bayán Kara Shan
4624
Yushu (Jyekundo)
Mekong
Chengtu
30°N

bul
Hindu Kush
7701
Chitral
Gilgit
3811
Kunlun Mountains
NANGCHEN JAPO
Changtu
Yaan
Kangting
Ipin
Red Basin

Jalalabad
KHYBER PASS
Peshawar
Islamabad
Rawalpindi
Srinagar
Leh
JAMMU & KASHMIR
ALING KANGRI 7315
TIBET
Salween
Batang
5297
Hsichang
Huitse
Yangtze (Kinsha)

Sialkot
Jammu
7756
7099
Nyenchen Tanglha Range
Lhasa
Tsangpo
Kunming
25°N

Shah
Faisalabad
3382
Lahore
Amritsar
Dehra Dun
Simla
NAMET
Shigatse
Tsangpo(Matsang)
Gyangtse
Chenkiang
Tengchung
3826

Multan
Sutlej
PUNJAB
Patiala
Saharanpur
ANNARURNA
MT.EVEREST 8079 8848
NEPAL
Katmandu
BHUTAN
Guwahati
Assam
Brahmaputra
Naga Hills
Myitkyina
Bhamo
3234

Bikaner
Bahawalpur
Meerut
Moradabad
Bareilly
Shahjahanpur
Gorakhpur
Darjeeling
Muzaffarpur
Rangpur
Shillong
2831
Kohima
Imphal
Indaw
Bawdwin

Delhi
New Delhi
Agra
Jaipur
Lucknow
Kanpur
Patna
Ganges
Bhagalpur
Berhampore
BANGLADESH
Dacca
Sylhet
Mawlaik
SHAN
Lashio
Shwebo

Jodhpur
Ajmer
Gwalior
Allahabad
Varanasi
Hazaribagh
Ranchi
Asansol
Jessore
Chittagong
Chin Hills
BURMA
STATES
Mandalay
Pakokku
LAOS
B.Houei Sai
20°N

Thar Desert
Kota
Jhansi
1225
Jamshedpur
Haora (Howrah)
Calcutta
BENGAL
Akyab
Chindwin
Arakan Yoma
Yenangyaung
Magwe
Chiang Rai
Chiang Mai
4007
Uttaradit

erabad
Rajkot
Ujjain
Bhopal
Vindhya Range
Jabalpur
Bilaspur
Mahanadi
Raipur
SUNDARBANS
Mouths of the Ganges
Hugli (Hooghly)
Cuttack
Cheduba
Toungoo
Prone
Thayetmyo
Pegu
Salween
Tak

Ahmadabad
Vadodara
Indore
Narmada
Satpura Range
Nagpur
1267
Bassein
Rangoon
Moulmein
Gulf of Martaban
15°N

Surat
157
Tapti
Akola
Gulf of Khambhat
Nasik
Godavari
1680
Vizianagaram
Vishakhapatnam
Pagoda Pt.
Ye
Tavoy
Bangkok

Bombay
Pune (Poona)
Warangal
Kakinada
Bay of

Sholapur
Hyderabad
Krishna
Vijayavada
Andaman Sea
200 m

Kolhapur
Belgaum
Kurnool
Nellore
Andaman Islands (India)
Mergui Arch.
1335
10°N

Hubli
Bellary
Bengal
200 m

Lakshadweep (Laccadive Islands)
Mangalore
Bangalore
Mysore
Nilgiri Hills 2633
Pondicherry
Madras
Coromandel Coast
Phuket I.
5°N

Kozhikode
Palghat Gap
Tiruchirapalli
Madurai
Nicobar Islands (India)
AN
OCEAN

Cochin
Jaffna
Trincomalee
Gal Oya
Banda Aceh
Sumatra

Trivandrum
Tirunelveli
SRI LANKA
Kandy
2524
Battioaloa

Colombo
Galle
©Oxford University Press

MALDIVE ISLANDS

Metres
5000
3000
2000
1000
500
300
200
100
Sea level
Land depression
Spot heights in metres

India and Sri Lanka

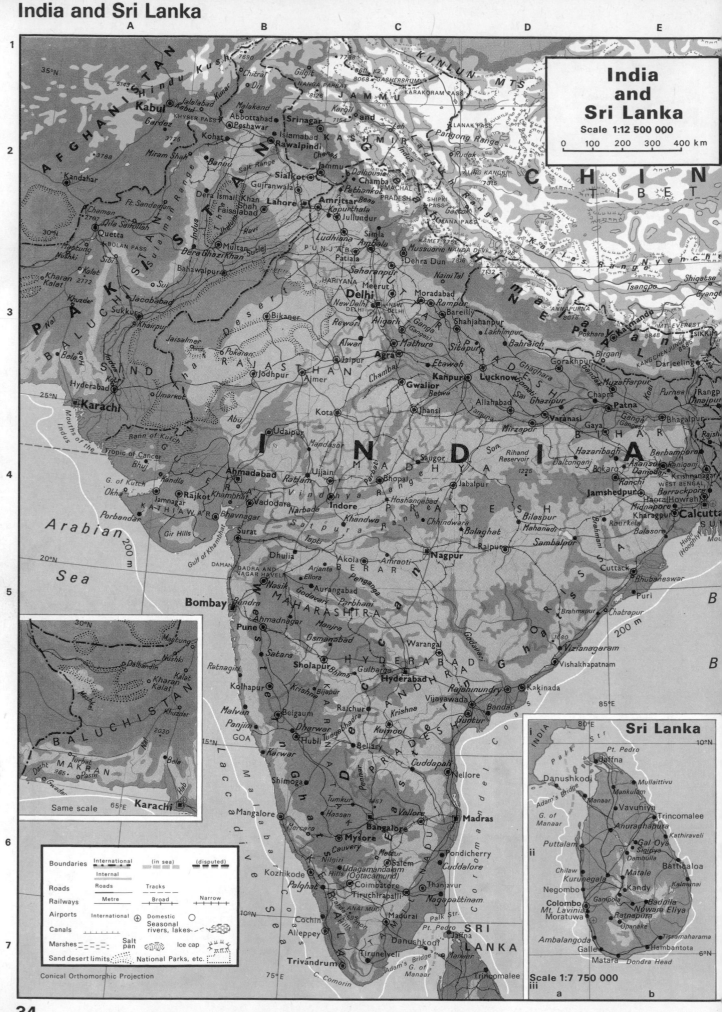

India and Sri Lanka
Scale 1:12 500 000
0 100 200 300 400 km

Sri Lanka
Scale 1:7 750 000

Conical Orthomorphic Projection

Boundaries International (in sea) (disputed)
Internal
Roads Roads Tracks
Railways Metre Broad Narrow
Airports International Domestic
Canals Seasonal rivers, lakes
Marshes Salt pan Ice cap
Sand desert limits National Parks, etc.

Same scale

34

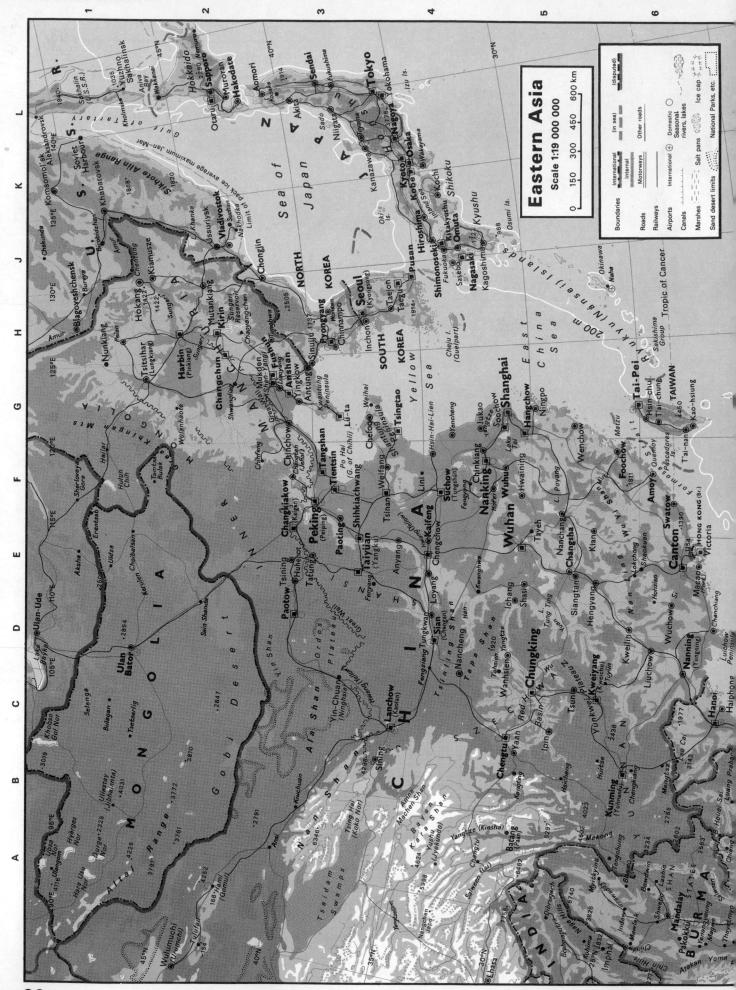

Eastern Asia

Scale 1:19 000 000

0 150 300 450 600 km

Boundaries	International	(in sea)	(disputed)
Roads	Internal	Motorways	Other roads
Railways	International		
Airports	Domestic	Seasonal rivers, lakes	
Canals	Salt pans	Ice cap etc.	
Marshes	Sand desert limits	National Parks, etc.	

36

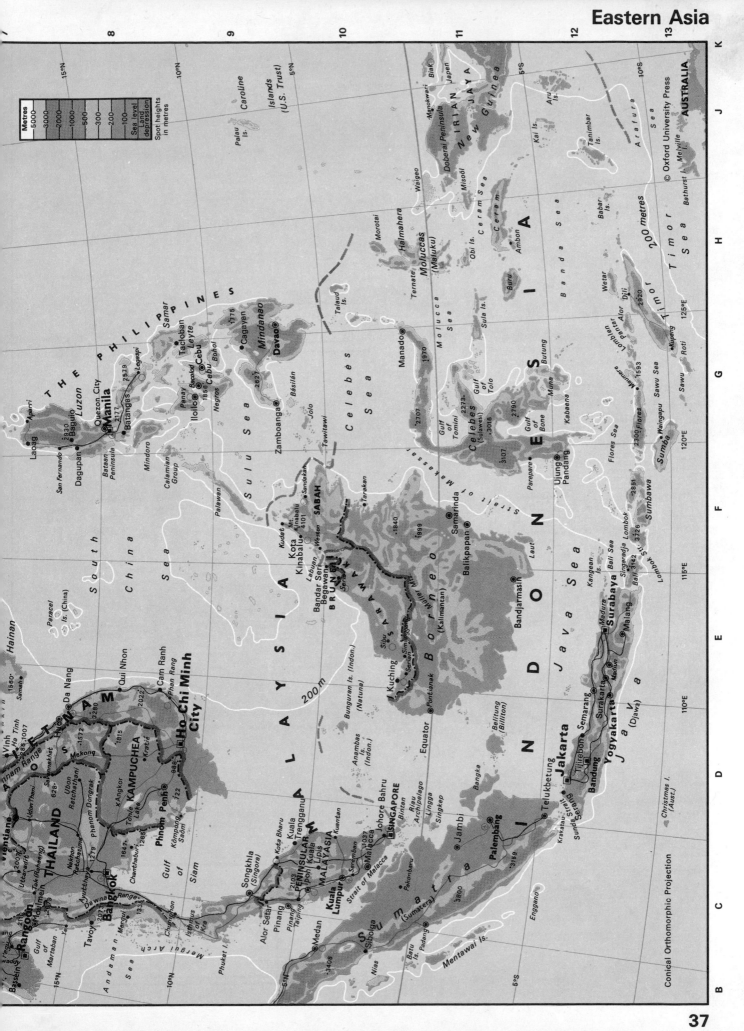

Metres
5000
3000
2000
1000
500
300
200
100
Sea level
Land
depression
Spot heights
in metres

K

Caroline

Islands
(U.S. Trust)

Palau Is.

J

Manokwari Japen

Biak

IRIAN JAYA

Doberai Peninsula

New Guinea

Waigeo

Misoöl

Aru
Is.

Kai Is.

Tanimbar
Is.

Melville I.

Bathurst I.

AUSTRALIA

H

Morotai

Halmahera

Ternate

Moluccas
(Maluku)

Obi   Ceram Sea

Ceram

Ambon

Buru

Banda Sea

Babar

Wetar

Timor

Sea

200 metres

G

Manado

Molucca
Sea

Sula Is.

Butung

2920

Alor

Dili

Kupang

Roti

Sawu

A

I

N

I

Gulf
of
Tomini

2707

2273

Celebes
(Sulawesi)

3016

2790

Gulf
of
Bone

Muna

Kabaena

Flores Sea

2300 Flores

Sawu Sea

Waingapu Sumba

F

Celebes
Sea

Zamboanga

Bāsilán

Jolo

Tawitawi

1970

3107

Parepare

Ujung
Pandang

2851

Lombok

3142

Sumbawa

3726

Bali
Strait of Makassar

Philippines

Samar

Tacloban

Leyte

Cebu

Bohol

1775

Cagayan

Mindanao

2627

Davao

THE PHILIPPINES

Luzon

Quezon City

Manila

Batangas

2177

Baguio

2930

Laoag

Aparri

San Fernando

Dagupan

Bataan
Peninsula

Iloilo

Bacolod

Cebu

1856

Panay

Negros

2579

Legaspi

Mindoro

Calamian
Group

Palawan

Kudat

Mt.
Kinabalu
4101

Kota
Kinabalu

Labuan   Weston

SABAH

Sandakan

Tarakan

1840

1999

Samarinda

Balikpapan

Laut

Bandjarmasin

Kangean

Singaradja

Madura

Surabaya

Malang

Semarang

Surakarta

Yogyakarta

Madiun

Bandung

Tjilebon

Jakarta

Serang

Telukbetung

2851

Kedang

2790

Maumere

1593

E

Hainan

South

China

Sea

Paracel
Is. (China)

Parapel
Is.

Qui Nhon

Cam Ranh

Phan Rang

Da Nang

1580

Samah

Ho Chi Minh
City

200 m

Sibu

Sin

Kuching

Seriani

Pontianak

Borneo
(Kalimantan)

I   N   D   O   N

Belitung
(Billiton)

Java Sea

Java (Djawa)

Bangka

Bintan

Singkep

Lingga

Riau
Archipelago

Anambas
Is. (Indon.)

Bunguran Is. (Indon.)
(Natuna)

Sibu

Serian

Schwaner Mts.

BRUNEI
Bandar Seri
Begawan

SARAWAK

D

VIETNAM

Mekong

KAMPUCHEA

X.Angkor

Tonle Sap
Lake

1265

Kompong
Saôm

Phnom Penh

722

Kratié

889

1815

2022

1572

Vinh

Ha Tinh

1007

1288

3280

Annam Range

Vientiane

LAOS

Udon Thani

Ubon
Ratchathani

628

Nakhon
Ratchasima

Pharom Dongrak

Kuala
Trengganu

Johore Bahru

SINGAPORE

PENINSULAR
MALAYSIA

Kuala
Lipis

Kuantan

Seremban

3037

Malacca

Strait of Malacca

Pekanbaru

Jambi

Palembang

Sunda Strait

Krakatau Strait

3159

Christmas I.
(Aust.)

Equator

5°S

10°S

C

THAILAND

2007

Uttaradit

Tak (Raheng)

1779

Nakhon
Sawan

Ayutthaya

1647

Chanthaburi

Bangkok

2103

1335

Chumphon

Isthmus
of Kra

Songkhla
(Singora)

Pinang
Pinang

Taiping

Ipoh

Kuala
Lumpur

Alor Setar

Kota Bharu

Medan

3408

Nias

Batu
Is.

Sibolga

Padang

Sumatra
(Sumacera)

3880

3805

Enggano

Bengkulu

Mentawai Is.

B

Rangoon

Bassein

Basseiny

Gulf
of
Martaban

Moulmein

Tavoy

Mergui

Mergui Arch.

Phuket I.

Andaman

Sea

2603

Dawna
Range

Bilugyan

Gulf
of
Siam

15°N

10°N

5°N

0°

90°E

95°E

100°E

105°E

110°E

115°E

120°E

125°E

8   9   10   11   12   13

Conical Orthomorphic Projection

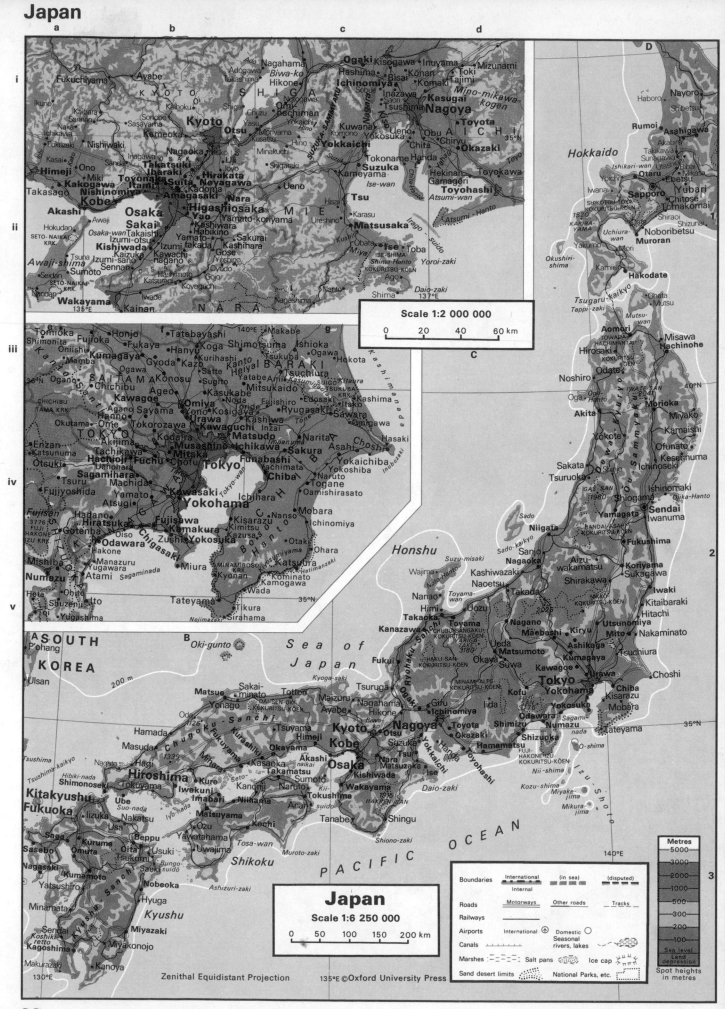

Japan

Scale 1:2 000 000

0   20   40   60 km

Japan

Scale 1:6 250 000

0   50   100   150   200 km

Boundaries	International	(in sea)	(disputed)
	Internal		
Roads	Motorways	Other roads	Tracks
Railways			
Airports	International ⊕	Domestic ○	
Canals	├──┤	Seasonal rivers, lakes	
Marshes	╌╌╌╌	Salt pans	Ice cap
Sand desert limits		National Parks, etc.	

Metres
5000
3000
2000
1000
500
300
200
100
Sea level
Land depression
Spot heights in metres

Zenithal Equidistant Projection   135°E ©Oxford University Press

Australasia: Rainfall and Physical

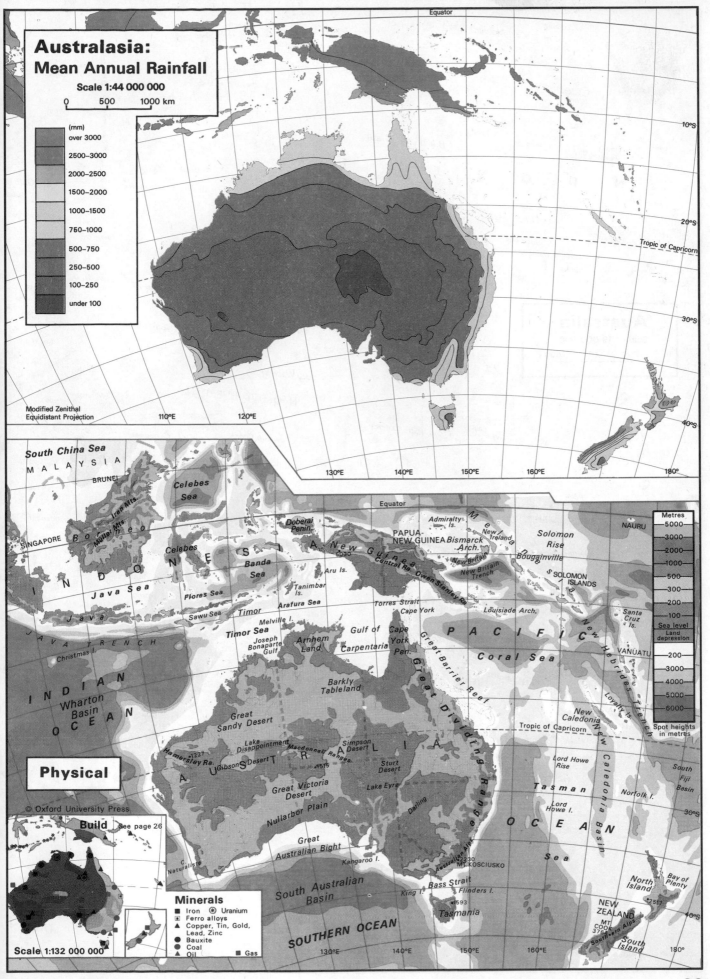

Australasia: Mean Annual Rainfall

Scale 1:44 000 000

0   500   1000 km

(mm)
- over 3000
- 2500–3000
- 2000–2500
- 1500–2000
- 1000–1500
- 750–1000
- 500–750
- 250–500
- 100–250
- under 100

Modified Zenithal Equidistant Projection

Equator

Tropic of Capricorn

10°S
20°S
30°S
40°S

110°E   120°E   130°E   140°E   150°E   160°E   180°

Physical

© Oxford University Press

South China Sea

MALAYSIA

BRUNEI

Iran Mts.

SINGAPORE

Muller Mts.

Borneo

Celebes Sea

INDONESIA

Celebes

Banda Sea

Java Sea

Java

Flores Sea

Sawu Sea

JAVA TRENCH

Christmas I.

INDIAN OCEAN

Wharton Basin

Timor Sea

Melville I.

Joseph Bonaparte Gulf

Arnhem Land

Arafura Sea

Tanimbar Is.

Timor

Aru Is.

Doberai Penin.

New Guinea

Central Ra.

PAPUA NEW GUINEA

5030

Owen Stanley Ra.

Admiralty Is.

New Ireland

Bismarck Arch.

New Britain

New Britain Trench

Torres Strait

Cape York

Gulf of Carpentaria

Cape York Pen.

Great Barrier Reef

Louisiade Arch.

Solomon Rise

Bougainville

SOLOMON ISLANDS

PACIFIC

Coral Sea

New Hebrides Trench

NAURU

Santa Cruz Is.

VANUATU

Loyalty Is.

New Caledonia

New Caledonia Basin

Tropic of Capricorn

Barkly Tableland

Great Sandy Desert

Hamersley Ra.

1227

Gibson Desert

Lake Disappointment

Macdonnell Ranges

Simpson Desert

1515

Sturt Desert

Great Victoria Desert

Lake Eyre

AUSTRALIA

Nullarbor Plain

Darling

Great Australian Bight

C. Naturaliste

Kangaroo I.

South Australian Basin

SOUTHERN OCEAN

Lord Howe Rise

Lord Howe I.

Tasman

Sea

Norfolk I.

OCEAN

South Fiji Basin

30°S

Great Dividing Range

Australian Alps

2230

MT.KOSCIUSKO

Bass Strait

King I.

Flinders I.

1593

Tasmania

North Island

Bay of Plenty

NEW ZEALAND

2517

MT. COOK 3764

Southern Alps

South Island

40°S

130°E   140°E   150°E   160°E   180°

Minerals

- ■ Iron
- ⊠ Ferro alloys
- ▲ Copper, Tin, Gold, Lead, Zinc
- ● Bauxite
- ● Coal
- ▲ Oil
- ■ Gas
- ⊕ Uranium

Build   See page 26

Scale 1:132 000 000

Metres
- 5000
- 3000
- 2000
- 1000
- 500
- 300
- 200
- 100
- Sea level
- Land depression
- 200
- 3000
- 4000
- 5000
- 6000

Spot heights in metres

Australia

Scale 1:19 000 000

0   200   400   600 km.

B   C   D   E   F   G

Equator

Samarinda

Gulf of Tomini   Molucca Sea

Strait of Makassar

2279   Sula Is.   Obi Is.   990

Tolo Bay   3016   Moluccas   3019   Ceram

Celebes (Sulawesi)   1731   Ambon

Buru

Gulf of Bone

Ujung Pandang   2871   Muna   Kabaena   Butung

Kangean Is.   200 metres

Flores Sea   Sorong   Misoöl   Doberaï Penin.   Manokwari   Biak   Japen

Kaimana   2239   IRIAN   New   Djayapura   Aitape   Wewak

5030   DJAJA PEAK   4700   JAYA   3860   Central Range   Guinea   PAPUA

Banda Sea   Kai Is.   Aru Is.   Fly   Gulf of Papua

Wetar   Lomblen   Alor   Tanimbar Is.   Dolak I.   C. Vals   Merauke

5°S   Bali Sea   3142   3726   2851   Sumbawa   2300   Flores   Dili   2920   Timor   Arafura Sea

Lombok   999   Waingapu   Kupang   Roti   Torres Strait   Thursday I.   C. York   714

Lombok Str.   Sumba   Suvu   Suvu Sea   Pantar   597   Weipa   Cape York   586   Great

10°S   Timor Sea   Melville I.   Bathurst I.   Darwin   Gulf of   Groote Eylandt   Cooktown   1387   Mitchell

Joseph Bonaparte Gulf   Rum Jungle   Arnhem Land   Carpentaria   Wellesley Is.   Normanton   Croydon   Gilbert   Herb

A   C. Talbot   Daly   Katherine   NORTHERN   Forsayth   Norman

3   Wyndham   Victoria   Birdum   Flinders   Cloncurry   Hughenden

C. Leveque   Daly Waters   Barkly Plateau   Camooweal   Mount Isa   QUEENSL

15°S   Yampi Sound   Ord   Tennant Creek   TERRITORY   Dajarra   Winton

Dampier Land   Derby   936   Halls Creek   1510   Longreach   Barcoo

Broome   Fitzroy   Alice Springs   Yaraka

200 metres   Great Sandy Desert   Macdonnell Ranges   Simpson Desert   Quilpie

Port Hedland   80 Mile Beach   MT. GOLDSWORTHY   707   1515   Oodnadatta   Cooper Creek   Cunnamulla

20°S   Monte Bello Is.   133   L. Mackay   SOUTHERN   Marree   Lake Eyre   1059   Sturt Desert

Marble Bar   Lake Disappointment   342   994   W E S T E R N   Mt. Eba   Leigh Creek   Lake Frome   Darling

Exmouth Gulf   Fortescue   Hamersley Ra.   1227   Gibson Desert   A U S T R A L I A   Tarcoola   L. Torrens   Woomera

Ashburton   A U S T R A L I A   564   Great Victoria Desert   Ooldea   Lake Gairdner   Iron Knob   Broken Hill

5   Carnarvon   Wiluna   594   Ceduna   Whyalla   Quorn   933

Dirk Hartog I.   Murchison   Meekatharra   565   Nullarbor Plain   Forrest   Eucla   Port Pirie   Flinders Range   Murray   Mildura

25°S   Mt. Magnet   Leonora   Laverton   Port Augusta   Lofty Ra.   Murrumb

Geraldton   Kalgoorlie   Zanthus   Great   Port Lincoln   Spencer Gulf   Adelaide   Swan River   Ec

6   Coolgardie   Southern Cross   Norseman   Australian Bight   C. Catastrophe   Murray Bridge   VICTO   Lach

30°S   Perth   Northam   585   Kangaroo I.   Bendigo

Fremantle   Esperance   Recherche Archipelago   1167   Ballarat

C. Naturaliste   Bunbury   1109   Mt. Gambier   Geelong

7   C. Leeuwin   Albany   Warrnambool   Melbourne

I N D I A N   O C E A N   King I.

35°S   Bur   MT.

8   Zenithal Equidistant Projection   TASMANIA

115°E   120°E   125°E   130°E   135°E   140°E

40

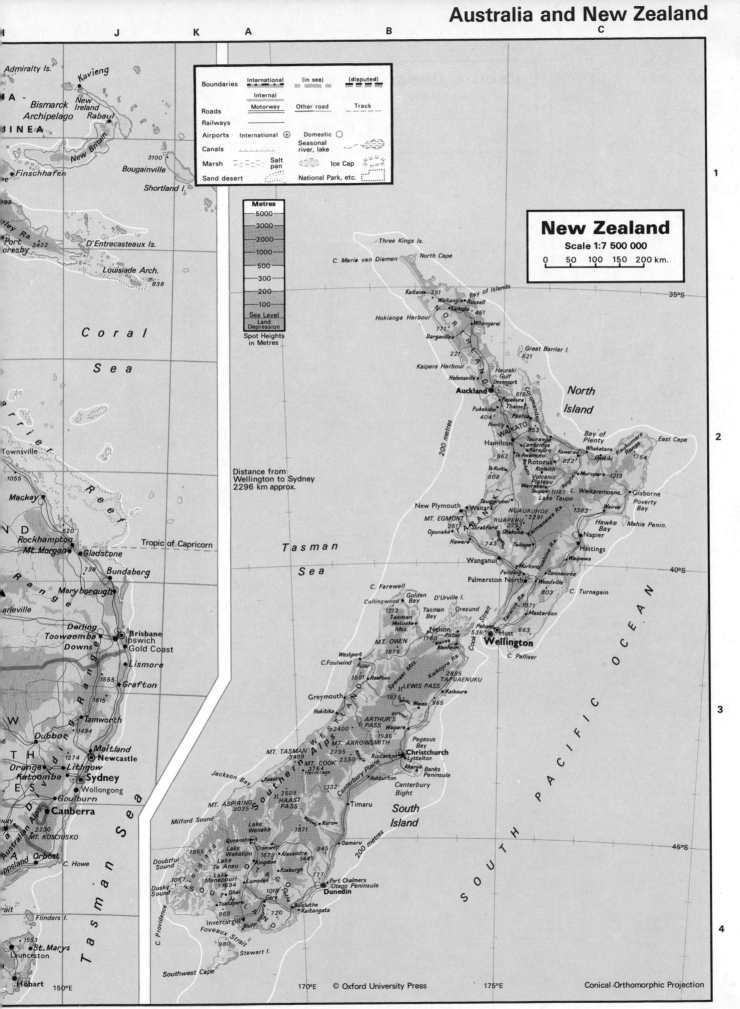

I J K A B C

Admiralty Is.
Kavieng
New Ireland
Bismarck Archipelago
Rabaul
JINEA
New Britain
Finschhafen
3100
Bougainville
Shortland I.

Three Kings Is.
C. Maria van Diemen   North Cape

ley Ra
Port oresby   3422
D'Entrecasteaux Is.
Louisiade Arch.
838

Metres
5000
3000
2000
1000
500
300
200
100
Sea Level
Land Depression
Spot Heights in Metres

New Zealand
Scale 1:7 500 000
0   50   100   150   200 km.

Kaitaia 751   Bay of Islands
Waitangi Russell
Kaikohe • 461
Hokianga Harbour   Whangarei
Dargaville   771
221

35°S

C o r a l

S e a

Kaipara Harbour
Helensville
Hauraki Gulf
Devonport
Auckland
Pukekohe Papakura Thames
404 Paeroa
Huntly
WAIKATO 853

Great Barrier I.
621

North Island

rrier Reef
Townsville
1055

Mackay

Hamilton
Te Awamutu Cambridge
962 Karapiro
Te Kuiti Rotorua
808 Kinleith
Volcanic
Plateau
Wairakei
Taupo 1087
Lake Taupo

Bay of Plenty
Tauranga Whakatane
Kawerau Opotiki
822 Murupara
1213
L. Waikaremoana
NGAURUHOE
1383

East Cape
Raukumara Range
1754

620
Rockhampton
Mt. Morgan   Gladstone
738 Bundaberg

New Plymouth Waitara
MT. EGMONT Taranaki
2517 Stratford
Opunake Ohakune
Hawera 743

RUAPEHU
2791
Taihape
Kaimanawa Ra.
Raetihi

Gisborne
Poverty Bay
Wairoa
Mahia Penin.
Hawke Bay
Napier
Hastings
Waipawa

Maryborough
arleville

T a s m a n

S e a

Tropic of Capricorn

Distance from
Wellington to Sydney
2296 km approx.

Wanganui
Feilding Morton
Palmerston North Dannevirke
Woodville
803

C. Turnagain

40°S

ND
Darling Brisbane
Toowoomba Ipswich
Downs Gold Coast
Lismore

C. Farewell
Collingwood Golden Bay
1213
Tasman Motueka
Mts.
MT. OWEN Nelson
1876 1760

D'Urville I.
Tasman Bay Oresund
Waimea Picton
Wairau Blenheim

Tararua Ra.
1571 Masterton
Pahiatua
663
536
Wellington
Hutt

C. Palliser

1555
Grafton
1615

Westport
C. Foulwind Buller
Reefton 1501
Greymouth
Hokitika
ARTHUR'S
PASS 2400

Spenser Mts.
LEWIS PASS
TAPUAENUKU
2885
Kaikoura Ra.
Kaikoura
1875 Waiau
Waiau 965
Hurunui
Waipara

Cook Strait

Tamworth
1494
Dubbo
Maitland
1274 Newcastle
Orange Lithgow
Katoomba Sydney
Wollongong
Goulburn
Canberra
2230
MT. KOSCIUSKO

MT. TASMAN 1935
3498 MT. ARROWSMITH
MT. COOK 2795 2330
3764
Hermitage
Jackson Bay Haast
1332
MT. ASPIRING 2508
3035 HAAST
PASS
Milford Sound

Pegasus Bay
Riccarton **Christchurch**
Lyttelton
Akaroa Banks
Peninsula
Ashburton
Canterbury
Bight

South Island

Orbost
C. Howe

Doubtful Sound
1067
Dusky Sound
869
C. Providence

Queenstown
Lake
Wanaka
Lake
Wakatipu Cromwell
1679 Alexandra
Lake
Te Anau Kingston 1449
1694 Roxburgh
Lake
Manapouri 777
Ohai 1018
720
Gore
Tuatapere
980 Bluff
Invercargill
Foveaux Strait
Stewart I.
Southwest Cape

Milton 945 Oamaru
Kurow
1871

Balclutha
Kaitangata
Dunedin
Port Chalmers
Otago Peninsula

200 metres

Timaru

45°S

S O U T H   P A C I F I C   O C E A N

Flinders I.
1593
St. Marys
Launceston
Hobart

150°E   170°E   © Oxford University Press   175°E   Conical Orthomorphic Projection

1

2

3

4

Pacific Ocean

Scale 1:63 000 000

0 km 500   1000   1500   2000

Ocean Currents
→ Warm currents
⇢ Cold currents

Metres
5000
3000
2000
1000
500
300
200
100
Sea Level
Land depression
−200
−3000
−4000
−5000
−6000

Spot heights in metres

Modified Zenithal Equidistant Projection

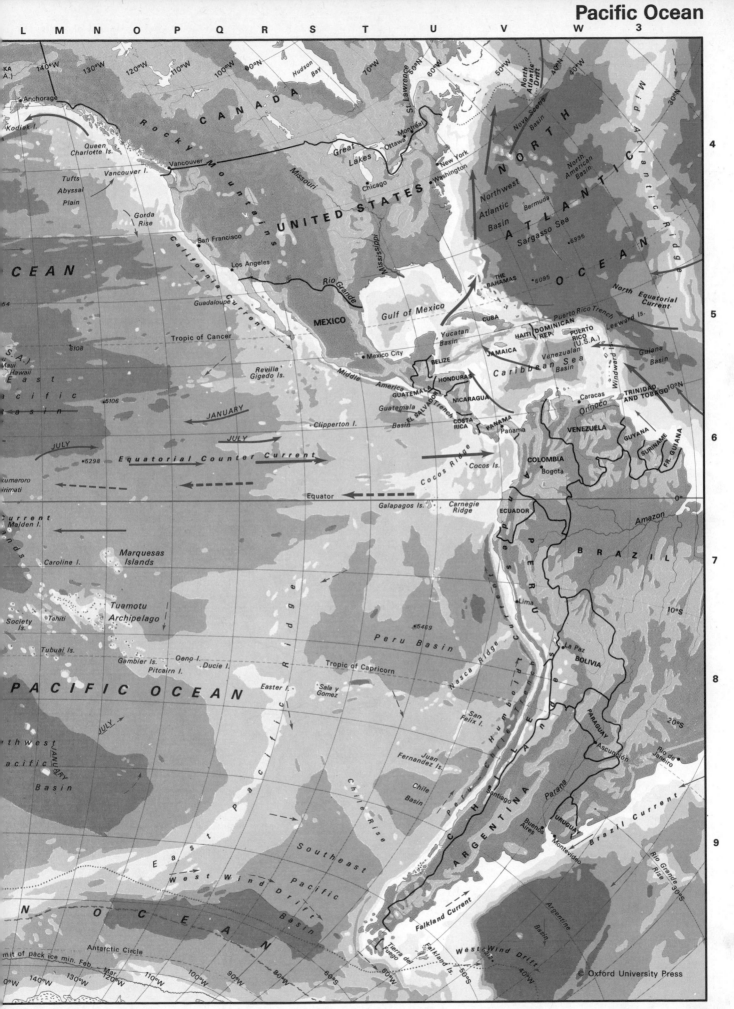

L M N O P Q R S T U V W 3

140°W 130°W 120°W 110°W 100°W 80°N 70°W 60°W 50°W

4

ALA.S.
K.A.)
Anchorage
Kodiak I.
Queen
Charlotte Is.
Vancouver
Vancouver I.
Tufts
Abyssal
Plain
Gorda
Rise
San Francisco
Los Angeles
Guadaloupe Current

CANADA

Rocky Mountains

Hudson Bay

Great Lakes

St. Lawrence

Montréal
Ottawa
Chicago
New York
Washington

UNITED STATES

Missouri
Mississippi
Rio Grande

NORTH ATLANTIC OCEAN

North Atlantic Drift

Nova Scotia Basin

Northwest
Atlantic
Basin

North
American
Basin

Bermuda

Sargasso Sea

•6995

Mid Atlantic Ridge

30°N

•6095

North Equatorial Current

5

OCEAN

54

Tropic of Cancer

MEXICO
Mexico City

5108

Revilla
Gigedo Is.

U.S.A.)
Maui
Hawaii

East

Pacific

Basin

5106

JANUARY

JULY

5298

Equatorial Counter Current

JULY

Gulf of Mexico

THE
BAHAMAS

CUBA

Yucatan
Basin

HAITI
DOMINICAN
REP.

PUERTO
RICO
(U.S.A.)

Puerto Rico Trench

Leeward Is.

Guiana
Basin

JAMAICA

Venezuelan
Basin

Caribbean Sea

Windward Is.

TRINIDAD
AND TOBAGO

North
Equatorial
Current

BELIZE

Middle

America

GUATEMALA

HONDURAS

Guatemala
Basin

EL SALVADOR

NICARAGUA

COSTA
RICA

Trench

Clipperton I.

PANAMA
Panama

Cocos Ridge

Cocos Is.

Caracas
Orinoco

VENEZUELA

GUYANA

SURINAME

FR. GUIANA

6

COLOMBIA
Bogota

Amazon

10°N

0°

umaroro
irimati

Current
Malden I.

Caroline I.

Marquesas
Islands

Equator

Galapagos Is.

Carnegie
Ridge

ECUADOR

BRAZIL

7

Society
Is.
Tahiti

Tuamotu
Archipelago

Lima

PERU

10°S

Tubuai Is.

Gambier Is.

Oeno I.
Ducie I.
Pitcairn I.

5469

Peru Basin

La Paz
BOLIVIA

Tropic of Capricorn

8

PACIFIC OCEAN

Easter I.

Sala y
Gomez

Nasca Ridge

PARAGUAY
Ascunción

20°S

San
Felix I.

Juan
Fernandez Is.

Chile
Basin

Rio de
Janeiro

thwest
acific
Basin

JULY

JANUARY

East

Pacific

Ridge

Chile Rise

Santiago

Parana

ARGENTINA

CHILE

Humboldt Current

Peru Current

Buenos
Aires

Montevideo

URUGUAY

Brazil Current

Rio Grande Rise

30°S

9

Southeast

Pacific

Basin

West Wind Drift

N   OCEAN

Falkland Current

Tierra del
Fuego

Falkland Is.

West Wind Drift

Argentine
Basin

Antarctic Circle

mit of pack ice min. Feb

Mar

60°S

© Oxford University Press

140°W 130°W 120°W 110°W 100°W 90°W 80°W 60°W 50°W 40°W

North and South America: Physical

Scale 1:44 000 000

0   1000   2000 km

Metres	
5000	
3000	
2000	
1000	
500	
300	
200	
100	
Sea level	
Land depression	
200	
3000	
4000	
5000	
6000	

Spot heights in metres

UNITED KINGDOM
IRELAND

NORTH ATLANTIC OCEAN

West European Basin

PEAK 5344

Mid Atlantic Ridge

Cape Verde Basin

Tropic of Cancer

Azores

Reykjanes Ridge

Arctic Circle

ICELAND

GREENLAND

Labrador Basin

Newfoundland

Limit of pack ice - min.

Limit of pack ice - max.

Nova Scotia Basin

BERMUDA (U.K.)

Sargasso Sea •6995

Baffin Bay

Baffin Island

Labrador Peninsula

Northwest Atlantic Basin

•6095

Ungava Pen.

St. Lawrence

Hudson

Puerto Rico Trench

PUERTO RICO

LEEWARD Is.
BARBUDA
ANTIGUA
ST. KITTS-
NEVIS
DOMINICA

Hudson Bay

CANADA

Lake Winnipeg

Great Lakes

Appalachians

THE BAHAMAS

TURKS & CAICOS IS. (U.K.)

HAITI
DOMINICAN
REPUBLIC

Polar Ice
N. Magnetic Pole
Queen Elizabeth
Islands 1981

Arctic Ocean

Victoria Island

Banks Island

75°N

Mackenzie

Peace

Missouri

Platte

UNITED STATES

Maximum extent of glaciation

Mississippi

CUBA

JAMAICA

Caribbean Sea

Yucatan Basin

ALASKA (U.S.A.)

Yukon

Fraser

Rocky Mountains

Snake

Colorado

Rio Grande

Gulf of Mexico

Yucatan

MEXICO

Columbia

Vancouver I.

Queen Charlotte Is.

Gulf of Alaska

Kodiak Island

Bering Sea

Aleutian Islands

60°N

BELIZE
HONDURAS
GUATEMALA
EL SALVADOR

Middle America

Revilla Gigedo Is.

Guadaloupe

Tropic of Cancer

Clipperton I.

NORTH PACIFIC OCEAN

45°N

30°N

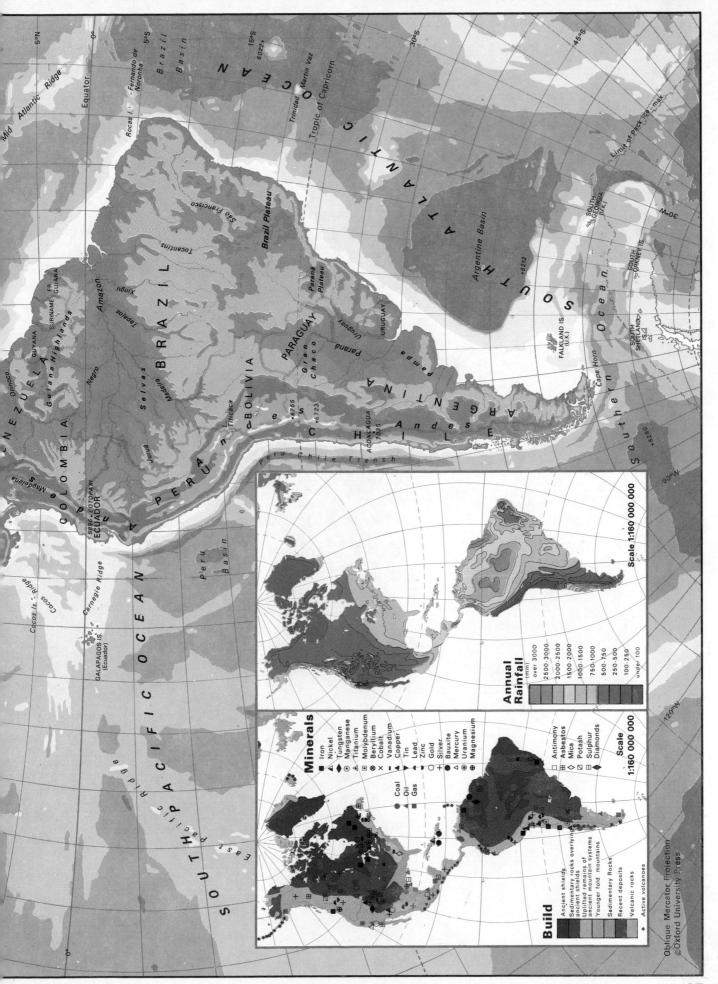

46

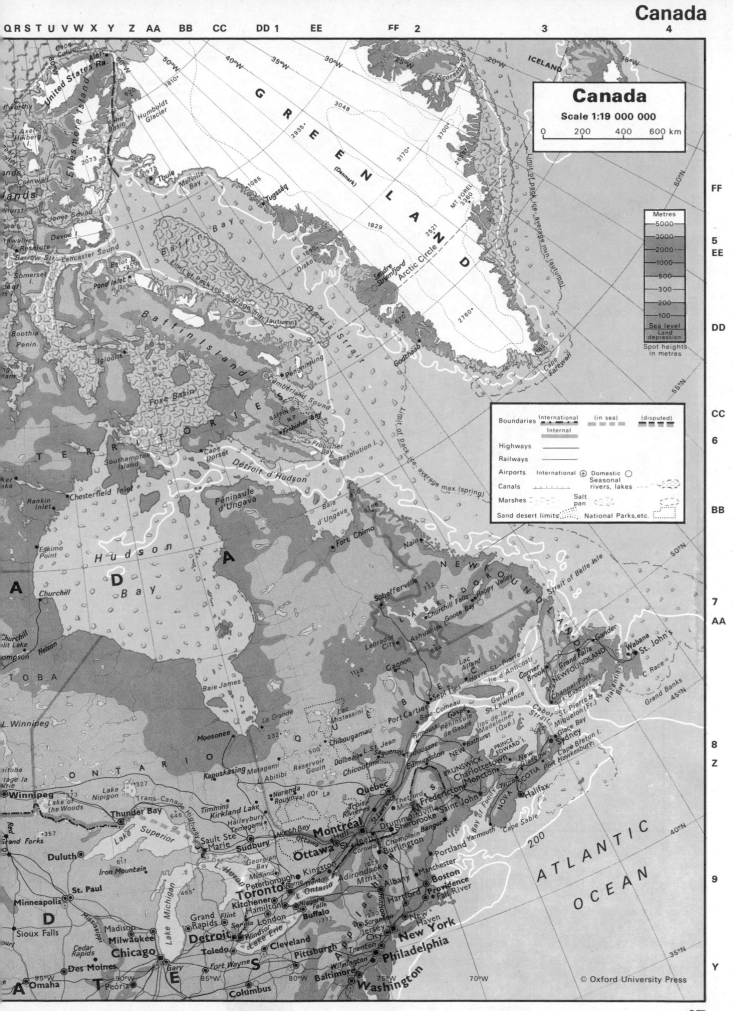

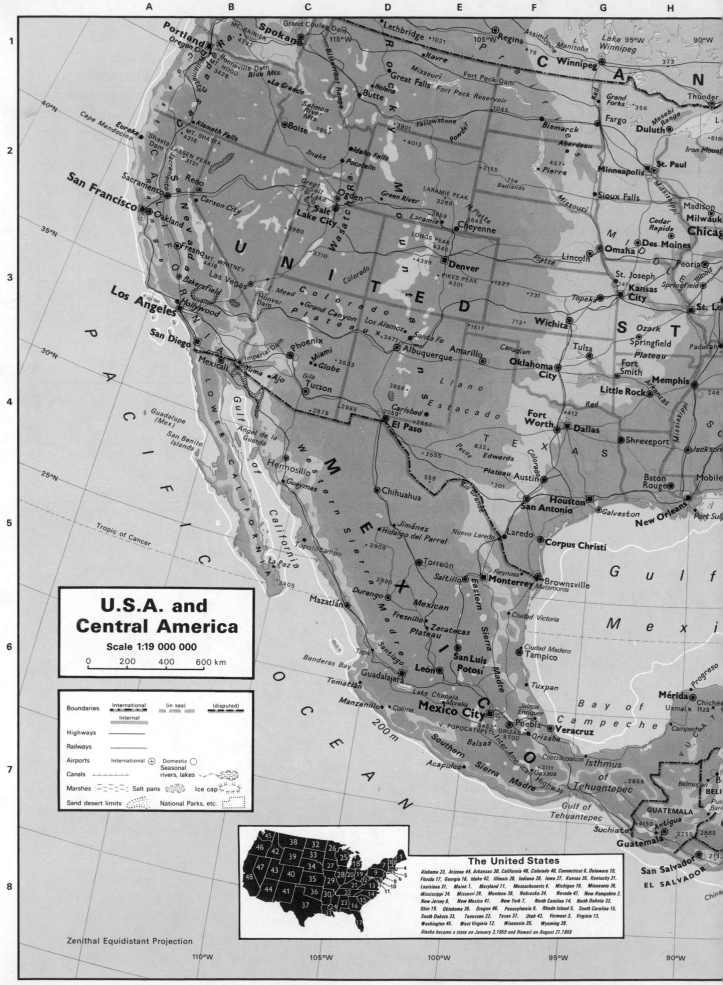

U.S.A. and
Central America

Scale 1:19 000 000

0   200   400   600 km

Boundaries   International   (in sea)   (disputed)
             Internal
Highways
Railways
Airports   International ⊕   Domestic ○
Canals   Seasonal
                             rivers, lakes
Marshes   Salt pans
Sand desert limits   National Parks, etc.

The United States
Alabama 23, Arizona 44, Arkansas 30, California 48, Colorado 40, Connecticut 6, Delaware 10,
Florida 17, Georgia 16, Idaho 42, Illinois 28, Indiana 20, Iowa 27, Kansas 35, Kentucky 21,
Louisiana 31, Maine 1, Maryland 11, Massachusetts 4, Michigan 18, Minnesota 26,
Mississippi 24, Missouri 29, Montana 38, Nebraska 34, Nevada 47, New Hampshire 2,
New Jersey 8, New Mexico 41, New York 7, North Carolina 14, North Dakota 32,
Ohio 19, Oklahoma 36, Oregon 46, Pennsylvania 9, Rhode Island 5, South Carolina 15,
South Dakota 33, Tennessee 22, Texas 37, Utah 43, Vermont 3, Virginia 13,
Washington 45, West Virginia 12, Wisconsin 25, Wyoming 39.
Alaska became a state on January 3, 1959 and Hawaii on August 21, 1959

Zenithal Equidistant Projection

48

K   L   M   N   O   P   Q   R

Moosonee 80°W 232 75°W Lac Mistassini Sept Îles Gulf of St. Lawrence Channel-Port aux Basques Miquelon (Fr.) C. Race 55°W 50°W 45°W 1

Kapuskasing Gaspé 1268 Gaspé Peninsula Magdalen Is. PRINCE EDWARD I. Sydney Mines Placentia Bay 40°N

S. Porcupine Timmins L. Abitibi L. St. Jean Gouin Res. Tadoussac Edmundston Charlottetown Pictou Canso Sydney

Kirkland Lake Quebec Trois Rivieres Fredericton Moncton SCOTIA 35°N 2

Cobalt Montreal 1605 Thetford Mines Saint John Halifax

Sault Ste. Marie Sudbury Ottawa L. Champlain Bangor Bay of Fundy Cape Sable 200 m.

Lake Huron Georgian Bay Midland Kingston Burlington MT. WASHINGTON Portland

Toronto Hamilton L. Ontario Rochester Albany Manchester

Grand Rapids Flint Niagara Falls Syracuse Utica Hartford Boston Providence 3

Detroit Windsor Buffalo Scranton New Haven Fall River Cape Cod Long Island

Toledo Lake Erie Cleveland 776 Pittsburgh Jersey City New York

Fort Wayne 724 Trenton Philadelphia

Indianapolis Columbus Wilmington Baltimore Washington Delaware Bay

Cincinnati 1481 Richmond Newport News Chesapeake Bay

Louisville Lexington Charleston James Norfolk Cape Hatteras 4

Nashville Bristol 1265 Winston-Salem Raleigh

Knoxville MT. MITCHELL 2036 Charlotte

Chattanooga 632 Columbia Wilmington

Gadsden Atlanta Augusta Charleston

Birmingham Macon Savannah

Columbus Montgomery

Jacksonville

Daytona Beach

Tampa Cape Canaveral Melbourne

Lake Okeechobee Palm Beach

Miami

Key West Florida Keys Straits of Florida

Havana Matanzas Santa Clara Andros Eleuthera Cat I. San Salvador (Watling) Tropic of Cancer 5

Pinar del Rio C U B A Cienfuegos Holguin Long I. THE BAHAMAS Acklins I.

Camagüey 1799 Great Inagua Caicos Islands (Br.)

Santiago de Cuba Guantánamo Windward Passage Turks Is. (Br.)

Montego Bay Cap-Haitien HAITI Santiago DOMINICAN REPUBLIC San Juan 6

JAMAICA Kingston Port-au-Prince Les Cayes Santo Domingo PUERTO RICO

Spanish Town Hispaniola Mayaguez

Caribbean Sea

200 m 7

URAS Trujillo Segovia C. Gracias a Dios

ucigalpa NICARAGUA Matagalpa

Managua Lake Nicaragua 8

COSTA San José Puerto Limón Colón

RICA Puntarenas Portobello

Panama Canal Colón G. of Darien P A N A M A Panama COLOMBIA Turbo Cucuta

Sta. Marta Pt. de Gallinas Aruba (Neth.) Curaçao (Neth.) Willemstad Bonaire (Neth.)

Barranquilla Maracaibo Cabimas Valencia Caracas La Guaira

Cartagena Magdalena Lake of Maracaibo Barquisimeto Maracay Calabozo

Gulf of Venezuela 853 VENEZUELA Orinoco

Cord. de Mérida Ciudad Bolívar

70°W 65°W 60°W 85°W

ATLANTIC OCEAN

BERMUDA

200 m

W E S T I N D I E S

Greater Antilles Lesser Antilles

Anegada Passage Virgin Is. Sombrero Anguilla St. Martin (Fr. & Neth.) 15°N

St. Croix (U.S.) Sombrero passage ST. KITTS NEVIS BARBUDA ANTIGUA

St. Thomas (U.S.) Arecibo Montserrat Guadeloupe (Fr.) Basse-Terre

La Romana Ponce Mona Passage Leeward Islands Marie-Galante (Fr.) DOMINICA

Les Saintes Fort de France Martinique (Fr.)

Windward Islands ST. LUCIA 7

ST. VINCENT BARBADOS Bridgetown

Grenadines GRENADA Tobago

Margarita Is. Port of Spain TRINIDAD & TOBAGO 10°N San Fernando

Cumaná Barcelona Maturin Tucupita

GUYANA Georgetown Mackenzie

© Oxford University Press

Panama Canal inset

ATLANTIC   Gaillard Cut (Culebra)   PACIFIC
Maximum elevation 95 m

Minimum depth 12 m

Sea level   Sea level   Sea level

0   15   30   45   60   75km

Gatun Locks 3 pairs	Pedro Miguel Locks 1 pair	Miraflores Locks 2 pairs
Length 305 m	Length 305 m	Length 305 m
Width 34 m	Width 34 m	Width 34 m
Total Lift 26 m	Total Lift 9·3 m	Total Lift 16·6 m

Panama Canal
1 cm to 15 km approx.

ATLANTIC OCEAN

80°W Colón

Gatun Locks

P A N A M A

Gatun Lake CANAL ZONE

Pedro Miguel Locks Miraflores Locks

Balboa Panama 9°N

PACIFIC OCEAN

PANAMA: The canal, opened in 1914, is 80 km long, including approaches (actual canal 64 km). Minimum depth 12 m, minimum width 152 m (Gaillard Cut). Time of passage 8 hours. In 1978 12 677 vessels used the canal carrying 142 518 288 tonnes of cargo. In 1978 the Canal Zone became Panamanian territory but the U.S.A. will operate the Canal until 1999.

Metres scale

Metres
5000
3000
2000
1000
500
300
200
100
Sea level
Land depression

Spot heights in metres

Eastern
United States

Scale 1:8 000 000

0   100   200km

Boundaries
International   (in sea)   (disputed)
Internal
Roads   Limited access   Other highways   Tracks
Railways
Airports   International ⊕   Domestic ○
Canals
Marshes   Salt Pan   Seasonal rivers, lakes   Ice cap
Sand desert limits   National Parks etc.

Conical Orthomorphic Projection

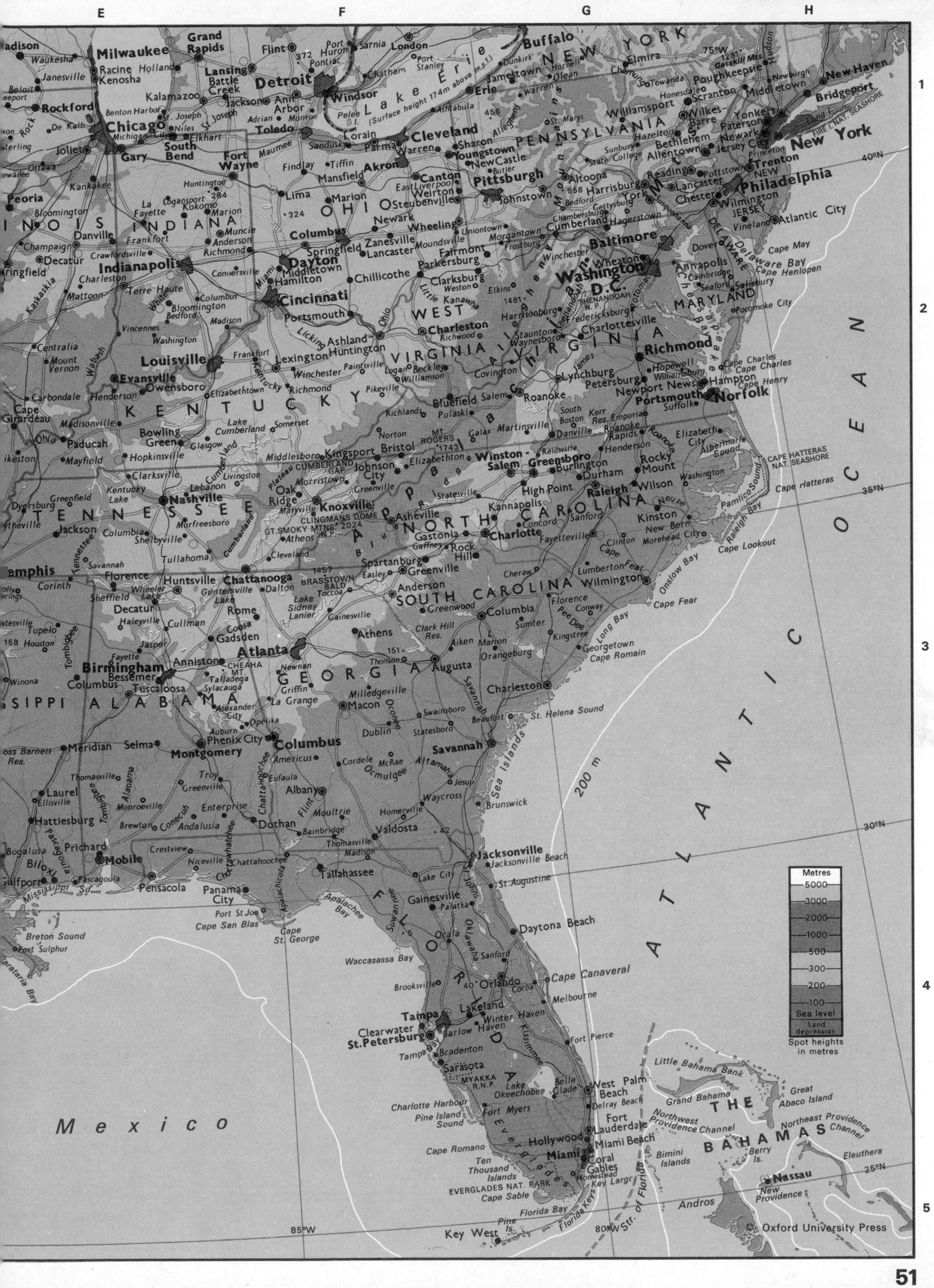

E
F
G
H
1
2
3
4
5
Milwaukee
Waukesha
Janesville
Beloit
Racine
Kenosha
Rockford
De Kalb
Chicago
Joliet
Gary
Peoria
Bloomington
Champaign
Danville
Decatur
Kankakee
Grand Rapids
Holland
Kalamazoo
Lansing
Battle Creek
Jackson
Benton Harbor
St. Joseph
Niles
Elkhart
South Bend
Fort Wayne
Michigan City
Flint
Port Huron
Sarnia
London
Pontiac
Detroit
Windsor
Ann Arbor
Adrian
Monroe
Toledo
Chatham
Lake Erie
(Surface height 174m above m.s.l.)
Pelee I.
Lorain
Cleveland
Sandusky
Parma
Akron
Warren
Sharon
Youngstown
New Castle
Butler
Pittsburgh
Johnstown
Erie
Ashtabula
Buffalo
Dunkirk
Jamestown
Olean
Hornell
Elmira
Corning
Towanda
NEW YORK
PENNSYLVANIA
Williamsport
Wilkes-Barre
Scranton
Hazelton
Bethlehem
Allentown
Sunbury
State College
Altoona
Harrisburg
York
Lancaster
Reading
Pottstown
Chester
Philadelphia
Trenton
Princeton
NEW JERSEY
Atlantic City
Vineland
Wilmington
Poughkeepsie
Newburgh
Middletown
New Haven
Bridgeport
Yonkers
Paterson
Newark
Jersey City
New York
FIRE I. NAT. SEASHORE
Long Island
Catskill Mts.
Hudson
75°W
40°N
Maumee
Findlay
Tiffin
Mansfield
Lima
Marion
OHIO
Columbus
Springfield
Dayton
Middletown
Hamilton
Cincinnati
Zanesville
Lancaster
Newark
Chillicothe
Portsmouth
Canton
East Liverpool
Weirton
Steubenville
Wheeling
Moundsville
Uniontown
Morgantown
Fairmont
Parkersburg
Clarksburg
Weston
Elkins
Cumberland
Frostburg
Hagerstown
Chambersburg
Gettysburg
Bedford
Baltimore
Washington D.C.
Wheaton
Winchester
Annapolis
Cambridge
Seaford
Salisbury
Dover
DELAWARE
Delaware Bay
Cape May
Cape Henlopen
MARYLAND
Pocomoke City
Chesapeake Bay
Huntington
Logansport
Kokomo
Marion
La Fayette
INDIANA
ILLINOIS
Muncie
Anderson
Richmond
Indianapolis
Crawfordsville
Connersville
Terre Haute
Charleston
Mattoon
Bloomington
Columbus
Bedford
Vincennes
Washington
Madison
Springfield
Centralia
Mount Vernon
Evansville
Owensboro
Henderson
Carbondale
Cape Girardeau
Paducah
Mayfield
Louisville
Frankfort
Lexington
Winchester
Richmond
Elizabethtown
KENTUCKY
Bowling Green
Hopkinsville
Madisonville
Glasgow
Lake Cumberland
Somerset
Paintsville
Pikeville
Ashland
Huntington
Charleston
Richwood
WEST VIRGINIA
Logan
Beckley
Williamson
Bluefield
Pulaski
Richlands
Norton
Kingsport
Bristol
Johnson City
Elizabethton
Middlesboro
CUMBERLAND GAP
MT. ROGERS 1743
Galax
Martinsville
Harrisonburg
Staunton
Waynesboro
Charlottesville
Fredericksburg
SHENANDOAH N.P.
VIRGINIA
Richmond
Hopewell
Williamsburg
Petersburg
Lynchburg
Roanoke
Salem
Covington
Newport News
Hampton
Norfolk
Portsmouth
Suffolk
Cape Charles
Cape Henry
South Boston
Kerr Res.
Emporia
Danville
Roanoke Rapids
Elizabeth City
Albemarle Sound
CAPE HATTERAS NAT. SEASHORE
Cape Hatteras
Pamlico Sound
Washington
Winston-Salem
Greensboro
Reidsville
Burlington
Durham
Henderson
Rocky Mount
Wilson
Raleigh
High Point
Statesville
Kannapolis
Concord
Charlotte
Gastonia
Sanford
Fayetteville
NORTH CAROLINA
Kinston
New Bern
Morehead City
Raleigh Bay
Cape Lookout
Onslow Bay
Clinton
Lumberton
Cape Fear
Wilmington
Knoxville
Asheville
Maryville
Oak Ridge
Morristown
Greeneville
CLINGMANS DOME 2024
GT. SMOKY MTNS. N.P.
Athens
Cleveland
Chattanooga
Nashville
Lebanon
Murfreesboro
Clarksville
Kentucky Lake
TENNESSEE
Dyersburg
Jackson
Columbia
Shelbyville
Tullahoma
Memphis
Corinth
Savannah
Florence
Sheffield
Decatur
Huntsville
Wheeler Lake
Guntersville Lake
Dalton
Rome
Cullman
Gadsden
Anniston
Birmingham
Bessemer
Tuscaloosa
Tupelo
Columbus
Talladega
Sylacauga
CHEAHA MT.
Alexander City
ALABAMA
MISSISSIPPI
Meridian
Selma
Montgomery
Auburn
Opelika
Phenix City
Columbus
Troy
Greenville
Enterprise
Dothan
Andalusia
Brewton
Laurel
Ellisville
Hattiesburg
Prichard
Mobile
Biloxi
Gulfport
Pascagoula
Pensacola
Crestview
Niceville
Panama City
Port St Joe
Cape San Blas
Cape St. George
Apalachee Bay
Tallahassee
BRASSTOWN BALD 1457
Toccoa
Gainesville
Lake Sidney Lanier
Athens
Atlanta
Newnan
Griffin
La Grange
GEORGIA
Macon
Milledgeville
Augusta
Thomson
Clark Hill Res.
Dublin
Swainsboro
Statesboro
Savannah
Americus
Albany
Cordele
McRae
Ocmulgee
Altamaha
Jesup
Waycross
Brunswick
Sea Islands
Moultrie
Homerville
Valdosta
Thomasville
Bainbridge
Spartanburg
Greenville
Easley
Anderson
Greenwood
Rock Hill
Gaffney
SOUTH CAROLINA
Columbia
Cheraw
Florence
Conway
Pee Dee
Sumter
Aiken
Marion
Orangeburg
Kingstree
Georgetown
Cape Romain
Long Bay
Charleston
Beaufort
St. Helena Sound
Jacksonville
Jacksonville Beach
St. Augustine
Lake City
Madison
Gainesville
Palatka
Ocala
Daytona Beach
FLORIDA
Suwannee
Oklawaha
Sanford
Orlando
Cocoa
Cape Canaveral
Melbourne
Brooksville
Waccasassa Bay
Tampa
Lakeland
Winter Haven
Clearwater
St. Petersburg
Barlow
Tampa Bay
Bradenton
Sarasota
MYAKKA R.N.P.
Kissimmee
Fort Pierce
Lake Okeechobee
Belle Glade
West Palm Beach
Delray Beach
Fort Lauderdale
Hollywood
Miami
Miami Beach
Coral Gables
Homestead
Key Largo
Charlotte Harbour
Pine Island Sound
Fort Myers
Everglades
Cape Romano
Ten Thousand Islands
EVERGLADES NAT. PARK
Cape Sable
Florida Bay
Florida Keys
Key West
Pine Is.
Str. of Florida
80°W
85°W
30°N
25°N
35°N
200 m
Gulf of Mexico
Breton Sound
Port Sulphur
Barataria Bay
ATLANTIC OCEAN
THE BAHAMAS
Little Bahama Bank
Grand Bahama
Great Abaco Island
Northwest Providence Channel
Northeast Providence Channel
Bimini Islands
Berry Is.
Andros
Nassau
New Providence
Eleuthera
Metres
5000
3000
2000
1000
500
300
200
100
Sea level
Land depression
Spot heights in metres
© Oxford University Press

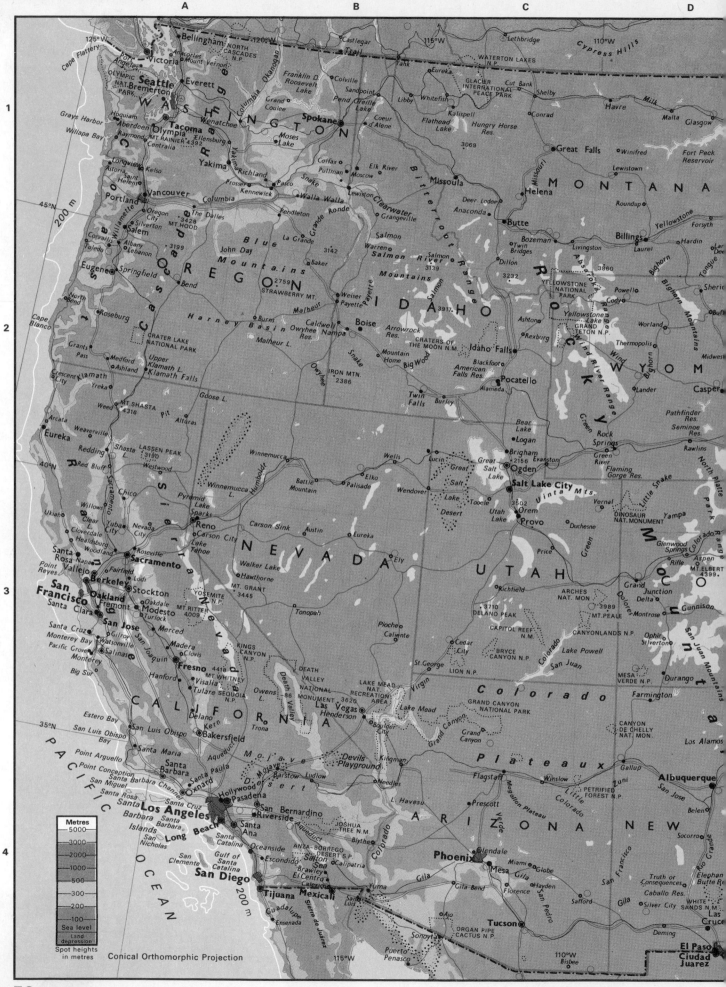

A   B   C   D

Metres
5000
3000
2000
1000
500
300
200
100
Sea level
Land
depression
Spot heights
in metres

Conical Orthomorphic Projection

52

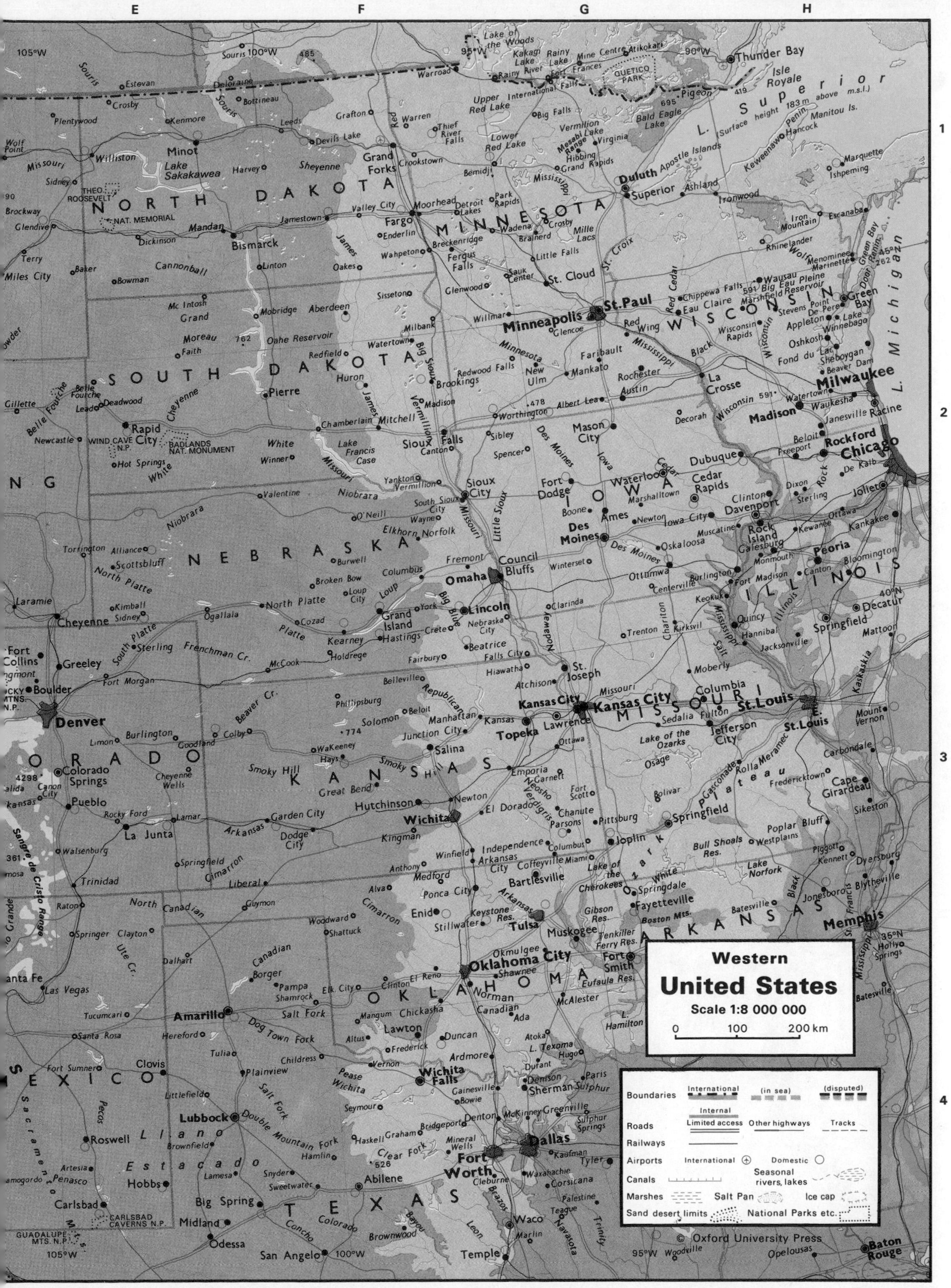

E F G H

Western United States

Scale 1:8 000 000

0   100   200 km

Boundaries	International	(in sea)	(disputed)
	Internal		
Roads	Limited access	Other highways	Tracks
Railways			
Airports	International ⊕	Domestic ○	
Canals		Seasonal rivers, lakes	
Marshes	Salt Pan	Ice cap	
Sand desert limits	National Parks etc.		

© Oxford University Press

States and regions: NORTH DAKOTA, SOUTH DAKOTA, MINNESOTA, WISCONSIN, NEBRASKA, IOWA, ILLINOIS, COLORADO, KANSAS, MISSOURI, OKLAHOMA, ARKANSAS, TEXAS, NEW MEXICO

Selected cities and places: Thunder Bay, Duluth, Superior, Minneapolis, St. Paul, Milwaukee, Madison, Chicago, Rockford, Fargo, Grand Forks, Bismarck, Mandan, Minot, Williston, Pierre, Rapid City, Sioux Falls, Sioux City, Des Moines, Omaha, Lincoln, Cedar Rapids, Davenport, Peoria, Springfield, Decatur, Denver, Boulder, Colorado Springs, Pueblo, Cheyenne, Kansas City, Topeka, Wichita, St. Louis, St. Joseph, Columbia, Jefferson City, Springfield, Tulsa, Oklahoma City, Fort Smith, Fayetteville, Memphis, Amarillo, Lubbock, Wichita Falls, Dallas, Fort Worth, Abilene, San Angelo, Odessa, Midland, Big Spring, Roswell, Carlsbad, Hobbs, Baton Rouge

L. Superior, L. Michigan, Lake Sakakawea, Oahe Reservoir, Missouri, Mississippi, Lake of the Woods, Rainy Lake

105°W   100°W   95°W   90°W

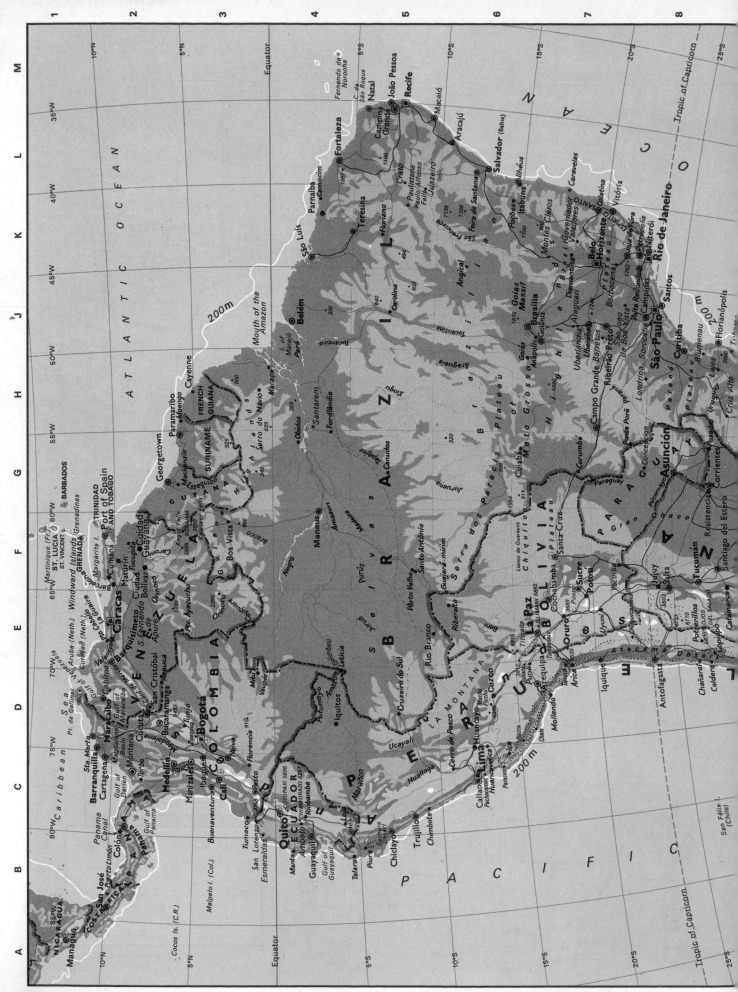

54

South America

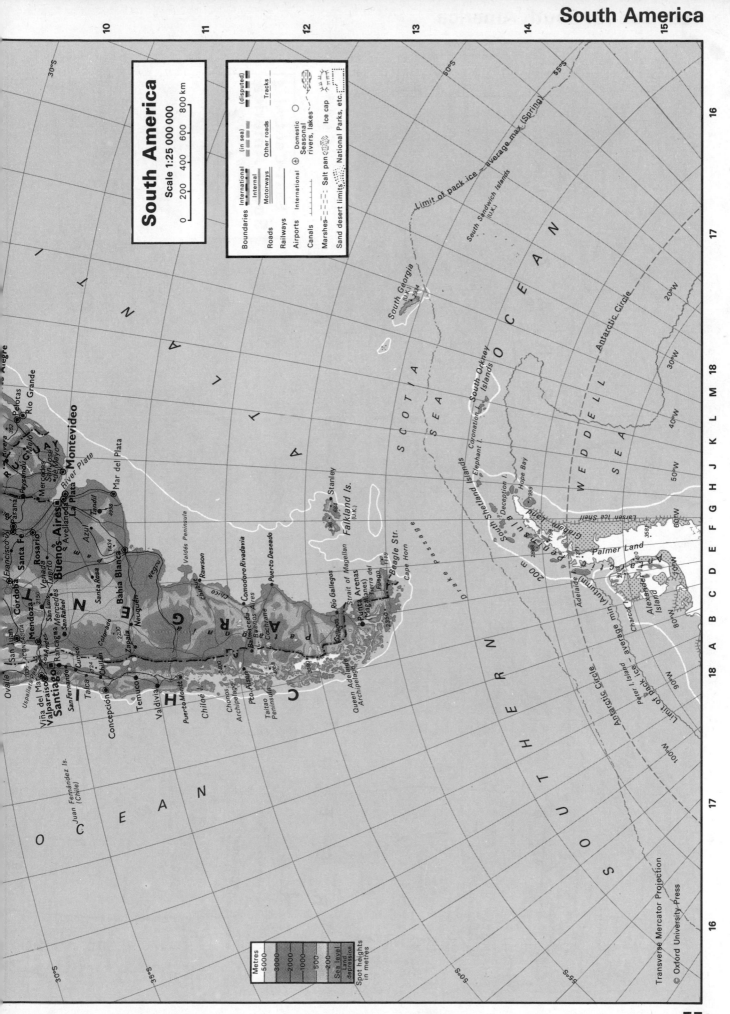

South America

Scale 1:25 000 000

0 200 400 600 800 km

Boundaries — International   (in sea)   (disputed)
  Internal

Roads — Motorways   Other roads   Tracks

Railways

Airports   ✈ International   ⊕ Domestic

Canals

Marshes — Salt pan — Seasonal rivers, lakes   ○ Ice cap

Sand desert limits — National Parks, etc.

Limit of pack ice — average max. (Spring)

South Sandwich Islands (U.K.)

South Georgia (U.K.)

S C O T I A   S E A

O C E A N

South Orkney Islands

Coronation I.

South Shetland Islands

Elephant I.

Deception I.

Hope Bay

W E D D E L L   S E A

Larsen Ice Shelf

Antarctic Circle

Graham Land

Palmer Land

A n t a r c t i c

Peter I. Island

Alexander Island

Charcot I.

Adelaide I.

Limit of pack ice — average min. (Autumn)

Antarctic Circle

S O U T H E R N

Drake Passage

Cape Horn

Beagle Str.

Stanley

Falkland Is. (U.K.)

Strait of Magellan

Tierra del Fuego

Punta Arenas (Magallanes)

Rio Gallegos

Gallegos

Queen Adelaide Archipelago

Taitao Peninsula

Chonos Archipelago

Chiloé I.

Puerto Montt

Valdivia

Temuco

Concepción

Talca

San Fernando

Santiago

Valparaíso

Viña del Mar

San Rafael

Curicó

Chillán

Rancagua

Los Andes

Mendoza

San Juan

Ovalle

San Luis

Venado

Río Cuarto

Córdoba

Santa Fe

Rosario

Paraná

Francisco

Buenos Aires

Avellaneda

La Plata

River Plate

Montevideo

Mar del Plata

Tandil

Azul

Bahía Blanca

Santa Rosa

Neuquén

Zapala

Comodoro Rivadavia

Puerto Deseado

Rawson

Chubut

Valdés Peninsula

Río Negro

Río Colorado

Río Chico

Pto. Aisén

Balmaceda

Juan Fernández Is. (Chile)

O C E A N

Río Grande

Pelotas

Alegre

A R G E N T I N A

A T L A N T I C

P A T A G O N I A

Rivera

Paysandú

Mercedes

Salto

Uspallata

Aconcagua 6960

Transverse Mercator Projection

© Oxford University Press

Metres
5000
3000
2000
1000
500
200
Sea level
Land depression

Spot heights in metres

55

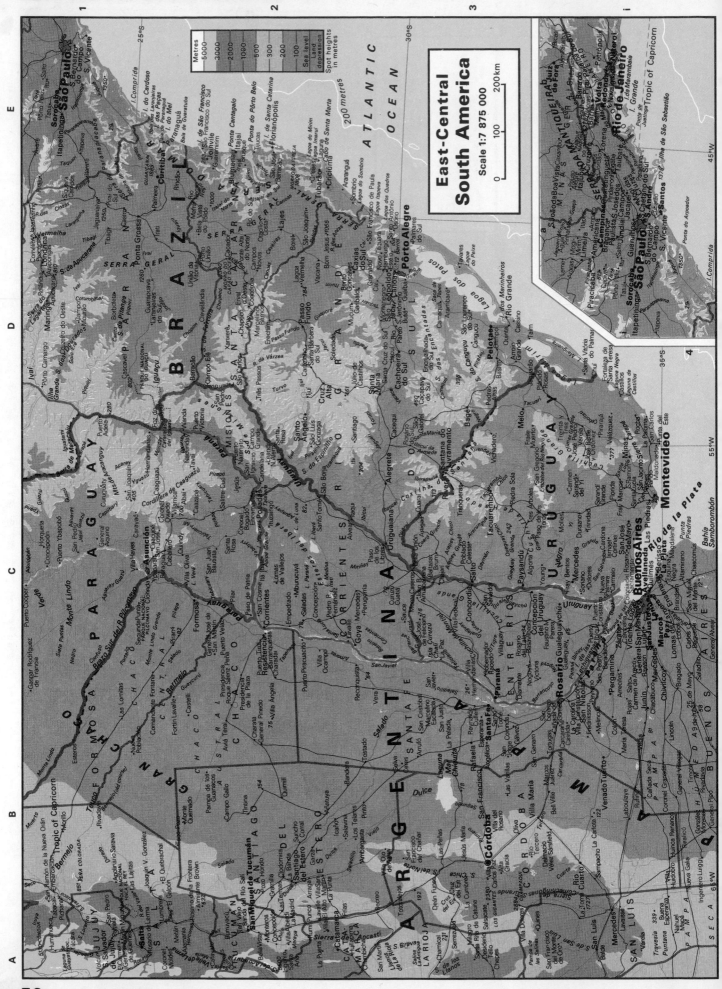

East-Central
South America

Scale 1:7 875 000

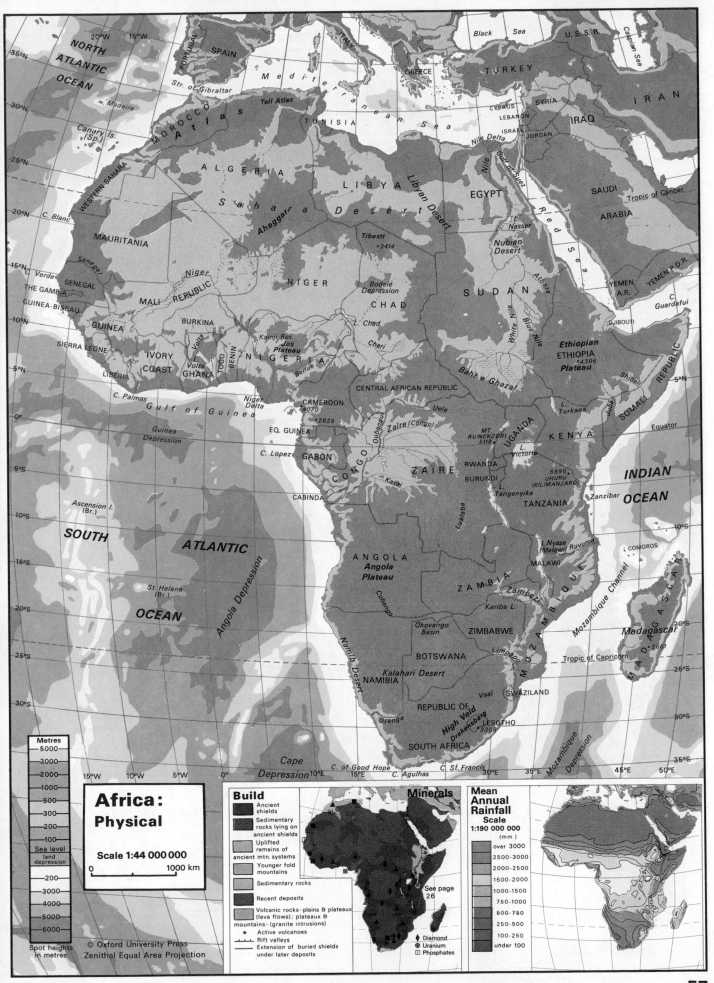

Africa: Physical

Scale 1:44 000 000

0   1000 km

Metres
5000
3000
2000
1000
500
300
200
100
Sea level
land
depression
200
3000
4000
5000
6000

Spot heights
in metres

© Oxford University Press
Zenithal Equal Area Projection

Build
- Ancient shields
- Sedimentary rocks lying on ancient shields
- Uplifted remains of ancient mtn. systems
- Younger fold mountains
- Sedimentary rocks
- Recent deposits
- Volcanic rocks - plains & plateaux (lava flows); plateaux & mountains - (granite intrusions)
- * Active volcanoes
- Rift valleys
- Extension of buried shields under later deposits

Minerals

See page 26

- ◆ Diamond
- ⊕ Uranium
- ⊞ Phosphates

Mean Annual Rainfall
Scale 1:190 000 000

(mm)
- over 3000
- 2500-3000
- 2000-2500
- 1500-2000
- 1000-1500
- 750-1000
- 500-750
- 250-500
- 100-250
- under 100

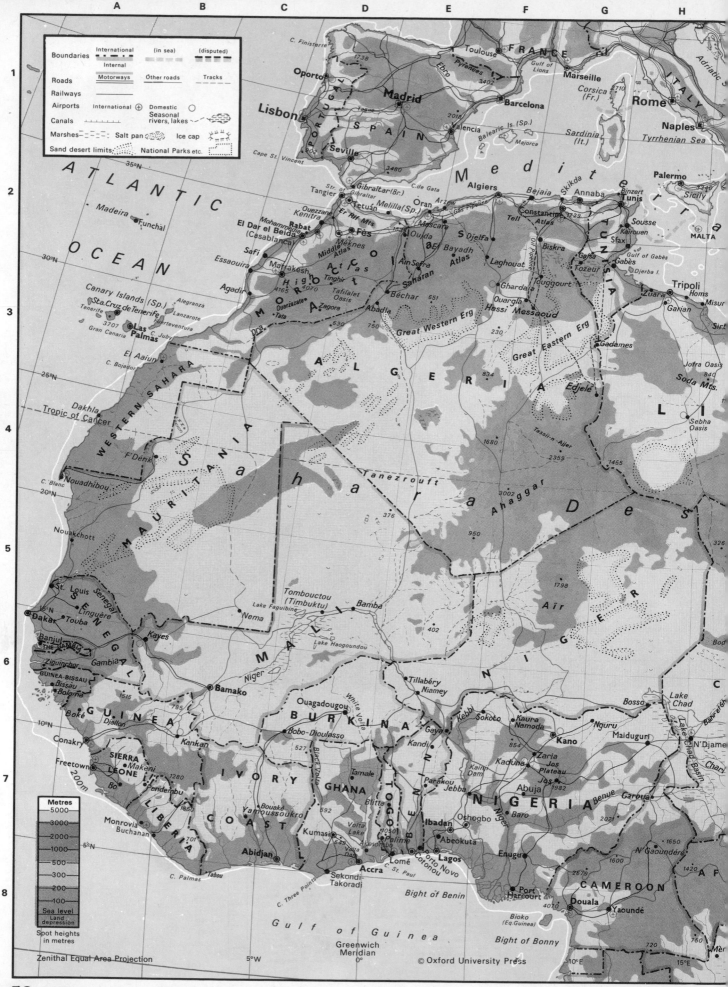

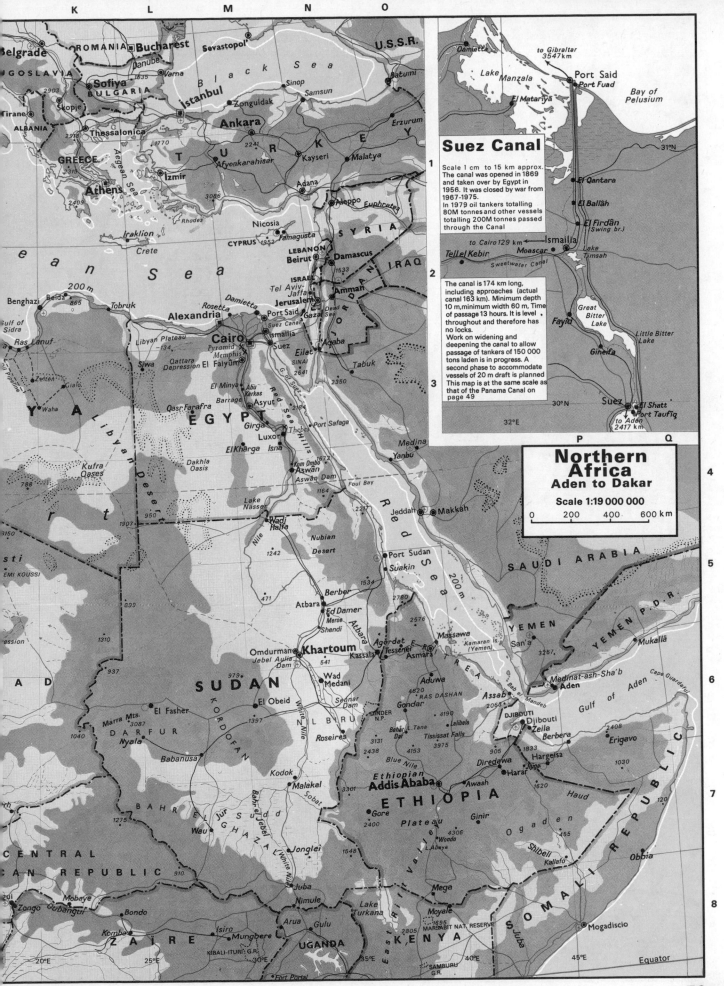

Suez Canal

Scale 1 cm to 15 km approx.
The canal was opened in 1869 and taken over by Egypt in 1956. It was closed by war from 1967-1975.
In 1979 oil tankers totalling 80M tonnes and other vessels totalling 200M tonnes passed through the Canal

The canal is 174 km long, including approaches (actual canal 163 km). Minimum depth 10 m, minimum width 60 m, Time of passage 13 hours. It is level throughout and therefore has no locks.
Work on widening and deepening the canal to allow passage of tankers of 150 000 tons laden is in progress. A second phase to accommodate vessels of 20 m draft is planned
This map is at the same scale as that of the Panama Canal on page 49

to Gibraltar 3547 km
Port Said
Port Fuad
Bay of Pelusium
Lake Manzala
Damietta
El Matariya
31°N
El Qantara
El Ballah
El Firdân (Swing br.)
to Cairo 129 km → Ismailia
Tel el Kebir
Moascar
Sweetwater Canal
Lake Timsah
Great Bitter Lake
Fayîd
Little Bitter Lake
Gineifa
30°N
Suez
El Shatt
Port Taufiq
to Aden 2417 km
32°E

Northern Africa
Aden to Dakar
Scale 1:19 000 000

0   200   400   600 km

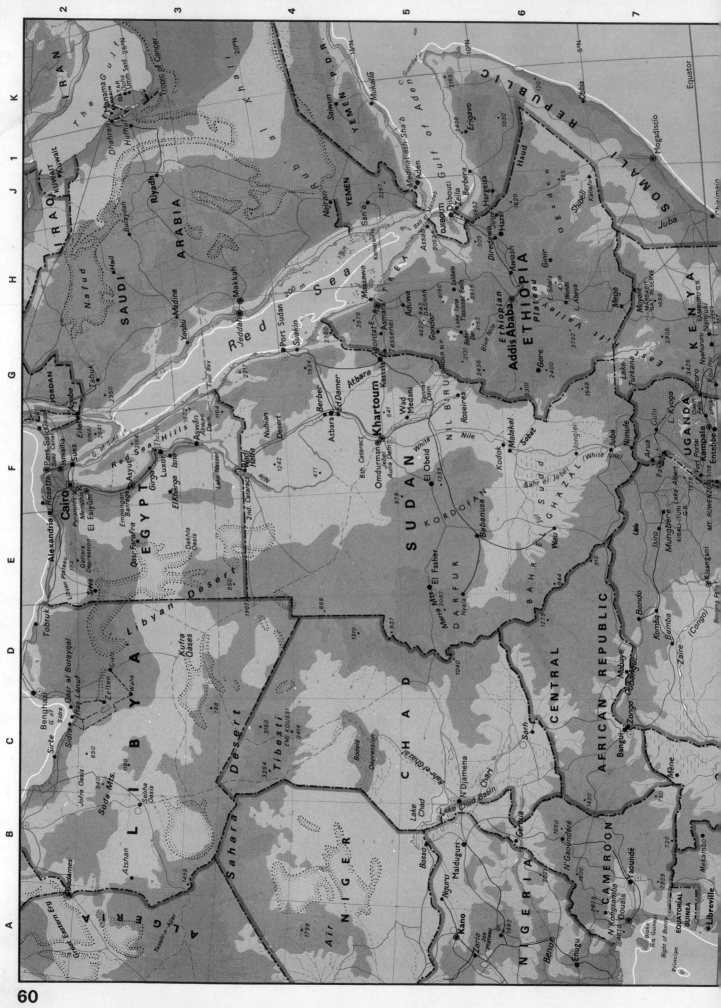

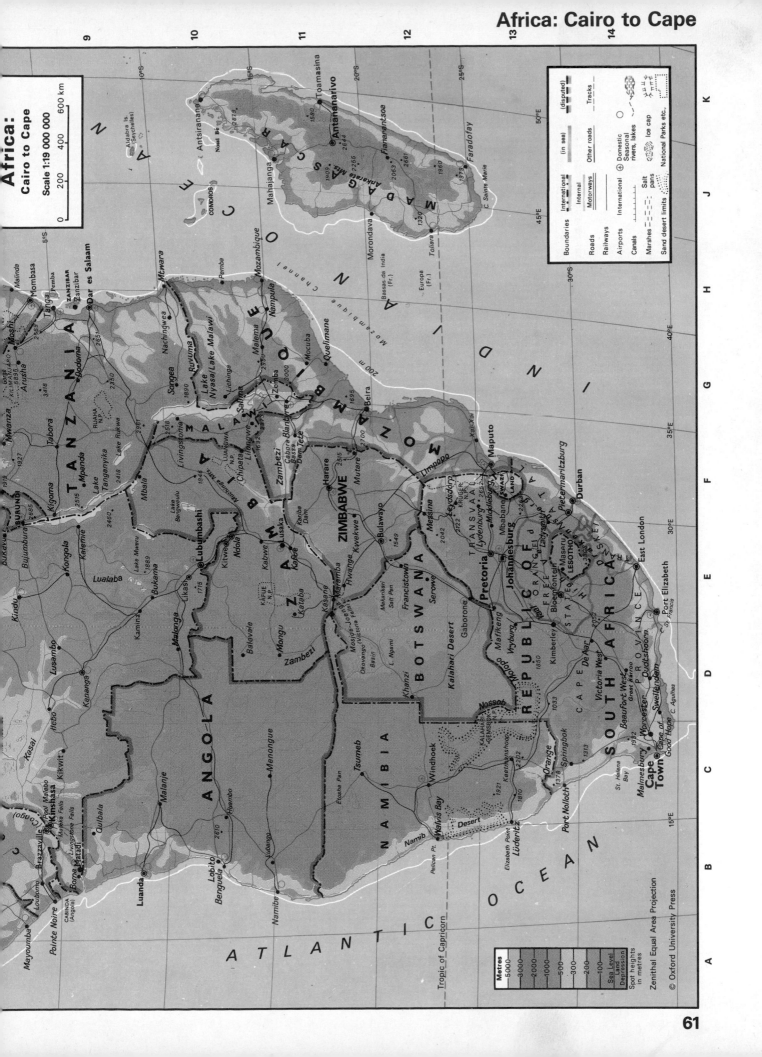

Africa:
Cairo to Cape

Scale 1:19 000 000

0   200   400   600 km

© Oxford University Press

Zenithal Equal Area Projection

Boundaries
International ————— (in sea) ·········· (disputed) ─·─·─
Internal ─·─·─

Roads
Motorways ═════
International ─────
Other roads
Tracks

Railways ─────
Airports ⊕ Domestic
Canals
Marshes
Salt pans
⊙ Seasonal rivers, lakes
ice cap
Sand desert limits
National Parks etc.

Metres
5000
3000
2000
1000
500
200
100
Sea Level
Land Depression

Spot heights in metres

sbury: England 13 F3
ner, Lake: Canada 46 O4
ham: England 13 H2
& r., Scotland 17 D4
Point of: Man 14 B2
thaya: Thailand 37 C8
baydzhan S.S.R.: S.R. 30 F5
es: is., Atl. O 10 H4
, Sea of: U.S.S.R. 30 D4
Argentina 55 F11
Loch: Scotland 16 C3
r Is.: Indonesia 37 H12
acombe Bay: Eng. 12 C4
el Mandeb: str., ca/Asia 58 O6
ne Lake: Canada 46 K6
don: Iraq 32 E4
u: Romania 22 E3
lod: Philippines 37 G8
p: England 14 D3
joz: Spain 21 A5
n: Switzerland 25 B2
n: Old state, nan F.R. 25 B2
n-Baden: Ger. F.R. 25 B2
schl: Austria 25 C2
Kissingen: F.R. 24 C1
Kreuznach: F.R. 24 B2
ands Nat. nument: U.S.A. 53 E2
Mergentheim: nan F.R. 24 B2
Reichenhall: nan F.R. 25 C2
lla: Sri Lanka 34 b ii
n Bay: Canada 47 X2
n Bay: U.S.A. 50 C4
n I.: Canada 47 U2
n I. Nat. Park: ada 47 W4
, Brazil 56 D3
nalstown: Rep. 15 E4
y Point: England 12 B3
HDAD: Iraq 32 D4
eria: Sicily 23 B5
io: Philippines 37 G7
AMAS, THE: 49 –
walpur: Pakistan 34 B3
see Salvador 54 L6
Samborombón, Argentina 56 C4
Blanca: Argentina 55 F11
ich: India 34 D3
RAIN 32 F5
el Ghazal: r., Chad 58 J6
el Ghazal: ., Sudan 59 L7
el Jebel (White : r., Sudan 59 M7
das Laranjeiras: Brazil 56 E2
de Guaratuba Brazil 56 E2
de Paranaguá: Brazil 56 E2
Mare: Romania 22 D3
Comeau: town, ada 47 W7
borough: Rep. 15 E3
r., England 13 F1
ridge: Ga, U.S.A. 51 F3
Hungary 22 C3
: N. Dak., U.S.A. 53 E1
: Oreg., U.S.A. 52 B2
Lake: sett., Can. 47 Q4
sfield: U.S.A. 52 B3
well: England 13 E1
U.S.S.R. 30 F5
& lake, Wales 12 C2
hat: India 34 D4
ava, U.S.S.R. 30 C5
nov: U.S.S.R. 30 E3
ore: India 34 E4
on, Lake: Hungary 22 C3
a: Panama 49 Ins
ggan: Irish Rep. 15 E3
y Point: Scot. 17 E5
tha: N.Z. 41 A4
: Argentina 56 A3
Eagle Lake: A. 53 G1
ck: England 13 F3
see Basel 25 B2
ic Is.: Med. Sea 21 C5
Belgium 24 B1
rand: Norway 18 A3
, Indonesia 37 E12
n Mts.: Bulgaria 23 D4
sir: Turkey 23 E5
apan: Indonesia 37 F11
a: Indonesia 37 F12
ash: & lake, S.R. 31 M4
trae: Scotland 17 C4
at: Australia 40 G8
er: Scotland 16 E2
y Is.: Antarctica 42 F13
a: Irish Rep. 15 B2
amore: Irish Rep. 15 D2
asloe: Irish Rep. 15 C3
collig: Irish Rep. 15 C5
robe: Irish Rep. 15 B3
skelligs Bay: Rep. 15 A5
ay: Irish Rep. 15 E2
ofey: Irish Rep. 15 D2
unnion: Rep. 15 B4
astle: N. Ireland 15 E1
lare: N. Ireland 15 F2
avid Head: pt., Irish Rep 15 A4
Ballyhaunis: Irish Rep. 15 C3
Ballyhoura Hills: Irish Rep. 15 C4
Ballyjamesduff: Irish Rep. 15 D3
Ballymahon: Irish Rep. 15 D3
Ballymena: N. Ireland 15 E2
Ballymoney: N. Ireland 15 E1
Ballymote: Irish Rep. 15 C2
Ballyshannon: Irish Republic 15 C2
Ballyteige Bay: Irish Rep. 15 E4
Balmaceda: Chile 55 D13
Balmoral Castle: Scot. 16 E2
Balovale: Zambia 61 D10
Balsas: r., Mexico 48 G6
Balta: U.S.S.R. 22 E3
Baltasar Brum: Uru. 56 C3
Baltic Sea: 19 C4
Baltimore: U.S.A. 51 G2
Baltinglass: Irish Rep. 15 E4
Baltrum: i., Ger. F.R. 24 B1
Baluchistan: Prov., Pak. 34 A3
BAMAKO: Mali 58 D6
Bamba: Mali 58 E5
Bamberg: German F.R. 24 C2
Bampton: England 12 C4
Banagher: Irish Rep. 15 D3
Banbridge: N. Ireland 15 E2
Banbury: England 13 E2
Banchory: Scotland 16 F2
Banda Aceh: Indonesia 31 P9
Banda del Río Salí: Argentina 56 A2
Bandai-asahi-kokuritsu-kōen: N.P., Japan 38 C2
Bandar: India 34 D5
Bandar Abbās: Iran 32 G5
*Bandar-e-Shāh: Iran 30 G6
Bandar Khomeini: Iran 32 F5
BANDAR SERI BEGAWAN: Brunei 37 E10
Banda Sea: Indonesia 37 H12
Bandera: Argentina 56 B2
Banderas Bay: Mexico 48 E5
Bandırma: Turkey 23 E4
Bandjarmasin: Indon. 37 E11
Bandon: & r., Irish Rep. 15 C5
Bandra: India 34 B5
Bandung: Indonesia 37 D12
Banff: & nat. park., Can. 46 M6
Banff: Scotland 16 F2
Bangalore: India 34 C6
Bangka: i., Indon. 37 D11
BANGKOK: Thailand 37 C8
BANGLADESH 34/35 –
Bangor: N. Ireland 15 F2
Bangor: U.S.A. 49 N1
Bangor: Wales 12 B1
BANGUI: Cen. Afr. Rep. 59 J8
Bangweulu, Lake: Zambia 61 E10
Ban Houei Sai: Laos 36 C6
Baniyās: Syria 30 D6
Banja Luka: Yugoslavia 23 C4
BANJUL: The Gambia 58 B6
Banks I.: Canada 46 L2
Banks Peninsula: N.Z. 41 B3
Bann: r., Irish Rep. 15 E4
Bann: r., N. Ireland 15 E2
Bannu: Pakistan 34 B2
Banská Bystrica: Czech. 22 C3
Bantry: & bay, Irish Republic 15 B5
Banstead: England 13 F3
Banwy: r., Wales 12 C2
Baotou see Paotow 36 D2
Baradero: Argentina 56 C3
Baranovichi Slonim: U.S.S.R. 22 E2
Barataria Bay: U.S.A. 51 E4
Barbacena: Brazil 54 K8
BARBADOS: 49 P7
Barbuda: i., Leeward Is. 49 O6
Barcellona: Sicily 23 C5
Barcelona: Spain 21 C4
Barcelona: Venezuela 49 O7
Barcelonnette: France 25 B3
Barcoo: r., Australia 40 G5
Bardsey I.: Wales 12 B2
Bareilly: India 34 C3
Bareno: Italy 25 B2
Barents Sea: Arctic O. 28 –
Bari: Italy 23 C4
Barking: England 13 G3
Barkly Plateau Australia 40 F4
Bar-le-Duc: France 24 B2
Barletta: Italy 23 C4
Barlow Haven: U.S.A. 51 F4
Barmouth: & bay, Wales 12 B2
Barnard Castle: England 14 E2
Barnaul: U.S.S.R. 31 N3
Barnet: England 13 F3
Barnoldswick: England 14 D3
Barnsley: England 14 E3
Barnstaple: England 12 B3
Barnstaple (Bideford) Bay: England 12 B3
Baro: Nigeria 58 G7
Barquisimeto: Ven. 48 N7
Barra: & Sound, Scot. 16 A2
Barracão: Brazil 56 D2
Barracão: Brazil 56 E2
Barrackpore: India 34 E4
Barra do Piraí: Brazil 56 b i
Barra Head: pt. Scot. 16 A3
Barra Mansa: Brazil 56 b i
Barrancas: r., Argentina 56 C3
Barrancoso: r., Arg. 56 B3
Barranqueras: Arg. 56 C2
Barranquilla: Colombia 49 M7
Barreiro: Portugal 21 A5
Barretos: Brazil 54 J8
Barrhead: Scotland 17 D4
Barrie: Canada 47 U8
Barros, Lago dos: Brazil 56 D2
Barrow: r., Irish Rep. 15 E4
Barrow: U.S.A. 46 D2
Barrow, Point: U.S.A. 46 D2
Barrow-in-Furness: England 14 C2
Barrow Strait: Canada 47 R2
Barry: Wales 12 C3
Barstow: U.S.A. 52 B4
Bar-sur-Seine: France 25 A2
Barth: Wales 12 B2
Bartlesville: U.S.A. 50 C2
Barton-upon-Humber: England 14 F3
Barwell: England 13 E2
Basavilbasco: Argentina 56 C3
Basel (Bâle): Switz. 25 B2
Básilán: i., Phil. 37 G9
Basildon: England 13 G3
Basílio: Brazil 56 D3
Basingstoke: England 13 E3
Baskunchak: U.S.S.R. 30 F4
Basra: Iraq 32 E4
Bassano del Grappa: Italy 25 C2
Bassas da India: i., Indian Ocean 70 G12
Bassein: Burma 33 O7
Bassenthwaite Lake: England 14 C2
Basse-Terre: Guadeloupe 49 O8
Bass Strait: Australia 40/41 H8
Bassum: German F.R. 24 B1
Bastia: Corsica 21 a i
Bastogne: Belgium 24 B1
Bastrop: U.S.A. 50 D3
Bataan Penin: Phil. 37 G8
Batang (Paan): China 36 B5
Batangas: Phil. 37 G8
Batelito: r., Argentina 56 C2
Batesville, Ark., U.S.A. 50 D2
Batesville: Miss., U.S.A. 51 E3
Bath: England 12 D3
Bathgate: Scotland 17 E4
Bathurst: Canada 47 W7
Bathurst, Cape: Can. 46 K2
Bathurst I.: Australia 40 E3
Bathurst I.: Canada 47 Q1
Baton Rouge: U.S.A. 50 D3
Batticaloa: Sri Lanka 34 b ii
Battle: England 13 G4
Battle Creek: town., U.S.A. 51 E1
Battle Mountain: town., U.S.A. 52 B2
Batu Is.: Indonesia 37 B11
Batumi: U.S.S.R. 30 E5
Bautzen: German D.R. 24 C1
Bavaria: State, German F.R. 24 C2
Bavarian Alps: Ger. F.R. 25 C2
Bavarian Forest: mtns. & nat. park, Ger. F.R. 24 C2
Bawdwin: Burma 33 P6
Bawtry: England 14 E3
Bayadh: Algeria 58 F2
Bayan Kara Shan: ra., China 36 B4
Bay City: Tex., U.S.A. 50 C4
Baykal, Lake: U.S.S.R. 29 N7
Baykonur: U.S.S.R. 31 K4
Baymak: U.S.S.R. 31 H3
Bayonne: France 21 B4
Bayou: r., U.S.A. 50 C3
Bayreuth: German F.R. 24 C2
Baytown: U.S.A. 50 C4
Bâza: Spain 21 B5
Beachy Head: cape, England 13 G4
Beacon Hill: Wales 12 C2
Beaconsfield: England 13 F3
Beagle Strait: Arg./Chile 55 E14
Beaminster: England 12 D4
Bear Island: Arctic O. 28 D3
Bear Island: Irish Rep. 15 B5
Bear Lake: U.S.A. 52 C2
Bearsden: Scotland 17 D4
Beas: r., India 34 C2
Beatrice: U.S.A. 50 C1
Beaufort: U.S.A. 51 F3
Beaufort Sea: Arctic Ocean 46 G2
Beaufort West: S. Africa 61 D14
Beauly: & r., Scotland 16 D2
Beaumaris: Wales 12 B1
Beaumont: U.S.A. 50 D3
Beaune: France 25 A2
Beauvais: France 20 C3
Beaver Creek: U.S.A. 50 B2
Beaver Dam: town, U.S.A. 53 H2
Beccles: England 13 H2
Béchar: Algeria 58 E2
Beckley: U.S.A. 51 F2
Bedale: England 14 E2
Bedford: England 13 F2
Bedford: Ind., U.S.A. 51 E2
Bedford: Pa., U.S.A. 51 G1
Bedfordshire: Co., Eng. 13 F2
Bedlington: England 14 E1
Bedworth: England 13 E2
Bee, Loch: Scotland 16 A2
Beeston: England 13 E2
Beeville: U.S.A. 50 C4
Begovat: U.S.S.R. 31 K5
Behar Dar: Ethiopia 59 N6
Beida: Libya 59 K2
Beijing see Peking 36 F3
Beira see Sofala 61 F11
BEIRUT: Lebanon 30 D7
Beja: Portugal 21 A5
Békéscaba: Hungary 22 D3
Bela: Pakistan 34 A3
Bela Vista do Tôldo: Brazil 56 D2
Belaya: r., U.S.S.R. 30 H3
Belaya Tserkov: U.S.S.R. 22 F3
Belém: Brazil 54 J4
Belen: U.S.A. 52 D4
BELFAST: N. Ireland 15 F2
Belfast Lough: N. Ireland 15 F2
Belford: England 17 G4
Belfort: France 25 B2
Belgaum: India 34 B5
BELGIUM: 20 C2
Belgorod: U.S.S.R. 30 D3
BELGRADE: Yugoslavia 23 D4
Belitung (Billiton) i., Indonesia 37 D11
BELIZE: 48 J6
Belize: Belize 48 J6
Bellagio: Italy 25 B2
Bellano: Italy 25 B2
Bellary: India 34 C5
Bella Unión: Uruguay 56 C3
Bella Vista: Argentina 56 A2
Belleek: N. Ireland 15 C2
Belle Fourche: & r., U.S.A. 53 E2
Bellegarde: France 25 B2
Belle Glade: U.S.A. 51 F4
Belle Île-en-Mer: France 20 B3
Belle Isle, Strait of: Canada 47 Y6
Belleville: U.S.A. 50 C2
Bellingham: England 14 D1
Bellingham: U.S.A. 52 A1
Bellinzona: Switz. 25 B2
Belluno: Italy 25 C2
Bell Ville: Argentina 56 B3
BELMOPAN: Belize 48 J6
Belo Horizonte: Brazil 54 K7
Beloit: Kans., U.S.A. 50 C2
Beloit: Wis., U.S.A. 51 E1
Belousovka: U.S.S.R. 31 N3
Belper: England 13 E1
Beltra, Lough: Irish Rep. 15 B3
Bel'tsy: U.S.S.R. 22 E3
Belturbet: Irish Rep. 15 D2
Belyy Island: U.S.S.R. 29 K3
Bemidji: U.S.A. 53 F1
Ben Alder: mtn., Scot. 16 D3
Benavente: Spain 21 C4
Ben Avon: mtn., Scotland 16 E2
Benbane Head: cape, N. Ireland 15 E1
Benbecula: i., Scotland 16 A2
Ben Chonzie: mtn., Scotland 16 E3
Ben Cruachan: mtn., Scotland 16 C3
Bend: U.S.A. 52 A2
Ben Dearg: mtn., Scot. 16 D2
Bendery: U.S.S.R. 22 E3
Bendigo: Australia 40 G8
Ben Dorain: mtn., Scot. 16 O3
Ben Eighe: mtn., Scot. 16 C2
Ben Fhada: mtn., Scot. 16 C2
Bengal, Bay of: Ind. O. 33 –
Benghazi: Libya 59 K2
Benguela: Angola 61 B10
Ben Hope: mtn., Scot. 16 D1
Beni: r., Bolivia 54 E6
Benicarló: Spain 21 C4
Benidorm: Spain 21 B5
BENIN: 58 F7
Benin, Bight of: Gulf of Guinea 58 F8
Beni Saf: Algeria 21 B5
Ben Klibreck: mtn., Scotland 16 D1
Ben Lawers: mtn., Scot. 16 D3
Ben Ledi: mtn., Scot. 16 D3
Benllech: Wales 12 B1
Ben Lomond: mtn., Scotland 17 D3
Ben Loyal: mtn., Scot. 16 D1
Ben Macdhui: mtn., Scotland 16 E2
Ben Mhor: mtn., Scotland 16 B2
Ben More: mtn., Central Scotland 16 B3
Ben More: mtn., Mull, Scotland 16 D3
Ben More Assynt: mtn., Scotland 16 D1
Bennane Head: cape, Scotland 17 C4
Ben Nevis: mtn., Scotland 16 D3
Ben Rinnes: mtn., Scot. 16 E2
Bensersiel: Ger. F.R. 24 B1
Ben Sgritheall: mtn. Scotland 16 C2
Bensheim: German F.R. 24 B2
Ben Starav: mtn., Scot. 16 C3
Bentley: England 14 E3
Bento Gonçalves: Brazil 56 D2
Benton: Ark., U.S.A. 50 D3
Benton: Wis., U.S.A. 51 E1
Benue: r., Nigeria 58 H7
Ben Vorlich: mtn., Scot. 16 D3
Benwee Head: cape, Irish Rep. 15 B2
Ben Wyvis: mtn., Scotland 16 D2
Beppu: Japan 38 B3
Berar: geog. reg., India 34 C4
Berat: Albania 23 C4
Berber: Sudan 59 M5
Berbera: Somali Rep. 59 P8
Berchtesgaden: German F.R. 25 C2
Berdichev: U.S.S.R. 22 E3
Beregovo: U.S.S.R. 22 D3
Berezniki: U.S.S.R. 31 H2
Berezovo: U.S.S.R. 31 K1
Bergama: Turkey 23 E5
Bergamo: Italy 25 B2
Bergamo Alps: Italy 25 B2
Bergen: Norway 19 A3
Bergen op Zoom: Neth. 24 A1
Bergisch Gladbach: German F.R. 24 B1
Bergstrasse Odenwald Nat. Park: Ger. F.R. 24 B2
Berhampora: India 34 E4
*Berhampore: India 34 D5
Berisso: Argentina 56 C3
Berkåk: Norway 18 B33
Berkeley: U.S.A. 52 A3
Berkhamsted: England 13 F3
Berkshire: Co., England 13 E3
BERLIN: German D.R. 24 C1
Berlin: German F.R. 24 C1
Bermejo: r., Arg. 56 B1
Bermejo (old course): r., Argentina 56 B1
BERMUDA: 49 O3
BERN (Berne): Switz. 25 B2
Berne see BERN 25 B2
Berneray: i., Scotland 16 A2
Bernese Alps: Switz. 25 B2
Bernina Fass: Switz. 25 C2
Bernkastel: Ger. F.R. 24 B2
Berry Head: cape, Eng. 12 C4
Berry Island: Bahamas 51 G4
Bertraghboy Bay: Irish Rep. 15 B3
Berwick-upon-Tweed: England 17 G4
Berwyn: r., Wales 12 C2
Besançon: France 25 B2
Bessbrook: N. Ireland 15 E2
Bessemer: U.S.A. 51 E3
Bethel: U.S.A. 46 C4
Bethesda: Wales 12 B1
Bethlehem: U.S.A. 51 G1
Betwa: r., India 34 C3
Betws-y-Coed: Wales 12 C1
Beult: r., England 13 G3
Beverley: England 14 F3
Bewdley: England 12 D2
Bexhill: England 13 G4
Bexley: England 13 G3
Bezhitsa: U.S.S.R. 30 C3
Béziers: France 21 C4
Bhagalpur: India 34 E3
Bhamo: Burma 33 P6
Bhavnagar: India 34 B4
Bhima: r., India 34 C5
Bhopal: India 34 C4
Bhubaneswar: India 34 E4
Bhuj: India 34 B4
BHUTAN: 34/35 –
Biak: i., Indonesia 36 K11
Bialystok: Poland 22 D2
Biarritz: France 21 B4
Bibai: Japan 38 D1
Biberach: Ger. F.R. 25 B2
Bicas: Brazil 56 b i
Bicester: England 18 E3
Biddulph: England 12 D1
Bideford: England 12 B3
Bideford (Barnstaple) Bay: England 12 B3
Biebrza: r., Poland 22 D2
Biel: Switzerland 25 B2
Bielefeld: Ger. F.R. 24 B1
Biella: Italy 25 B2
Bieloveja Nat. Park: U.S.S.R. 22 D2
Bielsko-Biala: Pol. 22 C3
Big Bend Nat. Park: U.S.A. 50 B4
Big Black: r., U.S.A. 50 D3
Big Blue: r., U.S.A. 53 F2
Bigbury Bay: England 12 C4
Big Eau Pleine Reservoir: U.S.A. 53 H2
Big Falls: town, U.S.A. 53 G1
Biggar: Scotland 17 E4
Biggleswade: Eng. 13 F2
Bighorn: r., U.S.A. 52 D1
Bighorn Mountains: U.S.A. 52 D2
Big Sioux: r., U.S.A. 53 F2
Big Spring: town, U.S.A. 50 B3
Big Sur: U.S.A. 52 A3
Big Wood: r., U.S.A. 52 C2
Bihać: Yugoslavia 23 C4
Bihar: State, India 34 E4
Bijapur: India 34 C5
Bikaner: India 34 B3
Bilaspur: India 34 D4
Bilbao: Spain 21 B4
Billericay: England 13 G3
Billingham: England 14 E2
Billings: U.S.A. 52 D1
Billingshurst: England 13 F3
Billiton: i., see Belitung 37 D11
Bill of Portland: cape, England 12 D4
Bilo Gora: mtns., Yugoslavia 22 C3
Biloxi: U.S.A. 51 E3
Bimini Islands: The Bahamas 51 G4
Binevenagh: mtn., N. Ireland 15 E1
Bingen: Ger. F.R. 24 B2
Bingham: England 13 F2
Bingham: U.S.A. 52 C2
Bingley: England 14 E3
Bintan: i., Indon. 37 C10
Binzert: Tunisia 58 G1
Bioko: i., Equatorial Guinea 58 G8
Birdun: Australia 40 E4
Birganj: Nepal 34 E3
Birjand: Iran 32 G4
Birkenhead: England 14 C3
Birlad: Romania 22 E3
Birmingham: Eng. 13 E2
Birmingham: U.S.A. 51 E3
Birobidzhan: U.S.S.R. 29 Q8
Birr: Irish Rep. 15 D3
Bisai: Japan 38 c i
Bisbee: U.S.A. 52 D4
Biscay, Bay of: Fr./Sp. 20/21 –
Bishop Auckland: Eng. 14 E2
Bishopbriggs: Scot. 17 D4
Bishop's Castle: Eng. 12 C2
Bishop's Stortford: Eng. 13 G3
Bishop's Waltham: England 13 E4
Biskra: Algeria 58 G2
Bismarck: U.S.A. 53 E1
Bismarck Archipelago: Papua-New Guinea 40 J1
BISSAU: Guinea-Bissau 58 B6
Bistrita: Romania 22 D3
Bistrita: r., Rom. 22 E3
Bitola: Yugoslavia 23 D4
Bitterfeld: Ger. D.R. 24 C1
Bitterroot Range: U.S.A. 52 C1
Biwa-ko: lake, Japan 38 c i
Biysk: U.S.S.R. 31 O3
Black: r., Miss., U.S.A 50 D2
Blackburn: England 14 D3
Blackdown Hills: Eng. 12 C4
Blackfoot: U.S.A. 52 C2
Black Forest: Ger. F.R. 28 B2
Black Head: cape, England 12 A4
Black Head: cape, Irish Rep. 15 B3
Black Irtysh: r., Mong./U.S.S.R. 31 O4
Black Isle: penin., Scotland 16 D2
Blackmoor, Vale of: valley, England 12 D4
Black Mts.: Wales 12 C3
Blackpool: England 14 C3
Black Sea: 30 –
Blacksod Bay: Irish Republic 15 A2
Blackstairs Mt.: Irish Republic 15 E4
Black Volta: r., Ghana 58 E7
Blackwater: r., Eng. 13 G3
Blackwater: r., Cork/Wat., Irish Rep 15 D4
Blackwater: r., Meath, Irish Rep. 15 E3
Blackwater Reservoir: Scotland 16 D3
Blaenau Ffestiniog: Wales 12 C2
Blagoveshchensk: U.S.S.R. 29 P7
Blairgowrie: Scotland 16 E3
Blakeney Point: Eng. 13 H2
Blanc, Cape: Mauritania 58 B4
Blanc, Mont: France 25 B2
Blanco, Cape: U.S.A. 52 A2
Blandford Forum: Eng. 12 D4
Blanes: Spain 21 C4
Blantyre: Malawi 61 F11
Blarney: Irish Rep. 15 C5
Bled: Yugoslavia 22 B3
Blenheim: hist., Ger. F.R. 25 C2
Blenheim: N.Z. 41 B3
Bletchley: England 13 F2
Blida: Algeria 21 C5
Blitta: Togo 58 F7
Bloemfontein: South Africa 61 E13
Blois: France 20 C3
Bloody Foreland: cape, Irish Republic 15 C1
Bloomington: Ill., U.S.A. 51 E1
Bloomington: Ind., U.S.A. 51 E2
Bluefield: U.S.A. 51 F2
Blue Mountains: U.S.A. 52 B1/2
Blue Nile: r., Ethiopia 59 N6
Blue Ridge: U.S.A. 51 F2
Blue Stack Mts.: Irish Republic 15 C2
Bluff: N.Z. 41 A4
Blumenau: Brazil 56 E2
Blumenthal: Ger. F.R. 24 B1
Blyth: & r., England 14 E1
Blythe: r., England 13 H2
Blythe: U.S.A. 52 C4
Blytheville: U.S.A. 51 E2
Bo: Sierra Leone 58 C7
Boa Vista: Brazil 54 F3
*Bobo-Dioulasso: Upper Volta 58 E6
Bobruysk: U.S.S.R. 22 E2
Bocholt: Ger. F.R. 24 B1
Bochum: Ger. F.R. 24 B1
Bodele Depression: Chad 59 J5
Boden: Sweden 18 D2
Bodensee see Constance, Lake 25 B2
Bodensee Hegau Nature Pk: Ger. F.R. 25 B2
Boderg, Lough: Irish Republic 15 C3
Bodin: Norway 18 B2
Bodmin: England 12 B4
Bodmin Moor: England 12 B4
Bodø: Norway 18 B2
Bofin Lough: Irish Republic 15 D3
Bogalusa: U.S.A. 51 E3
Boggeragh Mts.: Irish Republic 15 C4
Bognor Regis: England 13 F4
Bog of Allen: Irish Republic 15 D3
BOGOTÁ: Colombia 54 D3
Bohemian Forest: mtns., Czech/Ger. F.R. 22 B3
Bohol: i., Philippines 37 G9
Boise: U.S.A. 52 B2
Bojador, Cape: W. Sahara 58 C3
Bokaro: India 34 E4
Boké: Guinea 58 C6
Boknafjorden: fd., Nor. 19 A4
Bol: Yugoslavia 23 C4
Bolama: Guinea-Bissau 58 B6
Bolan Pass: Pakistan 34 A3
Boldon: England 14 E2
Boleslawiec: Poland 22 C2

page 80

alia: Wash.,
A. 52 A1
al: Reg., Scot. 16/17 D3
al Pacific Basin:
ic Ocean 42 H6
al Range:
a-New Guinea 40 G2
al Siberian Plain:
S.R. 29 –
alonia: i., Greece 23 D5
: i. & sea, Indon. 37 H11
Argentina 56 B2
de Pasco: Peru 54 C6
a: Italy 25 C3
U.S.S.R. 19 E4
Budějovice:
hoslovakia 22 B3
o: Italy 23 C5
: Spain 21 A5
nes: mtns., Fr. 21 C4
buco: Argentina 56 B3
ile: Nigeria 57 C1
: Prov., Arg. 56 B2
Austral: geog.
Argentina 56 B2
Central: geog.
Argentina 56 C2
59 J6
Lake: Africa 58 H6
s-Laccadive
au: Indian O. 35 f v
e de l'Étoile:
France 25 B3
i: Argentina 56 C3
: Peru 54 D7
ns-sur-Marne: Fr. 24 A2
n-sur-Saôn: Fr. 25 A2
an: Pakistan 34 A2
ba: India 34 C2
bal: r., India 34 C3
berlain: U.S.A. 53 F2
bersburg: U.S.A. 51 G2
béry: France 25 B2
ical: Argentina 56 A3
onix: France 25 B2
pagne Pouilleuse:
reg., France 24 A2
paign: U.S.A. 51 E1
paqui: mtn., Arg. 56 B3
péry: Switz. 25 B2
plain, Lake:
A. 47 M1
ral: Chile 54 D9
hiang: China 36 E6
an (Sian):
36 D4
chun: China 36 H2
kiakow (Kalgan):
36 E2
sha: China 36 E5
tu: China 36 B4
el Islands: U.K. 12 a ii
haburi: Thailand 37 C8
te: U.S.A. 50 C2
Lake: U.S.S.R. 31 M3
angchen: China 36 H2
la, Lake: Max. 48 F5
yevsk: U.S.S.R. 30 F3
có: & r., Brazil 56 D2
a: India 34 D3
dai: Argentina 56 C2
a: Argentina 56 B2
ot I.: Antarc. 55 C17
England 12 D4
hou: U.S.S.R. 31 J6
r., Chad 58 J6
on: r., U.S.A. 50 D1
ury: England 13 E3
roi: Belgium 24 A1
s, Cape: U.S.A. 51 G2
ston: Ill., U.S.A. 51 E2
ston: S.C.
A. 51 F3
ston: W. Va.,
A. 51 F2
stown of
our: Scotland 16 E2
ville: Australia 41 H6
ville: France 24 A2
tte: U.S.A. 51 F2
tte Harbour:
51 F4
ttesville: U.S.A. 51 G2
ttetown: Can. 47 X7
llais, Monts du:
e 25 A2
ers Towers:
stralia 40 H5
es: France 20 C3
omús: Argentina 56 C4
aubriant: France 20 B3
audun: France 20 C3
auroux: France 20 C3
llerault: France 20 C3
am: Canada 51 F1
am: England 13 G3
am Is.: Pac. O. 42 H11
am Rise: Pac. O. 42 G11
apur: India 34 D5
ahoochee: & r.,
A. 51 E3
anooga: U.S.A. 51 E2
ens: England 13 G2
mont: France 20 D3
dle: Gtr. Man.,
and 14 D3
dle: Staffs., Eng. 13 E2
na Mt.: U.S.A. 51 E3
Czech. 24 C1
oksary: U.S.S.R. 30 F2
dar: England 12 D3
uba: i., Burma 33 O7
o: China 36 G3
(Quelpart) I.:
h Korea 36 H4
unda: U.S.S.R. 29 Q7
ken: U.S.S.R. 30 G6
f: r., Algeria 21 C5
ar-Tengiz,
: U.S.S.R. 31 J4
n: Poland 22 D2

Chelmsford: England 13 G3
Cheltenham: Eng. 12 D3
Chelyabinsk: U.S.S.R. 31 J2
Chelyuskin, Cape:
U.S.S.R. 29 N2
Chemnitz *see*
Karl-Marx-Stadt
Chemung: *r.*, U.S.A. 51 G1
Chenab: *r.*, Ind./Pak. 34 C2
Chengchow
(Zhengzhou): China 36 E4
Chengteh (Jehol):
China 36 F2
Chengtu (Chengdu):
China 36 C4
Chentung: China 36 J1
Chepes: Argentina 56 A3
Chepstow: Wales 12 D3
Cheraw: U.S.A. 51 G3
Cherbourg: France 20 B3
Cherchell: Algeria 21 C5
Cherdoyak: U.S.S.R. 31 N4
Cheremkhovo: U.S.S.R. 29 N7
Cherepovets: U.S.S.R. 30 D2
Chernogorsk: U.S.S.R. 31 P3
Chernovtsy: U.S.S.R. 22 E3
Chernyakhovsk:
U.S.S.R. 19 D5
Cherokees, Lake of the:
U.S.A. 50 D2
Cherrapunji: India 35 F3
Cherskiy Range:
U.S.S.R. 29 R4
Chertsey: England 13 F3
Chervonograd:
U.S.S.R. 22 D2
Cherwell: *r.*, England 13 E2
Chesapeake Bay:
U.S.A. 51 G2
Chesham: England 13 F3
Cheshire: *Co.*, Eng. 12 D1
Cheshunt: England 13 G3
Chesil Beach: Eng. 12 D4
Chester: England 12 D1
Chester: U.S.A. 51 G1
Chesterfield: England 13 E1
Chesterfield Inlet:
sett., Canada 47 R4
Chester-le-Street:
England 14 E2
Cheviot: *mtn.*, Eng. 17 F4
Cheviot Hills: Eng./
Scotland 17 F4
Chew Valley Lake:
England 12 D3
Cheyenne: & *r.*, U.S.A. 53 E2
Cheyenne Wells:
town, U.S.A. 53 E3
Chhindwara: India 34 C4
Chiang Mai: Thailand 36 B7
Chiang Rai: Thailand 36 B7
Chiari: Italy 25 B2
Chiba: & *Pref.*,
Japan 38 g iv
Chibougamau: Can. 47 V7
Chica, Sierra: *ra.*, Arg. 56 B3
Chicago: U.S.A. 51 E1
Chichagof I.: U.S.A. 46 H5
Chichén Itzá: Mex. 48 J5
Chichester: England 13 F4
Chichibu: Japan 38 f iv
Chichibu-tama-
kokuritsu-kōen:
nat. park, Japan 38 e iv
Chiclayo: Peru 54 C5
Chico: *r.*, Chubut,
Argentina 55 E12
Chico: *r.*, Tucuman,
Argentina 56 A2
Chico: U.S.A. 52 A3
Chicoutimi: Can. 47 V7
Chiemsee: *l.*, Ger. F.R. 25 C2
Chieti: Italy 23 B4
Chigasaki: Japan 38 f iv
Chihfeng: China 36 F2
Chihli, Gulf of (Po Hai):
China 36 F3
Chihuahua: Mexico 48 E4
Chilaw: Sri Lanka 34 a ii
CHILE: 54/55 –
Chile Basin: Pacific O. 43 R10
Chile Rise: Pacific O. 43 R11
Chillán: Chile 55 D11
Chillicothe: U.S.A. 51 F2
Chiloé Island: Chile 55 D12
Chiltern Hills: Eng. 13 F3
Chimborazo: *volc.*, Ec. 54 C4
Chimbote: Peru 54 C5
Chimkent: U.S.S.R. 31 K5
Chimo: China 36 D2
CHINA: 36 –
Chinandega: Nicaragua 48 J7
Chinchow: China 36 G2
Chindwin: *r.*, Burma 33 O6
Chingyuan *see* Paoting 36 F3
Chin Hills: & *Divis.*,
Burma 33 O6
Chinkiang: China 36 F4
Chinnampo: N. Korea 36 H3
Chioggia: Italy 25 C2
Chios: & *i.*, Greece 23 E5
Chipata: Zambia 61 F10
Chippenham: England 12 D3
Chippewa Falls:
town, U.S.A. 53 G2
Chipping Camden: Eng. 13 E2
Chipping Ongar: Eng. 13 G3
Chipping Norton: Eng. 13 E3
Chipping Sodbury: Eng. 12 D3
Chiquitos Plateau: Bol. 54 F7
Chiryu: Japan 38 d ii
Chisimaio: Somali Rep. 60 H8
Chita: Japan 38 c ii
Chita: & *Reg.*,
U.S.S.R. 29 O7
Chita-Hanto: *penin.*,
Japan 38 c ii
Chitose: Japan 38 D1
Chitral: Pakistan 34 B1
Chittagong: Bangl 35 F4
Chivilcoy: Argentina 56 B3

Choctawhatchee: *r.*,
U.S.A. 51 E3
Chofu: Japan 38 f iv
Choibalsan: Mongolia 36 E1
Cholet: France 20 B3
Chongjin: N. Korea 36 H2
Chongqing *see*
Chungking 36 D5
Chonos Arch.: Chile 55 D12
Chopim: *r.*, Brazil 56 D2
Chorley: England 14 D3
Choshi: Japan 38 g iv
Christchurch: England 13 E4
Christchurch: N.Z. 41 B3
Christmas I.: Indian O. 37 D13
*Christmas I.: Pacific O. 43 K6
Christmas Ridge:
Pacific Ocean 42 J6
Chu: & *r.*, U.S.S.R. 31 L5
Chubu-sangaku-
kokuritsu-kōen:
nat. park, Japan 38 C2
Chubut: *r.*, Argentina 55 E12
Chudleigh: England 12 C4
Chugoku-Sanchi:
mtns., Japan 38 B2
Chuguchak: China 31 N4
Chuí: Brazil 56 D3
Chukchi Sea:
U.S.S.R./Alaska 29 V3
Chulak-Tau: U.S.S.R. 31 L5
Chulmleigh: England 12 C4
Chulym: *r.*, U.S.S.R. 31 O2
Chumbicha: Argentina 56 A2
Chumphon: Thailand 37 B8
Chungking
(Chongqing): China 36 D5
Chuquicamata: Chile 54 E8
Chur (Coire): Switz. 25 B2
Churchill: Can. 47 R5
Churchill: *r.*, Canada 47 Q5
Churchill Falls: *sett.*,
Canada 47 X6
Church Stretton: Eng. 12 D2
Churn: *r.*, England 13 E3
Chuzu: Japan 38 c i
Cienfuegos: Cuba 49 K5
Cilician Gates:
pass, Turkey 30 C6
Cimarron: *r.*, U.S.A. 50 C2
Cincinnati: U.S.A. 51 F2
Cinzas, Rio das:
r., Brazil 56 D1
Cirencester: England 13 E3
Ciudad Acuña: Mex. 50 B4
Ciudad Bolivar: Ven. 49 O8
Ciudad Guayana: Ven. 54 F2
Ciudad Madero: Mex. 48 G5
Ciudad Real: Spain 21 B5
Ciudad Victoria: Mex. 48 G5
Civitavecchia: Italy 23 B4
Clach Leathad: *mtn.*,
Scotland 16 D3
Clacton-on-Sea: Eng. 13 H3
Claerwen Res.: Wales 12 C2
Clara: Irish Rep. 15 D3
Clare: *Co.*, Irish Rep. 15 B4
Clare: *r.*, Irish Rep. 15 B3
Clarecastle: Irish Rep. 15 C4
Clare I.: Irish Rep. 15 A3
Claremorris: Irish Rep. 15 C3
Clarinda: U.S.A. 50 C1
Clark Hill Reservoir:
U.S.A. 51 F3
Clark Point: Canada 51 F2
Clarksdale: U.S.A. 50 D3
Clarksville: U.S.A. 51 E2
Clausthal-Zellerfeld:
German F.R. 24 C1
Clay Cross: England 13 E1
Claydon: England 13 H2
Clayton: U.S.A. 53 E3
Clear Fork: *r.*, U.S.A. 50 C3
Clear I.: Irish Rep. 15 B5
Clear Lake: U.S.A. 52 A3
Clearwater: U.S.A. 51 F4
Clearwater: *r.*, U.S.A. 52 B1
Cleator Moor: England 14 C2
Cleburne: U.S.A. 50 C3
Cleethorpes: England 14 F3
Cleobury Mortimer:
England 12 D2
Clermont-Ferrand: Fr. 20 C3
Clès: Italy 25 C2
Clevedon: England 12 D3
Cleveland: *Co.*, Eng. 14 E2
Cleveland: Miss.,
U.S.A. 50 D3
Cleveland: Ohio, U.S.A. 51 F1
Cleveland: Tenn.,
U.S.A. 51 F2
Cleveland: Tex., U.S.A. 50 C3
Cleveland Hills: England 14 E2
Clevelândia: Brazil 56 D2
Cleveleys: England 14 C3
Clew Bay: Irish Rep. 15 B3
Clifden: Irish Rep. 15 B3
Clingmans Dome:
mtn., U.S.A. 51 F2
Clinton: Iowa, U.S.A. 50 D1
Clinton: N.C., U.S.A. 51 G3
Clinton: Okla., U.S.A. 50 C2
Clipperton I.: Pacific O. 43 P5
Clisham: *mtn.*, Scot. 16 B2
Clitheroe: England 14 D3
Clodomira: Argentina 56 B2
Cloghan: Irish Rep. 15 D3
Clogher: N. Ireland 15 D2
Clogher Head: *cape*,
Irish Rep. 15 E3
Clonakilty: Irish Rep. 15 C5
Cloncurry: Australia 40 G5
Clondalkin: Irish Rep. 15 E3
Clones: Irish Rep. 15 D2
Clonmel: Irish Rep. 15 D4
Clonnda: Argentina 56 C2
Clontarf: Irish Rep. 16 E3
Cloppenburg: Ger. F.R. 24 B1
Clovelly: England 12 B4
Cloverdale: U.S.A. 52 A3
Clovis: Calif., U.S.A. 52 D3

Clovis: N. Mex., U.S.A. 53 E4
Cluanie, Loch: Scot. 16 C2
Cluj: Romania 22 D3
Clun: *r.*, England 12 D2
Clun Forest: England 12 C2
Clutha: *r.*, N.Z. 41 A4
Clwyd: *r.*, & *Co.*,
Wales 12 C1
Clwydian Range: Wales 12 C1
Clyde: *r.*, Scotland 17 E4
Clyde, Firth of: *est.*,
Scotland 17 D4
Clydebank: Scotland 17 D4
Cnoc Moy: *mtn.*, Scot. 17 C4
Coalisland: N. Ireland 15 E2
Coalville: England 13 E2
Coast Mts.: Can. 46 J5
Coast Ranges: U.S.A. 52 –
Coatbridge: Scotland 17 D4
Coatzacoalcos: Mex. 48 H6
Cobh: Irish Rep. 15 C5
Coburg: German F.R. 24 C1
Cochabamba: Bolivia 54 E7
Cochem: German F.R. 24 B1
Cochin: India 34 C6
Cochrane, Lake:
Argentina/Chile 55 D13
Cockermouth: England 14 C2
Cock of Arran: *pt.*,
Scotland 17 C4
Cocoa: U.S.A. 51 F4
Cocos Islands: Ind. O. 35 h vi
Cocos Basin: Ind. O. 35 h v
Cocos Islands: Ind. O. 35 h vi
Cocos Islands: Pac. O. 54 A2
Cocos Ridge: Pac. O. 43 R6
Cod, Cape: U.S.A. 47 N1
Cody: U.S.A. 52 D2
Coeur d'Alene: U.S.A. 52 B1
Coffeyville: U.S.A. 50 C2
Cognac: France 20 B3
Coimbatore: India 34 C6
Coimbra: Portugal 21 A4
Coire: *see* Chur 25 B2
Colatina: Brazil 54 K7
Colby: U.S.A. 50 B2
Colchester: England 13 G3
Coldstream: Scotland 17 F4
Coleford: England 12 D3
Coleraine: N. Ireland 15 E1
Colfax: U.S.A. 52 B1
Colgrave Sound:
Shetland Islands 16 c i
Colima: Mexico 48 F6
Coll: *i.*, Scotland 16 B3
Colmar: France 25 B2
Coln: *r.*, England 13 E3
Colne: England 14 D3
Colne: *r.*, England 13 G3
Colne Point: England 13 H3
Cologne (Köln):
German F.R. 24 B1
COLOMBIA: 54 –
COLOMBO: Sri Lanka 34 a ii
Colón: Argentina 56 B3
Colón: Panama 49 *Ins.*
Colonia del Rosario
Sacramento: Uru. 56 C3
Colonsay: *i.*, Scot. 17 B3
Colorado: *r.*, Argentina 56 E11
Colorado: *State* & *r.*,
U.S.A. 52-3 D3
Colorado: *r.*, Tex.,
U.S.A. 50 C4
Colorado Plateaux:
U.S.A. 52 C3
Colorado Springs:
town, U.S.A. 53 E3
Columbia: Mo., U.S.A. 50 D2
Columbia: S.C., U.S.A. 51 F3
Columbia: Tenn.,
U.S.A. 51 E2
Columbia: *r.*,
Can./U.S.A. 46 L7
Columbia, Cape: Can. 47 V0
Columbia Mts.:
Canada 46 L/M6
Columbus: Ga., U.S.A. 51 F3
Columbus: Ind., U.S.A. 51 E2
Columbus: Ka., U.S.A. 50 D2
Columbus: Miss.,
U.S.A. 51 E3
Columbus: Nebr.,
U.S.A. 53 F2
Columbus: Ohio,
U.S.A. 53 F2
Colville: U.S.A. 52 B1
Colville Lake: Can. 46 K3
Colwyn Bay: Wales 12 C1
Comandante Fontana:
Argentina 56 C2
Combe Martin: England 12 B3
Comber: N. Ireland 15 F2
Comechingones, Sierra
de: *ra.*, Argentina 56 B3
Comeragh Mts.: Irish
Republic 15 D4
Comilla: Bangladesh 35 F4
Communism, Mt.:
U.S.S.R. 31 L6
Como: & *lake*, Italy 25 B2
Comodoro Rivadavia:
Argentina 55 E13
Comorin, Cape: India 34 C7
*Comoro Is.: Indian O. 61 H10
Compiègne: France 20 C3
Comprida, Ilha: *i.*,
Brazil 56 E1
CONAKRY: Guinea 58 C7
Concepción:
Corrientes, Argentina 56 C2
Concepción: Tucumán,
Argentina 56 A2
Concepción: Chile 55 D11
Concepción: Paraguay 56 C1
Concepción del
Uruguay: Argentina 56 C3
Conception, Point:
U.S.A. 52 A4
Concho: *r.*, U.S.A. 50 B3
Concord: U.S.A. 51 F2

Concordia: Argentina 56 C3
Concórdia: Brazil 56 D2
Condor: *mtn.*, Arg. 56 A1
Confuso: *r.*, Paraguay 56 C1
Congleton: England 12 D1
CONGO: 61 D8
Congo (Zaïre): *r.*,
Congo/Zaïre 61 C8
Conisbrough: England 14 E3
Connah's Quay: Wales 12 C1
Connecuh: *r.*, U.S.A. 51 E3
Connemara: *dist.*,
Irish Rep. 15 B3
Connersville: U.S.A. 51 E2
Conrad: U.S.A. 52 C1
Conroe: U.S.A. 50 C3
Consett: England 14 E2
Constance, Lake
(Bodensee): Switz./
German F.R. 25 B2
Constanta: Romania 23 E4
Conway: U.S.A. 51 G3
Conwy: Wales 12 C1
Cooch Behlar: India 35 F3
Cook, Mt.: N.Z. 41 B3
Cook Is.: Pacific O. 42 K8
Cookstown: N. Ireland 15 E2
Cook Strait: N.Z. 41 B3
Cooktown: Australia 40 H4
Coolgardie: Australia 40 C7
Cooper Creek: Austl. 40 G6
Coosa: *r.*, U.S.A. 51 E3
Cootehill: Irish Rep. 15 D2
COPENHAGEN:
Denmark 19 B4
Copiapo: Chile 54 D9
Coppermine: Canada 46 N3
Coquet: *r.*, England 14 E1
Coral Gables: U.S.A. 51 F4
Corbridge: England 14 D2
Corby: England 13 F2
Cordele: U.S.A. 51 F3
Cordillera Cantabrica:
ra., Spain 21 A4
Cordillera Central:
ra., Spain 21 A4
Cordillera de Caaguazú:
ra., Paraguay 56 C2
Cordillera de Mérida:
ra., Venezuela 49 M8
Cordilleras Béticas:
ra., Spain 21 B5
Córdoba: & *Prov.*,
Argentina 56 B3
Cordoba: Spain 21 B5
Cordova: U.S.A. 46 F4
Corinth: & *gulf*,
Greece 23 D5
Corinth: U.S.A. 51 E3
Cork: & *Co.*, Irish
Republic 15 C5
Cork Harbour: Irish
Republic 15 C5
Corlu: Turkey 23 E4
Cornélio Procópio:
Brazil 56 D1
Corner Brook: Can. 47 Y7
Cornwall: Canada 47 V7
Cornwall: *Co.*, England 12 B4
Cornwall, Cape: U.K. 12 d iii
Cornwall I.: Can. 47 R1
Cornwallis I.: Can. 47 Q1
Coromandel Coast:
India 34 D6
Coromandel Range:
New Zealand 41 C2
Coronation Gulf: Can. 46 N3
Coronation I.: S. Ork. Is. 55 J16
Coronda: Argentina 56 B3
Coronel Bogado: Par. 56 C2
Coronel Granada: Arg. 56 B3
Coronel Moldes: Arg. 56 A2
Coronel Oviedo: Par. 56 C2
Corpus Christi: & *bay*,
U.S.A. 50 C4
Corraun Penin: Irish
Republic 15 B3
Correen Hills: Scot. 16 F2
Corrib Lough: Irish
Republic 15 B3
Corrientes: & *Prov.*,
Argentina 56 C2
Corrientes: *r.*, Arg. 56 C2
Corse, Cap: Corsica 21 a i
Corsham: England 12 D3
Corsica: *i.*, Med. Sea 21 a i
Corsicana: U.S.A. 50 C3
Corte: Corsica 21 a i
Cortina d'Ampezzo: It. 25 C2
Corumbá: Brazil 54 G7
Corumbataí: *r.*, Braz. 56 D1
Corvallis: U.S.A. 52 A2
Corve: *r.*, England 12 D2
Corwen: Wales 12 C2
Coryton: England 13 G3
Cosenza: Italy 23 C5
Costa Brava: *coast*,
Spain 21 C4
Costa del Sol: *coast*,
Spain 21 B5
COSTA RICA: 49 –
Côte d'Or: *geog. reg.*,
France 25 A2
Côtes de Moselle:
hills, France 24 B2
Cothi: *r.*, Wales 12 B3
Cotonou: Benin 58 F7
Cotopaxi: *volc.*, Ec. 54 C4
Cotswolds: *hills*, Eng. 12 D3
Cottbus: German D.R. 24 C1
Cottenham: England 13 G2
Cottian Alps: Fr./It. 25 B3
Cottingham: England 14 F3
Cotulla: U.S.A. 50 C4
Council Bluffs: U.S.A. 50 C1
Coupar Angus: Scot. 16 E3
Courmeyeur: Italy 25 B2
Courtmascherry Bay:
Irish Republic 15 C5
Coventry: England 13 E2
Covilhã: Portugal 21 A4

Covington: U.S.A. 51 G2
Cowdenbeath: Scot. 17 E3
Cowes: England 13 E4
Cowley: England 13 E3
Coxilha de Santana:
hills, Braz./Uru. 56 C3
Cozad: U.S.A. 53 E2
Cracow: Poland 22 C3
Craignure: Scotland 16 C3
Crail: Scotland 16 F3
Craiova: Romania 23 D4
Cranbrook: England 13 G3
Cranleigh: England 13 F3
Cranwell: England 13 F1
Crater Lake Nat. Park:
U.S.A. 52 A2
Craters of the Moon
Nat. Monument:
U.S.A. 52 C2
Crato: Brazil 54 L5
Crawfordsville:
U.S.A. 51 E2
Crawley: England 13 F3
Crediton: England 12 C4
Cree: *r.*, Scotland 17 D5
Crema: Italy 25 B2
Cremona: Italy 25 C2
Cres: *i.*, Yugoslavia 23 B4
Crescent City:
U.S.A. 52 A2
Crestview: U.S.A. 51 E3
Crete: *i.* & *sea*, Greece 23 D5
Creus, Cap: Spain 21 C4
Crewe: England 12 D1
Crewkerne: England 12 D4
Criccieth: Wales 12 B2
Criciúma: Brazil 56 E2
Cricklade: England 13 E3
Crieff: Scotland 16 E3
Crimea: *penin.*,
U.S.S.R. 30 C4
Cromalt Hills: Scot. 16 D2
Cromarty: & *firth*, Scot. 16 D2
Cromer: England 13 H2
Cromwell: N.Z. 41 A4
Crook: England 14 E2
Crookston: U.S.A. 53 F1
Croom: Irish Rep. 15 C4
Crosby: England 14 C3
Crosby: Minn., U.S.A. 53 G1
Crosby: N. Dak.,
U.S.A. 53 E1
Cross Fell: Eng. 14 D2
Crosshaven: Irish Rep. 15 C5
Cross Hill: N. Irel. 15 D2
Crossmaglen: N. Irel. 15 E2
Crossmolina: Irish Rep. 15 B2
Crotone: Italy 23 C5
Crouch: *r.*, England 13 G3
Crowborough: England 13 G3
Crowland: England 13 F2
Crowle: England 14 F3
Crowsnest Pass: Can. 46 N7
Croydon: Australia 40 G4
Croydon: England 13 F3
Crozet Basin: Ind. O. 35 d viii
Crozet Islands: Ind. O. 35 d ix
Cruz Alta: Brazil 56 D2
Cruz del Eje: & *r.*, Arg. 56 B3
Cruzeiro: Brazil 56 b i
Cruzeiro do Oeste:
Brazil 56 D1
Cruzeiro do Sul:
Brazil 54 D5
Cuaró Grande: *r.*, Uru. 56 C3
Cuarto: *r.*, Argentina 56 B3
CUBA: 49 –
Cubatão: Brazil 56 a i
Cuchilla de Haedo:
hills, Uruguay 56 C3
Cuchilla de Montiel:
hills, Argentina 56 C3
Cuchilla Grande:
hills, Argentina 56 C3
Cuchilla Grande:
hills, Uruguay 56 C3
Cuckfield: England 13 F3
Cucuta: Colombia 49 M8
Cuddalore: India 34 C6
Cuddapah: India 34 C6
Cuenca: Spain 21 B4
Cuiabá: Brazil 54 G7
Cuillin Hills: Scot. 16 B2
Cullen: Scotland 16 F2
Cullin, Lough: Irish
Republic 15 B3
Cullman: U.S.A. 51 E3
Cullompton: England 12 C4
Culm: *r.*, England 12 C4
Culoz: France 25 B2
Culter Fell: *hill*,
Scotland 17 E4
Culvain: *mtn.*, Scot. 16 C3
Cumaná: Venezuela 49 O7
Cumberland: U.S.A. 51 G2
Cumberland: *r.*, U.S.A. 51 E2
Cumberland Gap:
U.S.A. 51 F2
Cumberland, Lake:
U.S.A. 51 E2
Cumberland Plateau:
U.S.A. 51 E2
Cumberland Sound:
Canada 47 W3
Cumbernauld: Scot. 17 E4
Cumbrian Mts.:
England 14 C2
Cumnock: Scotland 17 D4
Cuneo: Italy 25 B3
Cunnamulla: Australia 40 H6
Cupar: Scotland 16 E3
Curaçao: *i.*, Neth.
Antilles 49 N7
Curicó: Chile 55 D11
Curitiba: Brazil 56 E2
Currane, Lough: Irish
Republic 15 B5
Curuguaty: Paraguay 56 C1
Curuzú Chalí, Isla:
Argentina 56 C3
Curuzu Cuatiá: Arg. 56 C2

page 80

* See page 80

: Somali Rep. 59 P6
i., Scot. 16 A2
Loch: Scot. 16 B1
Prov., Eth. 59 O6
r., Irish
alic 15 D4
n: Ger. F.R. 24 C2
Mts.: Mor. 58 D2
mtn., Irish
alic 15 C1
ead: cape,
Republic 15 A2
Oeste: Braz. 56 D2
rge: mtns., Ger.
Czech. 24 C1
n: Turkey 30 E6
: Denmark 19 A4
ba: U.S.A. 53 H1
Luxembourg 24 B2
ege: Ger. F.R. 24 C1
lido: U.S.A. 52 B4
England 13 F3
England 14 F2
Scotland 17 E4
una: Sweden 19 C4
Point: town,
la 47 R4
ir: Turkey 30 C6
aldas: Ec. 54 C3
nce: Australia 40 C7
nza: Argentina 56 B3
o Santo: State,
54 K8
Finland 19 D3
a Negra: Arg. 56 C4
ira: Morocco 58 D2
Ger. F.R. 24 B1
uibo: r., Guyana 54 G3
Co., England 13 G3
len: Ger. F.R. 25 B2
Brazil 56 D2
azy: Canada 46 P6
Bay: U.S.A. 52 A3
: Paraguay 56 B1
s del Iberá:
ps, Argentina 56 C2
England 14 E2
an S.S.R.:
.R. 19 E4
gom: Hungary 22 C3
de Berre: lag.,
e 25 B3
de Vaccarès:
France 25 A3
n: India 34 C3
PIA: 59 N7
ian Plateau: Eth. 59 N7
Loch: Scotland 16 C3
Mt.: volc., Sicily 23 B5
England 13 F3
Pan: salt
Namibia 61 C11
an Apennines:
, Italy 25 C3
a: i., Greece 23 D5
Australia 40 D7
a: U.S.A. 50 D3
a: U.S.A. 51 E3
a Reservoir:
A. 50 C2
e: U.S.A. 52 A2
e: U.S.A. 50 D3
: Belgium 24 B1
ates: r., Asia 32 D4
a: Calif., U.S.A. 52 A2
a: Mont., U.S.A. 52 B1
a: Nev., U.S.A. 52 B3
ort: Neth. 24 A1
on: U.S.A. 52 C2
ville: U.S.A. 51 E2
r., Scotland 16 D2
ode: r., England 13 E3
st, Mt.: China/
al 34 E3
t: U.S.A. 52 A1
ades, The:
nps, U.S.A. 51 F4
ades Nat. Park:
A. 51 F4
am: England 13 E2
France 25 B2
Portugal 21 A5
x: France 20 C3
Loch: Scotland 16 C2
, England 12 C3
: England 12 C4
or Forest: reg.,
and 12 C3
or Nat. Park: Eng. 12 C3
uth: England 12 C4
uth Gulf: Austl. 40 A5
England 13 H2
outh: Scotland 17 F4
eninsula: Scot. 16 B1
Lake: Australia 40 F6
g: Norway 19 B3
Loch: Scotland 16 C2
a: Italy 25 C3
e Is.: Atl. O. 10 K1
nes: Norway 19 A3
sta: Sweden 19 C3
bine, Lake: Ma'i 58 E5
anks: U.S.A. 46 F4
ury: U.S.A. 53 F2
eld: U.S.A. 52 A3
rd: England 13 E3
ead: cape, N.
nd 15 E1
sle: Scot. 11 C1
ont: U.S.A. 51 F1
U.S.A. 53 E1
bad: Afghanistan 31 L6
ham: England 13 G2
nye: U.S.S.R. 31 L1
, England 12 B4
nberg: Ger. D.R. 24 C1
hberg: Sweden 19 B4

Falkirk: Scotland 17 E4
Falkland Is.: Atlantic O. 55 G14
Falköping: Sweden 19 B4
Fall River: *city*, U.S.A. 47 M1
Falls City: U.S.A. 50 C1
Falmouth: *& bay*, Eng. 12 A4
Falun: Sweden 19 C3
Famagusta: Cyprus 32 B3
Fana: Norway 19 A3
Fannich, Loch: Scot. 16 D2
*Fanning I.: Pacific O. 42 K6
Fano: Italy 25 C3
Faradofay: Madagascar 61 J12
Farah: Afghanistan 32 H4
Farasan Is.: Red Sea 32 D7
Fareham: England 13 E4
Farewell: U.S.A. 46 E4
Farewell, Cape: Grnld. 47 BB5
Farewell, Cape: N.Z. 41 B3
Fargo: U.S.A. 53 F1
Faribault: U.S.A. 53 G2
Faringdon: England 13 E3
Farmington: U.S.A. 52 D3
Farnborough: England 13 F3
Farnham: England 13 F3
Farnworth: England 14 D3
Faro: Portugal 21 A5
Fårön: *i.*, Sweden 19 C4
Farrar: *r.*, Scot 16 D2
Farsund: Norway 19 A4
Fastov: U.S.S.R. 22 E2
Fauske: Norway 18 C2
Faustino M. Parera: Argentina 56 C3
Faversham: England 13 G3
Fawley: England 13 E4
Faxa Bay: Iceland 18 a ii
Fayette: U.S.A. 51 E3
Fayetteville: Ark., U.S.A. 50 D2
Fayetteville: N.C., U.S.A. 51 G2
Fayid: Egypt 59 *Ins.*
F'Dérik: Mauritania 58 C4
Feale: *r.*, Irish Rep. 15 B4
Fear, Cape: U.S.A. 51 G3
Fecagh, Lough: Irish Republic 15 B3
Fécamp: France 20 C3
Feilding: N.Z. 41 C3
Feira de Santana: Brazil 54 L6
Feldkirch: Austria 25 B2
Feliciano: *r.*, Arg. 56 C3
Felixstowe: England 13 H3
Feltre: Italy 25 C2
Femund: *lake*, Norway 18 B3
Fengsiang: China 36 D4
Fengyang: China 36 F4
Fens, The: *reg.*, Eng. 13 F2
Fenyang: China 36 E3
Feolin Ferry: Scot. 17 B4
Ferbane: Irish Rep. 15 D3
Fergana: U.S.S.R. 31 L5
Fergus Falls: *town*, U.S.A. 53 F1
Fermanagh: *Co.*, N. Ireland 15 D2
Fermoy: Irish Rep. 15 C4
Fernando de Noronha: *i.*, Brazil 54 M4
Ferrara: Italy 25 C3
Fès: Morocco 58 E2
Fethard: Irish Rep. 15 D4
Fetlar: *i.*, Shetland Is. 16 c i
Ffestiniog: Wales 12 B2
Ffoiest Fawr: *hills*, Wales 12 C3
Fianarantsoa: Malagasy Republic 61 I12
Fichtelgebirge: *mtns.*, German F.R. 24 C1
Fidenza: Italy 25 C3
Fier: Albania 23 C4
Fife: *reg.*, Scotland 17 E3
Fife Ness: *pt.*, Scot. 16 F3
Figile: *r.*, Irish Rep. 15 D3
Figueira da Foz: Port. 21 A4
Figueras: Spain 21 C4
FIJI: 42 G8
Filey: England 14 F2
Filton: England 12 D3
Finca el Rey, Parque Nacional: Argentina 56 B1
Findhorn: Scotland 16 E2
Findlay: U.S.A. 51 F1
Finisterre, Cape: Spain 21 A4
FINLAND: 18/19 –
Finland, Gulf of: Finland/U.S.S.R. 19 E4
Finnmarksvidda: *plat.*, Norway 18 D2
Finschhafen: Papua-New Guinea 40 H2
Finspång: Sweden 19 C4
Finsteraarhorn: *mtn.*, Switzerland 25 B2
Fintona: N. Ireland 15 D2
Fionn, Loch: Scotland 16 C2
Fionnphort: Scotland 16 B3
Fiordland: *dist.*, N.Z. 41 A4
Fire Island National Seashore: U.S.A. 51 H1
Firenze *see* Florence 25 C3
Fishguard: Wales 12 B3
Fitzroy: *r.*, Australia 40 C4
Flagstaff: U.S.A. 52 C3
Flåm: Norway 19 A3
Flamborough Head: *cape*, England 14 F2
Flaming George Reservoir: U.S.A. 52 D2
Flanders: *Prov.*, Belg. 24 A1
Flathead Lake: U.S.A. 52 C1
Flattery, Cape: U.S.A. 52 A1
Fleet: England 13 F3
Fleet: *r.*, Scotland 16 D2
Fleetwood: England 14 C3
Flekkefjord: Norway 19 A4
Flers: France 20 B3
Flinders: *r.*, Australia 40 G4

Flinders Island: Australia 41 H9
Flinders Range: Austl. 40 F7
Flin Flon: Canada 46 P6
Flint: U.S.A. 51 F1
Flint: *r.*, U.S.A. 51 F3
Flint: Wales 12 C1
Flora: Norway 18 A3
Florence (Firenze): It. 25 C3
Florence: Ala., U.S.A. 51 E3
Florence: Ariz., U.S.A. 52 C4
Florence: S.C. U.S.A. 51 G3
Florencia: Colombia 54 C3
Flores: *i. & sea*, Indon. 37 G12
Floreshty: U.S.S.R. 22 E3
Floriano: Brazil 54 K5
Florianópolis: Brazil 56 E2
Florida: Uruguay 56 C3
Florida: *State*, U.S.A. 51 F4
Florida Bay: U.S.A. 51 F4
Florida Keys: *is.*, U.S.A. 51 F4
Florida, Straits of: The Bahamas/U.S.A. 51 G4
Florina: Greece 23 D4
Flushing: Netherlands 24 A1
Fly: *r.*, Papua-New Guinea 40 G2
Fochabers: Scotland 16 E2
Focsani: Romania 22 E3
Foel Wen: *mtn.*, Wales 12 C2
Foggia: Italy 23 C4
Fohnsdorf: Austria 22 B3
Foinaven: *mtn.*, Scot. 16 D1
Foligno: Italy 23 B4
Folkestone: England 13 H3
Fond du Lac: Can. 46 O5
Fond du Lac: U.S.A. 53 H2
Foochow (Fuzhou): China 36 F5
Forcalquier: France 25 B3
Fordingbridge: England 13 E4
Fordlândia: Brazil 54 G4
Forel, Mt.: Greenland 47 DD3
Foreland: *pt.*, England 13 E4
Foreland Point: Eng. 12 C3
Forfar: Scotland 16 F3
Forli: Italy 25 C3
Formby: England 14 C3
Formentera: *i.*, Balearic Is. 21 C5
Formosa: *& Prov.*, Arg. 56 C2
Formosa Strait: China/Taiwan 36 F6
Forres: Scotland 16 E2
Forrest: Australia 40 D7
Forrest City: U.S.A. 50 D2
Forsayth: Australia 40 G4
Fortaleza: Brazil 54 L4
Fortaleza de Santa Teresa: Uruguay 56 D3
Fort Augustus: Scot. 16 D2
Fort Chimo: Canada 47 W5
Fort Chipewyan: Can. 46 N5
Fort Collins: U.S.A. 53 D2
FORT DE FRANCE Martinique 49 O7
Fort Dodge: U.S.A. 50 D1
Fortescue: *r.*, Austl. 40 B5
Fort Frances: Canada 53 G1
Forth: *r.*, Scotland 17 D3
Forth, Firth of: *est.*, Scotland 17 F3
Fortín Lavalle: Arg. 56 B2
Fort Lauderdale: U.S.A. 51 F4
Fort Liard: Canada 46 L4
Fort McMurray: Can. 46 N5
Fort McPherson: Can. 46 J3
Fort Madison: U.S.A. 50 D1
Fort Morgan: U.S.A. 53 E2
Fort Myers: U.S.A. 51 F4
Fort Nelson: Can. 46 L5
Fort Norman: Canada 46 L4
Fort Peck Reservoir: U.S.A. 52 D1
Fort Pierce: U.S.A. 51 F4
Fort Portal: Uganda 60 F7
Fort Providence: Can. 46 M4
Fort Resolution: Can. 46 N4
Fortrose: Scotland 16 D2
Fort Sandeman: Pak. 34 A2
Fort Scott: U.S.A. 50 D2
Fort Shevchenko: U.S.S.R. 30 G5
Fort Simpson: Canada 46 L4
Fort Smith: Canada 46 N4
Fort Smith: U.S.A. 50 D2
Fort Sumner: U.S.A. 53 E4
Fort Wayne: U.S.A. 51 E1
Fort William: Scot. 16 C3
Fort William *see* Thunder Bay 47 S7
Fort Worth: U.S.A. 50 C3
Fort Yukon: U.S.A. 46 F3
Forssa: Finland 19 D3
Forsyth: U.S.A. 52 D1
Fougères: France 20 B3
Foula: *i.*, Shetland Is. 16 a i
Foul Bay: Red Sea 59 N4
Foulness: *i. & cape*, England 13 G3
Foulwind, Cape: N.Z. 41 B3
Fourmies: France 20 C2
Foveaux Strait: N.Z. 41 A4
Fowey: *& r.*, England 12 B4
Foxe Basin: Canada 47 U3
Foxford: Irish Rep. 15 B3
Foyle, Lough: N. Irel. 15 D1
Foynes: Irish Rep. 15 B4
Foz do Iguaçu: Brazil 56 D2
Fraile Muerto: Uru. 56 D3
FRANCE: 20/21 –
Franche Comté: *Old Prov.*, France 25 B2
Francis Case, Lake: U.S.A. 53 F2
Francistown: Botswana 61 E12
Franconian Heights: *hills*, German F.R. 24 C2

Franconian Jura: *mtns.*, German F.R. 24 C2
Frankfort: Ind., U.S.A. 51 E1
Frankfort: Ky., U.S.A. 51 F2
Frankfurt am Main: German F.R. 24 B1
Frankfurt an der Oder: German D.R. 24 C1
Franklin D. Roosevelt Lake: U.S.A. 52 B1
Franz Josef Land: *is.*, Arctic Ocean 28-9 H1
Fraser: *r.*, Canada 46 L6
Fraserburgh: Scotland 16 G2
Fray Bentos: Uru. 56 C3
Fray Marcos: Uru. 56 C3
Fredericia: Denmark 19 A4
Frederick: U.S.A. 50 C3
Fredericksburg: U.S.A. 51 G2
Fredericktown: U.S.A. 51 D2
Fredericton: Canada 47 W7
Frederikshavn: Den. 19 B4
Fredriksson: Argentina 56 B3
Fredrikstad: Norway 19 B4
Freeport: Ill., U.S.A. 51 E1
Freeport: Tex., U.S.A. 50 C4
FREETOWN: Sierra Leone 58 C7
Freiburg im Breisgau: German F.R. 25 B2
Freising: Ger. F.R. 25 C2
Fréjus: France 25 B3
Fremantle: Australia 40 B7
Fremont: Calif., U.S.A. 52 A3
Fremont: U.S.A. 53 F2
FRENCH GUIANA 54 H3
Frenchman Creek: U.S.A. 53 E2
Fresnillo: Mexico 48 F5
Fresno: U.S.A. 52 B3
Freudenstadt: Ger. F.R. 25 B2
Frías: Argentina 56 A2
Fribourg: Switzerland 25 B2
Friedrichshafen: German F.R. 25 B2
Friesland: *Prov.*, Neth. 24 B1
Frio: *r.*, U.S.A. 50 C4
Frisa, Loch: Scotland 16 B3
Frobisher Bay: *town & bay*, Canada 47 W4
Frodsham: England 12 D1
Frohavet: *bay*, Norway 18 A3
Frome: England 12 D3
Frome: *r.*, Dorset, Eng. 12 D4
Frome: *r.*, Here. & Worcs., England 12 D2
Frome, Lake: Austl. 40 G7
Frosinone: Italy 23 B4
Frostburg: U.S.A. 51 G2
Frøya: *i.*, Norway 18 A3
Frunze: U.S.S.R. 31 L5
Frýdek-Místek: Czech. 22 C3
Fuchu: Japan 38 f iv
Fuerteventura: *i.*, Canary Islands 58 C3
Fuji-hakone-izu-kokuritsu-kōen: *nat. park*, Japan 38 C3
Fujioka: Japan 38 f iii
Fuji-san (Fujiyama): *mtn.*, Japan 38 e iv
Fujisawa: Japan 38 f iv
Fujishiro: Japan 38 g iv
Fujiyama *see* Fuji-san 38 e iv
Fujiyoshida: Japan 38 e iv
Fukaya: Japan 38 fiii
Fukuchiyama: Japan 38 b i
Fukui: Japan 38 C2
Fukuoka: Japan 38 B3
Fukushima: Japan 38 D2
Fukuyama: Japan 38 B3
Fukuzaki: Japan 38 a ii
Fulda: *& r.*, Ger. F.R. 24 B1
Fulton: U.S.A. 51 D1
Funabashi: Japan 38 f iv
Funchal: Madeira 58 B2
Fundy, Bay of: Can. 47 W8
Furka Pass: Switz. 25 B2
Fürth: German F.R. 24 C2
Fushun: China 36 G2
Fuzhou *see* Foochow 36 F5
Fyn: *i.*, Denmark 19 B4
Fyne, Loch: Scot. 17 C3

G

Gabès: *& gulf*, Tunisia 58 H2
GABON 61 B8
GABORONE Botswana 61 E12
Gabrovo: Bulgaria 23 E4
Gadames: Libya 58 G2
Gadsden: U.S.A. 51 E3
Gaeta: Italy 23 B4
Gaffney: U.S.A. 51 F2
Gafsa: Tunisia 58 G2
Gagnon: Canada 47 W6
Gail: *r.*, Austria 25 C2
Gailey: *r.*, Irish Rep. 15 B4
Gainsborough: England 14 F3
Gainesville: Fla., U.S.A. 51 F4
Gainesville: Ga., U.S.A. 51 F3
Gainesville: Tex., U.S.A. 50 C3
Gairdner, L.: Austl. 40 F7
Gairloch: *& loch*, Scotland 16 C2
Galapagos Is.: Pac. O. 43 Q7
Galashiels: Scotland 17 F4
Galati: Romania 22 E3
Galax: U.S.A. 51 F2
Galena: U.S.A. 46 D4
Galesburg: U.S.A. 50 D1
Galipoli: Italy 23 C4
Gallan Head: *cape*, Scotland 16 A1
Gallarate: Italy 25 B2
Galle: Sri Lanka 34 b ii

Gallegos: *r.*, Arg. 55 D14
Galley Head: *cape*, Irish Republic 15 C5
Gallinas, Punta: *pt.*, Colombia 49 M7
Gällivare: Sweden 18 D2
Galloway, Mull of: *penin.*, Scotland 17 D5
Gallup: U.S.A. 52 D3
Gal Oya: Sri Lanka 34 b ii
Galston: Scotland 17 D4
Galtee Mts.: Irish Republic 15 C4
Galtymore: *mtn.*, Irish Republic 15 C4
Galveston: *& bay*, U.S.A. 50 D4
Gálvez: Argentina 56 B3
Galway: *& Co.*, Irish Republic 15 B3
Galway Bay: Irish Republic 15 B3
Gamagōri: Japan 38 d ii
GAMBIA, THE 58 B6
Gambia: *r.*, The Gambia/Senegal 58 C6
Gambier Islands: Pacific Ocean 43 M9
Gambrill State Park: U.S.A. 54 C5
Gampola: Sri Lanka 34 b ii
Gand *see* Ghent 24 A1
Gandak: *r.*, India 34 D3
Gander: Canada 47 Z7
Ganga (Ganges): *r.*, Bangladesh/India 34-5 E4
Ganges: *r.*, *see* Ganga 34 E3
Ganges, Mouths of the: Bangladesh/India 34/35 E4
Gap: France 25 B3
Garda: *& lake*, It. 25 C2
Garden City: U.S.A. 50 B2
Gardez: Afghanistan 34 A2
Gardner I.: Phoenix Is. 42 H7
Gare, Lough: Irish Rep. 15 C3
Gargano, Cape: Italy 23 C4
Garian: Libya 58 H2
Garibaldi: Brazil 56 D2
Garmisch: Ger. F.R. 25 C2
Garnett: U.S.A. 50 C2
Garonne: *r.*, France 21 B4
*Garoua: Cameroun 58 H7
Garrison: N. Ireland 15 C2
Garrock Head: *cape*, Scotland 17 C4
Garron Point: N. Irel. 15 F1
Garron Point: Scot. 16 F3
Garry: *r.*, Scotland 16 D3
Garry Lake, Canada 46 P4
Garry, Loch: Scot. 16 D2
Garstang: England 14 D3
Gartok: China 34 D2
Garvagh: N. Ireland 15 E2
Gary: U.S.A. 51 E1
Garza: Argentina 56 B2
Gasconade: *r.*, U.S.A. 50 D2
Gasherbrum: *mtn.*, India 34 C1
Gaspar Rodríguez de Francia: Paraguay 56 C1
Gaspé: *& penin.*, Can. 47 X7
Gas-san: *mtn.*, Japan 38 C2
Gastonia: U.S.A. 51 F2
Gata, Cabo de: *cape*, Spain 21 B5
Gatchina: U.S.S.R. 19 F4
Gateshead: England 14 E2
Gatehouse of Fleet: Scotland 17 D5
Gatun Lake: *& locks*, Panama 49 *Ins.*
*Gauhati: India 35 F3
Gävle: Sweden 19 C3
Gaya: India 34 E4
Gaya: Niger 58 F6
Gaziantep: Turkey 30 D6
Gdańsk: *& gulf*, Pol. 22 C2
Gdynia: Poland 22 C2
Gediz: *r.*, Turkey 23 E5
Geelong: Australia 40 G8
Geeraardsbergen: Belg. 24 A1
Geesthacht: Ger. F.R. 24 C1
Geilo: Norway 19 A3
Geiranger: Norway 18 A3
Geissen: German F.R. 24 B1
Gela: Sicily 23 B5
Gelibolu: Turkey 23 E4
Gelligaer: Wales 12 C3
Gelsenkirchen: Ger. F.R. 24 B1
General Alvear: Arg. 56 C4
General Aquino: Par. 56 C1
General José de San Martin: Argentina 56 C2
General Martin Miguel de Güemes: Arg. 56 A1
General Pico: Arg. 56 B4
General Pinedo: Arg. 56 B2
General San Martin: Argentina 56 C3
General Villegas: Arg. 56 B4
Geneva: Switzerland 25 B2
Geneva, Lake of (Léman, Lac): Switz./France 25 B2
Genissiat Dam: France 25 B2
Genoa (Genova): *& gulf*, Italy 25 B3
GEORGETOWN: Guyana 49 P8
Georgetown: U.S.A. 51 G3
Georgia: *state*, U.S.A. 51 F3
Georgian Bay: Canada 47 T7
Georgian S.S.R.: U.S.S.R. 30 E5
Georgiu-Dezh: U.S.S.R. 30 D3
Gera: German D.R. 24 C1
Geraldton: Australia 40 A6

GERMAN DEMOCRATIC REPUBLIC: 24
GERMAN FEDERAL REPUBLIC: 24
Gerona: Spain 21 C4
Gerrards Cross: Eng. 13 F3
Gettysburg: U.S.A. 51 G2
Ghaghara: *r.*, India 34 D3
GHANA: 58 E7
Ghardaia: Algeria 58 F2
Ghazipur: India 34 D3
Ghent (Gand): Belg. 24 A1
Gheorghe Gheorghiu-Dej: Romania 22 E3
Gialo: Libya 59 K3
Giant's Causeway: *rocks*, N. Ireland 15 E1
GIBRALTAR: 21 A5
Gibraltar, Strait of: Africa/Europe 21 A5
Gibson Desert: Austl. 40 C/D5
Gibson Reservoir: U.S.A. 50 C2
Giddings: U.S.A. 50 C3
Gifu: Japan 38 C2
Gigha I.: Scotland 17 C4
Gijón: Spain 21 A4
Gila: *r.*, U.S.A. 52 C4
Gila Bend: *town*, U.S.A. 52 C4
Gilbert: *r.*, Austl. 40 G4
Gilbert Islands: *now*: KIRIBATI 42 G7
Gilgit: India 34 B1
Gill, Lough: Irish Republic 15 C2
Gillette: U.S.A. 53 D2
Gillingham: Kent, Eng. 13 G3
Gillingham: Wilts., Eng. 12 D3
Gilroy: U.S.A. 52 A3
Gineifa: Egypt 59 *Ins.*
Ginir: Ethiopia 59 O7
Gippsland: *geog. reg.*, Australia 41 H8
Girdle Ness: *pt.*, Scotland 16 F2
Girga: Egypt 59 M3
Gir Hills: India 34 B4
Gironde: *est.*, France 20 B3
Girton: England 13 G2
Girvan: Scotland 17 D4
Gisborne: N.Z. 41 C2
Giurgiu: Bulgaria 23 E4
Givors: France 25 A2
Gjinokastër: Albania 23 D4
Gjøvik: Norway 19 B3
Glace Bay: *town*, Canada 47 Y7
Glacier International Peace Park: U.S.A. 52 C1
Gladbeck: German F.R. 24 B1
Gladstone: Australia 41 J5
Glåma: *r.*, Norway 19 B3
Glarus: Switzerland 25 B2
Glascarnoch, Loch: Scotland 16 D2
Glasgow: Scotland 17 D4
Glasgow: Ky., U.S.A. 51 E2
Glasgow: Mont., U.S.A. 52 D1
Glas Maol: *mtn.*, Scot. 16 E3
Glass: *r.*, Scotland 16 D2
Glastonbury: England 12 D3
Glauchau: Ger. D.R. 24 C1
Glazov: U.S.S.R. 30 G2
Glen: *r.*, England 13 F2
Glen Coe: *valley*, Scotland 16 D3
Glencoe: U.S.A. 53 G2
Glencolumbkille: Irish Republic 15 C2
Glendale: U.S.A. 52 C4
Glendive: U.S.A. 53 E1
Glengad Head: *cape*, Irish Republic 15 D1
Glen Mór: *valley*, Scotland 16 D2
Glen More Nat. Forest Park: Scot. 16 E2
Glenrothes: Scotland 17 E3
Glen Roy: *valley*, Scot. 16 D3
Glen Spean: *valley*, Scotland 16 C3
Glenties: Irish Rep. 15 C2
Glentrool Nat. Forest Park: Scotland 17 D4
Glenwood: U.S.A. 53 F1
Glenwood Springs: *town*, U.S.A. 52 D3
Glin: Irish Rep. 15 B4
Gliwice: Poland 22 C2
Globe: U.S.A. 52 C4
Glossop: England 14 E3
Gloucester: England 12 D3
Gloucestershire: *Co.*, England 12 D3
Glyder Fawr: *mtn.*, Wales 12 B1
Gmunden: Austria 25 C2
Gniezno: Poland 22 C2
Goa: *Union Territ.*, India 34 B5
Goat Fell: *mtn.*, Scot. 17 C4
Gobernador Racedo: Argentina 56 B3
Gobi Desert: China/Mongolia 36 C2
Godalming: England 13 F3
Godavari: *r.*, India 34 C5
Godmanchester: Eng. 13 F2
GODTHAAB: Greenland 47 AA4
Goiânia: Brazil 54 J7
Goiás: Brazil 54 H7
Goiás Massif: Brazil 54 J7
Goio-Erê: *r.*, Brazil 56 D1
Gojo: Japan 38 b ii
Gol: Norway 19 A3
Golden Bay: N.Z. 41 B3
Goldsworthy, Mt.: Australia 40 B5

e page 80

* See page 80

y Islands 16 d iv
ger: Norway 18 A3
e: England 14 C3
: Ger. F.R. 24 B1
: Králové: Czech. 22 C2
ng: China 36 C5
u: Taiwan 36 G6
ai-lien: China 36 F4
ga: *r.*, Peru 54 C5
oo: Angola 61 C10
avelica: Peru 54 C6
ayo: Peru 54 D6
India 34 C5
all: England 13 E1
rsfield: Eng. 14 E3
svall: Sweden 18 C3
n: *r.*, U.S.A. 49 M1
n Bay: Can. 47 T5
ietnam 37 D7
: Spain 21 A5
: Spain 21 B4
f: Saudi Arabia 32 E5
nden: Austl. 40 G5
Town: Scilly Is. 12 c iv
U.S.A. 50 C3
ot: China 36 E2
oima: Arg. 56 A2
a Renancó: Arg. 56 B3
Canada 47 V7
, England 14 F3
Ger. F.R. 24 B1
Chih: *lake*,
a 36 F1
huaca: Argentina 56 A1
er: *est.*, Eng. 14 F3
erside: *Co.*, Eng. 14 F3
oldt: *r.*, U.S.A. 52 B2
doara: Rom. 22 D3
ARY: 22 C3
erford: England 13 E3
er Steppe:
S.R 31 L4
y Horse
rvoir: U.S.A. 52 C1
anby: England 14 F2
ück: *mtns.*,
an F.R. 24 B2
anton: Eng. 13 G2
ngdon: England 13 F2
ngton: U.S.A. 51 E1
: N.Z. 41 C2
: Scotland 16 F2
ville: Ala., U.S.A. 51 E3
ville: Tex., U.S.A. 50 C3
: U.S.A. 53 F2
, Lake: Canada/
A. 47 T7
pierpoint: Eng. 13 F4
ui: *r.*, N.Z. 41 B3
vik: Iceland 18 b i
varna: Sweden 19 B4
inson: U.S.A. 50 C2
N.Z. 41 C3
Belgium 24 B1
ning: China 36 F4
g (Yellow): *r.*,
a 36 E3
as Nor: *lake*,
golia 36 A1
England 14 D3
abad: *& State*,
34 C5
abad: Pak. 34 A3
: Hants., Eng. 13 E4
: Kent, Eng. 13 H3
a: Japan 38 B3
kää: Finland 19 D3

Romania 22 E3
n: Nigeria 58 F7
ê: Colombia 54 C3
ki: Japan 38 b ii
ki: *Pref.*, Japan 38 g iii
Lago: Argentina 56 C2
: *r.*, Brazil 56 C2
da Armada:
razil 56 C3
uitã: *r.*, Braz. 56 C3
caí: *r.*, Brazil 56 C2
& i.,
earic Islands 21 C5
Peru 54 C6
aquã: *r.*, Braz. 56 C2
: Argentina 56 B2
AND: 18 –
g: China 36 E4
r., Japan 38 a ii
ara: Japan 38 g iv
awa: Chiba,
an 38 f iv
awa: Hyogo,
an 38 a ii
omiya: Aichi,
an 38 c i
omiya: Chiba,
an 38 g iv
oseki: Japan 38 D2
el: U.S.A. 50 D3
: *State*,
.A. 52 C2
Falls: *city*,
.A. 52 C2
ll Pt.: Scot. 16 B2
a: U.S.S.R. 29 L4
Izane: Algeria 21 C5
ias: Sardinia 21 a ii
ik: Canada 47 T3
çu: *r.*, Brazil 56 D2
çu, Parque Nac.
Brazil 56 D2
emi: *r.*, Brazil 56 D1
Japan 38 C2
ni: Finland 18 E3
a: Japan 38 B3
iden: Neth. 24 A1
: *r.*, Neth. 24 B1
lmeer (Zuider
): Neth. 24 B1

Ijuí: *& r.*, Brazil 56 D2
Ikaria: *i.*, Greece 23 E5
Ikuno: Japan 38 a i
Ilchester: England 12 D4
Ilebo: Zaïre 61 D8
Ilfracombe: Eng. 12 B3
Ilha Grande: *i.*, Brazil 56 D1
Ilhéus: Brazil 54 L6
Ili: *r.*, China/U.S.S.R. 31 M5
Iliamna Lake: U.S.A. 46 D5
Ilkeston: England 13 E2
Ilkley: England 14 E3
Illimani: *mtn.*, Bol. 54 E7
Illinois: *State & r.*, U.S.A. 50-1 D/E1
Ilmen', Lake: U.S.S.R. 30 C2
Ilmenau: Ger. D.R. 24 C1
Ilminster: England 12 D4
Iloilo: Philippines 37 G8
Imabari: Japan 38 B3
Imandra, Lake: U.S.S.R. 18 F2
Imaruí, Lagoa: Braz. 56 E2
Imatra: Finland 18 E3
Imbanuma: *i.*, Japan 38 g iv
Immingham: England 14 F3
Imperia: Italy 25 B3
Imphal: India 35 F4
Inagawa: Japan 38 b ii
Inari: *& i.*, Finland 18 E2
Inazawa: Japan 38 c i
Inchard, Loch: Scot. 16 C1
Inchon: S. Korea 36 H3
Indal: *r.*, Sweden 18 C3
Indaw: Burma 33 P6
Independence: U.S.A. 50 C2
INDIA: 34/35 –
Indiana: *State*, U.S.A. 51 E1
Indianapolis: U.S.A. 52 E2
Indian Ocean: 35 –
Indirka: *r.*, U.S.S.R. 29 R3
INDONESIA: 37 –
Indore: India 34 C4
Indus: *r.*, India/Pak. 34 A3
Indus, Mouths of the: Pakistan 34 A4
Ingeniero Luiggi: Arg. 56 B4
Ingenio Santa Ana: Argentina 56 A2
Ingleborough: *mtn.*, England 14 D2
Ingolstadt: Ger. F.R. 25 C2
Inisbofin: *i.*, Irish Rep. 15 A3
Inishark: *i.*, Irish Rep. 15 A3
Inisheer: *i.*, Irish Rep. 15 B3
Inishmaan: *i.*, Irish Rep. 15 B3
Inishmore: *i.*, Irish Rep. 15 B3
Inishmurray: *i.*, Irish Republic 15 C2
Inishowen Peninsula: Irish Republic 15 D1
Inisturk: *i.*, Irish Republic 15 A3
Inkerman: U.S.S.R. 30 C5
Inland Sea *see* Seto-naikai 38 B3
Inn: *r.*, Austria 25 C2
Inner Hebrides: *is.*, Scotland 16 B2–3
Innerleithen: Scot. 17 E4
Inner Mongolia: *Aut. Reg.*, China 36 F2
Inner Sound: Scot. 16 C2
Innishowen Hd.: N. Ireland 15 E1
Innsbruck: Austria 25 C2
Inntal: *val.*, Aus. 25 C2
Inny: *r.*, England 12 B4
Inny: *r.*, Kerry, Irish Republic 15 A5
Inny: *r.*, Longford, Irish Republic 15 D3
Inowroclaw: Poland 22 C2
Inter-American Highway: Mexico 48 G8
Interlaken: Switz. 25 B2
International Falls: *town*, U.S.A. 53 G1
Inubo-zaki: *cape*, Japan 38 g iv
Inuvik: Canada 46 H3
Inuyama: Japan 38 c i
Invararay: Scot. 17 C3
Inverbervie: Scot. 16 F3
Invercargill: N.Z. 41 A4
Invergordon: Scot. 16 D2
Inverkeithing: Scot. 17 E3
Inverness: Scot. 16 D2
Inverurie: Scot. 16 F2
Inzai: Japan 38 g iv
Iona: *i.*, Scotland 16 B3
Ionian Is.: Greece 23 C5
Ionian Sea: Med. Sea 23 C5
Ionnina: Greece 23 D5
Ios: *i.*, Greece 23 E5
Iowa: *State & r.*, U.S.A. 50 D1
Iowa City, U.S.A. 50 D1
Ipin: China 36 C5
Ipoh: Malaysia 37 C10
Ipswich: Australia 41 J6
Ipswich: England 13 H2
Iquique: Chile 54 D8
Iquitos: Peru 54 D4
Irago-suido: *str.*, Japan 38 c ii
Iráklion: Crete 23 E5
IRAN: 32 F4
IRAQ: 32 D4
Irati: Brazil 56 D2
Irbīl: Iraq 30 E6
Irfon: *r.*, Wales 12 C2
IRISH REPUBLIC: 15 –
Irish Sea: Irel./Eng. 12 A2
Irkutsk: U.S.S.R. 29 N7
Iron, Lough: Irish Republic 15 D3
Iron Bridge: England 12 D2
Iron Gates: *gorge*, Rom./Yugo. 23 D4

Iron Knob: Austl. 40 F7
Iron Mountain: Idaho, U.S.A. 52 B2
Iron Mountain: *town*, U.S.A. 53 H1
Ironwood: U.S.A. 53 G1
Irrawaddy: *r.*, Burma 33 O7
Irthlingborough: Eng. 13 F2
Irtysh: *r.*, U.S.S.R. 31 L2
Irvine: Scotland 17 D4
Irvinestown: N. Irel. 15 D2
Iruya: *r.*, Arg. 56 B1
Isafjördhur: Ice. 18 a i
Isanzo: *r.*, Italy/ Yugoslavia 25 C2
Isar: *r.*, Ger. F.R. 25 C2
Isarco: *r.*, Italy 25 C2
Ise: Japan 38 c ii
Iseo, Lake: Italy 25 C2
Isère: *r.*, France 25 B2
Iserlohn: Ger. F.R. 24 B1
Ise-shima-kokuritsu-kōen: *nat. park*, Japan 38 c ii
Ise-wan: *bay*, Japan 38 c ii
Isfahan: Iran 32 F4
Ishikari-wan: *bay*, Japan 38 D1
Ishim: *r.*, U.S.S.R. 31 K3
Ishimbay: U.S.S.R. 30 H3
Ishinomaki: Japan 38 D2
Ishioka: Japan 38 g iii
Ishpeming: U.S.A. 53 H1
Isiro: Zaïre 60 E7
Iskâr: *r.*, Bulg. 23 D4
Iskenderun: Turkey 30 D6
Isla: *r.*, Scot. 16 E3
ISLAMABAD: Pak. 34 B2
Islands, Bay of: N.Z. 41 B2
Islay: *i.*, Scotland 17 B4
Isle: *r.*, England 12 D4
Isle Royale: *i.*, U.S.A. 53 H1
Ismael Cortinas: Uru. 56 C3
Ismailia: Egypt 59 M2
Isna: Egypt 59 M3
ISRAEL: 32 B4
Issyk-Kul': U.S.S.R. 31 M5
Istanbul: Turkey 23 E4
Istra (Istria): *penin.*, Yugoslavia 23 B3
Itabuna: Brazil 54 L6
Itá Ibaté: Argentina 56 C2
Itajaí: *& r.*, Brazil 56 E2
Itajaí do Norte: *r.*, Brazil 56 E2
Itajaí do Sul: *r.*, Brazil 56 E2
Itajaí Mirim: *r.*, Brazil 56 E2
Itajubá: Brazil 56 a i
Itako: Japan 38 g iv
ITALY: 25 C2
Itami: Japan 38 b ii
Itapetininga: *& r.*, Brazil 56 a i
Itapeva: Brazil 56 a i
Itapeva, Lagoa: Brazil 56 E2
Itapira: Brazil 56 a i
Itaqui: Brazil 56 C2
Itarare: *& r.*, Brazil 56 E1
Itatí, Lago: Arg. 56 C2
Itatiaja, Parque Nacional do: Brazil 56 b i
Itchen: *r.*, England 13 E3
Ithon: *r.*, Wales 12 C2
Ito: Japan 38 f v
Itu: Brazil 56 a i
Itu: *r.*, Brazil 56 C2
Ituim: *r.*, Brazil 56 D2
Ituzaingó: Arg. 56 C2
Ivaí: *r.*, Brazil 56 D1
Ivalo: Finland 18 E2
Ivano-Frankovsk: U.S.S.R. 22 D3
Ivanovo: U.S.S.R. 30 E2
Ivdel': U.S.S.R. 31 J1
IVORY COAST: 58 D7
Ivybridge: England 12 C4
Iwade: Japan 38 b ii
Iwaki: Japan 38 D2
Iwakuni: Japan 38 B3
Iwanai: Japan 38 D1
Iwanuma: Japan 38 D2
Iwate-san: *mtn.*, Japan 38 D2
Iyo-nada: *sea*, Japan 38 B3
Izhevsk: U.S.S.R. 30 G2
Izhma: *r.*, U.S.S.R. 28 H5
Izmir: Turkey 23 E5
Izumi: Japan 38 b ii
Izumi-otsu: Japan 38 b ii
Izumi-sano: Japan 38 b ii
Izu-Shoto: *arch.*, Japan 38 C3

J

Jabalpur: India 34 C4
Jablonet: Czech. 22 C2
Jaca: Spain 21 B4
Jacarei: Brazil 56 a i
Jacarézinho: Brazil 56 E1
Jáchymov: Czech. 24 C1
Jackson: Mich., U.S.A. 51 F1
Jackson: Miss., U.S.A. 50 D3
Jackson: Tenn., U.S.A. 51 E2
Jackson Bay: N.Z. 41 A3
Jacksonville: Fla., U.S.A. 51 F3
Jacksonville: Ill., U.S.A. 50 D2
Jacksonville Beach: *town*, U.S.A. 51 F3
Jacobabad: Pakistan 34 A3
Jacuí: *& r.*, Brazil 56 D2
Jaén: Spain 21 B5
Jæren: *geog. reg.*, Norway 19 A4
Jaffa *see* Tel Aviv-Jaffa 32 B4
Jaffna: Sri Lanka 34 b ll
Jaguarão: Brazil 56 D3
Jaguari: *r.*, Brazil 56 D2
Jaguariaíva: Brazil 56 E1
Jaguari-Mirim: *r.*, Brazil 56 a i
Jaipur: India 34 C3
Jaisalmer: India 34 B3
Jakhdhar: *mtn.*, Oman 32 G6
Jalalabad: Afghanistan 34 A2
Jalapa Enriquer: Mex. 48 G6
JAMAICA: 49 L6
Jambol: Bulgaria 23 E4
James: *r.*, S. Dak., U.S.A. 53 F1
James: *r.*, Va., U.S.A. 51 G2
James, Baie: *bay*, Canada 47 T6
Jamestown: N. Dak., U.S.A. 53 F1
Jamestown: N.Y., U.S.A. 51 G1
Jammu: India 34 B2
Jammu and Kashmir: *State*, disputed between India & Pak. 34 C2
Jamnagar: India 34 B4
Jamshedpur: India 34 E4
Janesville: U.S.A. 51 E1
JAPAN: 38 –
Japan, Sea of: Japan 36 J3
Japan Trench: Pac. O. 42 D3
Japen: *i.*, Indon. 37 K11
Jarrow: England 14 E2
Järvenpää: Finland 19 E3
Jaslo: Poland 22 D3
Jasper: U.S.A. 51 E3
Jasper Nat. Park: Canada 46 M6
Jauf: Saudi Arabia 32 C5
Java (Djawa): *i.*, Indon. 37 D12
Java Sea: Indon. 37 E12
Java Trench: Ind. O. 35 j v
Jaxartes: *r.*, *see* Syr Dar'ya 31 K5
Jebba: Nigeria 58 F7
Jebel Aulia Dam: Sudan 59 M5
Jedburgh: Scot. 17 F4
Jefferson City: U.S.A. 50 D2
Jega: Nigeria 67 A1
Jehol: *see* Chengteh 36 F2
Jejui Guazú: *r.*, Par. 56 C1
Jekabpils: U.S.S.R. 19 E4
Jelenia Góra: Pol. 22 C2
Jelgava: U.S.S.R. 19 D4
Jena: German D.R. 24 C1
Jerez: Spain 21 A5
Jerez de los Caballeros: Spain 21 A5
Jersey: *i.*, Chan. Is. 12 a ii
Jersey City: U.S.A. 51 H1
JERUSALEM: Israel 32 B4
Jessore: Bangladesh 34 E4
Jesup: U.S.A. 51 F3
Jesús: Paraguay 56 C2
Jesús María: Arg. 56 B3
Jethou: *i.*, Chan. Is. 12 a ii
Jhansi: India 34 C3
Jhelum: *r.*, Pak. 34 B2
Jibhalanta *see* Uliastay 36 B1
*Jidda: Saudi Arabia 32 C6
Jihlava: Czech. 22 C3
Jijiga: Ethiopia 59 O7
Jiménez: Mexico 48 E4
Jinan *see* Tsinan 36 F3
Jinja: Uganda 60 F7
João Pessoa: Brazil 54 L5
Joaquín V. González: Argentina 56 B2
Jodhpur: India 34 B3
Joensuu: Finland 18 E3
Jofra Oasis: Libya 58 H3
*Jogjakarta: Indon. 37 E12
Johannesburg: S. Afr. 61 E13
John Day: *r.*, U.S.A. 52 B2
John o'Groats: Scot. 16 E1
Johnson City: Tenn., U.S.A. 51 F2
Johnstone: Scotland 17 D4
Johnston I.: Pac. O. 42 J5
Johnston's Point: Scotland 17 C4
Johnstown: U.S.A. 51 G1
Johore Bahru: Mal. 37 C10
Joinvile: Brazil 56 E2
Jokkmokk: Sweden 18 C2
Joliet: U.S.A. 52 E1
Jolo: *i.*, Philippines 37 G9
Jonesboro: U.S.A. 50 D2
Jones Sound: Can. 47 S1
Jonglei: Sudan 59 M7
Jönköping: Sweden 19 B4
Joplin: U.S.A. 50 D2
JORDAN: 32 C4
Jordan: U.S.A. 54 D1
Jordão: *r.*, Brazil 56 D2
Jorhat: India 35 F3
Jos: *& plateau*, Nigeria 58 G6
José Battle y Ordóñez: Uru. 56 C3
José Pedro Varela: Uruguay 56 D3
Joseph Bonaparte Gulf: Austl. 40 D3
Joshua Tree Nat. Monument: U.S.A. 52 B4
Jostedalsbreen: *ice-cap*, Norway 18 A3
Jotunheimen: *mtns.*, Norway 18 A3
Joyces Country: *dist.*, Irish Republic 15 B3
Joyo: Japan 38 b ii
Juan B. Arruabarrena: Argentina 56 C3
Juan Fernández Is.: Pacific Ocean 55 C10
Juarez, Sierra de: *ra.*, Mexico 52 B4
Juatinga, Ponta de: *pt.*, Brazil 56 b i
Juazeiro: Brazil 54 K5
Juba: Sudan 59 M8
Juba: *r.*, Somali Rep. 59 O8
Juby, Cape: Canary Is. 58 C3
Júcar: *r.*, Spain 21 B5
Juist: *i.*, Ger. F.R. 24 B1
Juiz de Fora: Braz. 56 b i
Jujuy: *Prov.*, Arg. 56 A1
Jukao: China 36 G4
Juliaca: Peru 54 D7
Julian Alps: Italy/ Yugoslavia 25 C2
Jülich: Ger. F.R. 24 B1
Julier Pass: Switz. 25 B2
Júlio de Castilhos: Brazil 56 D2
Jullundur: India 34 C2
Jumilla: Spain 21 B5
Junction City: U.S.A. 50 C2
Jundiaí: Brazil 56 a i
Juneau: U.S.A. 46 J5
Jungfrau: *mtn.*, Switzerland 25 B2
Junín: Argentina 56 B3
Junsele: Sweden 18 C3
Junquiá: *r.*, Brazil 56 a i
Jur: *r.*, Sudan 59 L7
Jura: *i, & sound*, Scotland 17 C4
Jura, The: *mtns.*, Fr./Switz. 25 B2
Juruá: *r.*, Brazil 54 E5
Juruena: *r.*, Brazil 54 G6
Jüterbog: Ger. D.R. 24 C1
Jutland: *penin.*, *see* Jylland 19 A4
Jyekundo: *see* Yushu 36 B4
Jylland (Jutland): *penin.*, Denmark 19 A4
Jyväskylä: Finland 18 E3

K

Kabaena: *l.*, Indon. 37 G12
KABUL: *& r.*, Afghanistan 34 A2
Kabwe: Zambia 61 E10
Kadaň: Czechoslovakia 24 C1
Kadoma: Japan 38 b ii
Kaduna: Nigeria 58 G6
Kafue: Zambia 61 E11
Kafue Nat. Park: Zambia 61 E10
Kagoshima: Japan 38 B3
Kaibara: Japan 38 b i
Kaieteur Falls: Guyana 54 G2
Kaifeng: China 36 E4
Kai Is.: Indonesia 37 J12
Kaikohe: N.Z. 41 B2
Kaikoura: *& range*, New Zealand 41 B3
Kailas Range: China 34 D2
Kaimana: Indonesia 40 E1
Kaimanawa Ra.: N.Z. 41 C2
Kainan: Japan 38 b ii
Kainji Dam: Nigeria 58 F6
Kaipara Harbour: N.Z. 41 B2
Kairouen: Tunisia 58 H1
Kaiserslautern: German F.R. 24 B2
Kaitaia: N.Z. 41 B2
Kaitangata: N.Z. 41 A4
Kaizuka: Japan 38 b ii
Kajaani: Finland 18 E3
Kakagi, Lake: Can. 53 G1
Kakinada: India 34 D5
Kako: *r.*, Japan 38 a ii
Kakogawa: Japan 38 a ii
Kaktovik: U.S.A. 46 G2
Kalachinsk: U.S.S.R. 31 L2
Kalahari Desert: Botswana/Namibia 61 D12
Kalahari Gemsbok Nat. Park: S. Africa 61 C13
Kalamai: Greece 23 D5
Kalamazoo: U.S.A. 51 E1
Kalat: Pakistan 34 A3
Kalemie: Zaïre 61 E9
Kalevala: U.S.S.R. 18 F2
Kalgansee: Changkiakow 36 E2
Kalgoorlie: Australia 40 C7
Kalinin: U.S.S.R. 30 D2
Kaliningrad: U.S.S.R. 19 D5
Kalispell: U.S.A. 52 C1
Kalisz: Poland 22 C2
Kalix: *r.*, Sweden 18 D2
Kalimantan: *Prov.*, Indonesia 37 E11
Kallafo: Ethiopia 59 O7
Kall Lake: Sweden 18 B3
Kalmar: Sweden 19 C4
Kalmunai: Sri Lanka 34 b ii
Kaluga: U.S.S.R. 30 D3
Kalush: U.S.S.R. 22 D3
Kama: *r.*, U.S.S.R. 30 G2
Kamaishi: Japan 38 D2
Kamakura: Japan 38 f iv
Kamaran Is.: Yemen P.D.R. 32 D7
Kamchatka: *penin.*, U.S.S.R. 29 S6
Kamchatka Bay: U.S.S.R. 29 T6
Kamenets Podol'skiy: U.S.S.R. 22 E3
Kamenskoye: U.S.S.R. 29 T5
Kamensk-Uralskiy: U.S.S.R. 31 J2
Kameoka: Japan 38 b i
Kamet: *mtn.*, India 34 C2
Kameyama: Japan 38 c ii
Kamiiso: Japan 38 D1
Kamina: Zaïre 61 E9
Kamloops: Canada 46 L6
Kamogawa: Japan 38 g iv
KAMPALA: Uganda 60 F7
Kampen: Neth. 24 B1
KAMPUCHEA (Cambodia): 37 –
Kamyshin: U.S.S.R. 30 F3
Kamyshlov: U.S.S.R. 31 J2
Kanagawa: *Pref.*, Japan 38 f iv
Kananga: Zaïre 61 D9
Kanazawa: Japan 38 C2
Kandahar: Afghanistan 34 A2
Kandalaksha: U.S.S.R. 18 F2
Kandi: Benin 58 F6
Kandla: India 34 B4
Kandy: Sri Lanka 34 b ii
Kane Basin: Canada 47 V1
Kangaroo I.: Australia 40 F8
Kangchenjunga: *mtn.*, India/Nepal 34 E3
Kangean Is.: Indon. 37 F12
Kangting: China 36 C5
Kanin, Cape: U.S.S.R. 28 G4
Kankaanpää: Finland 18 D3
Kankakee: U.S.A. 51 E1
Kankan: Guinea 58 D6
Kannapolis: U.S.A. 51 F2
Kano: Nigeria 58 G6
Kanonji: Japan 38 B3
Kanoya: Japan 38 B3
Kanpur: India 34 D3
Kansas: *r.*, U.S.A. 50 C2
Kansas: *State*, U.S.A. 50 C2
Kansas City: Kans., U.S.A. 50 D2
Kansas City: Mo., U.S.A. 50 D2
Kansk: U.S.S.R. 31 Q2
Kanto Heiya: *plain*, Japan 38 f iii
Kanto Santi: *plain*, Japan 38 e iii
Kanturk: Irish Rep. 15 C4
Kao-hsiung: Taiwan 36 G6
Kaolan *see* Lanchow 36 C3
Kaposvár: Hungary 22 C3
Kapsukas: U.S.S.R. 19 D5
Kapurthala: India 34 C2
Kapuskasing: Canada 47 T7
Kara: U.S.S.R. 28 J4
Kara-Bogaz-Gol: *gulf*, U.S.S.R. 30 G5
Karabük: Turkey 30 C5
Karachi: Pakistan 34 A4
Karaganda: U.S.S.R. 31 L4
Karakoram Pass: China/India 34 C1
Kara Kum: *des.*, U.S.S.R. 31 H6
Karapiro: N.Z. 41 C2
Kara Sea: U.S.S.R. 28 J3
Kara-Tau: *ra.*, U.S.S.R. 31 K5
Karasu: Japan 38 c ii
Karaul: U.S.S.R. 29 L3
Karbala: Iraq 32 D4
Kärdla: U.S.S.R. 19 D4
Kargil: India 34 C2
Karhula: Finland 19 E3
Kariba Lake: *& dam & gorge*, Zambia/Zimb. 61 E11
Kariba-yama: *mtn.*, Japan 38 C1
Karigasniemi: Norway 18 E2
Karl-Marx-Stadt (Chemnitz): German Democratic Rep. 24 C1
Karlovac: Yugoslavia 23 C3
Karlovy Vary: Czech. 22 B2
Karlshamn: Sweden 19 B4
Karlskoga: Sweden 19 B4
Karlskrona: Sweden 19 C4
Karlsruhe: Ger. F.R. 24 B2
Karlstad: Sweden 19 B4
Karnataka: *State*, India 34 C6
Kárpathos: *i.*, Greece 23 E5
Karpenísion: Greece 23 D5
Kars: Turkey 30 E5
Kartaly: U.S.S.R. 31 J3
Kārūn: *r.*, Iran 32 E4
Karvina: Poland 22 C3
Karwar: India 34 B6
Kasai: Japan 38 a ii
Kasai: *r.*, Zaïre 61 C8
Kasane: Zambia 61 E11
Kasaoka: Japan 38 B3
Kasba Lake: Canada 46 P4
Kasese: Uganda 60 F7
Kāshān: Iran 32 F4
Kashgar *see* Sufu 33 L3
Kashihara: Japan 38 b ii
Kashima: Japan 38 g iv
Kashima-nada: *bay*, Japan 38 g iii
Kashiwa: Japan 38 f iv
Kashiwara: Japan 38 b ii
Kashiwazaki: Japan 38 C2
Kaskaskia: *r.*, U.S.A. 51 E2
Kasli: U.S.S.R. 31 J2
Kásos: *i.*, Greece 23 E5
Kassala: Sudan 59 N5
Kassel: Ger. F.R. 24 B1
Kasugai: Japan 38 c i
Kasukabe: japan 38 f iv
Kasumigaura: *lake*, Japan 38 g iii
Kataba: Zambia 61 E11
Kateríni: Greece 23 D4
Katherine: Australia 40 E3
Kathiawar: *State*, India 34 B4
Kathiraveli: Sri Lanka 34 b ii
KATMANDU: Nepal 34 E3
Katoomba: Austl. 41 J7
Katowice: Poland 22 C2
Katrine: *l.*, Scot. 16 D3
Katrineholm: Sweden 19 C4
Katsunuma: Japan 38 e iv
Katsuragi: Japan 38 b ii
Katsuura: Japan 38 g iv
Kattegat: *str.*, Denmark/Norway 19 B4

e page 80

Page ref.
Kauai: *i.*, Hawaiian Is. 43 K4
Kaufbeuren: Ger. F.R. 25 C2
Kaufman: U.S.A. 50 C3
Kaunas: U.S.S.R. 19 D5
Kaura Namoda: Nig. 58 G6
Kavacha: U.S.S.R. 29 T5
Kavaje: Albania 23 C4
Kavála: Greece 23 D4
Kavieng: Pap.-N.G. 40 J1
Kawachi-nagano: Japan 38 b ii
Kawagoe: Japan 38 f iv
Kawaguchi: Japan 38 f iv
Kawasaki: Japan 38 f iv
Kawerau: N.Z. 41 C2
Kayes: Mali 58 C6
Kayser: Turkey 30 D6
Kazach'ye: U.S.S.R. 29 Q3
Kazakh S.S.R.: U.S.S.R. 30/31 -
Kazakh Uplands: U.S.S.R. 31 L4
Kazalinsk: U.S.S.R. 31 J4
Kazan: U.S.S.R. 30 F2
Kazanlâk: Bulg. 23 E4
Kazatin: U.S.S.R. 22 E3
Kaziranga: India 35 F3
Kazo: Japan 38 f iii
Kazusa: Japan 38 g iv
Kéa: *i.*, Greece 23 D5
Keady: N. Ireland 15 E2
Keal, Loch: Scot. 16 B3
Kearney: U.S.A. 53 F2
Kebbi: *r.*, Nigeria 58 F6
Kebock Head: *c.*, Scot. 16 B1
Kecskemét: Hungary 22 C3
Keele: England 12 D1
Keeling Is.: *see* Cocos Is. 35 j vi
Keen, Mt.: Scotland 16 F3
Keeper Hill: Irish Republic 15 C4
Keflavík: Iceland 18 a ii
Keighley: England 14 E3
Keihoku: Japan 38 b i
Keith: Scotland 16 F2
Kelheim: Ger. F.R. 24 C2
Kells: Irish Republic 15 E3
Kelowna: Canada 46 M7
Kelsey Hd.: Eng. 12 A4
Kelso: Scotland 17 F4
Kelso: U.S.A. 52 A1
Kemerovo: U.S.S.R. 31 O2
Kemi: Finland 18 D2
Kemi: *l. & r.*, Fin. 18 E2
Kemijärvi: Finland 18 E2
Kempston: England 13 F2
Kempten: Ger. F.R. 25 C2
Kenai Peninsula: U.S.A. 46 E4
Kendal: England 14 D2
Kenilworth: Eng. 13 E2
Kenitra: Morocco 58 D2
Ken Loch: Scotland 17 D4
Kenmare: & *r.*, Irish Republic 15 B5
Kenmore: U.S.A. 53 E1
Kennett: U.S.A. 50 D2
Kennett: *r.*, Eng. 13 E3
Kennewick: U.S.A. 52 B1
Kennicott: U.S.A. 46 G4
Kenosha: U.S.A. 51 E1
Kent: *Co.*, England 13 G3
Kent, Vale of: England 13 G3
Kentucky: *State & r.*, U.S.A. 51E1/F1
Kentucky Lake: U.S.A. 51 E2
KENYA: 60 G7
Kenya, Mt.: Kenya 61 G8
Keokuk: U.S.A. 50 D1
Kerala: *State*, India 34 C6
Kerch': U.S.S.R. 30 D4
Kerguelen Islands: Southern Ocean 35 e ix
Kerguelen Plateau: Southern Ocean 35 f x
Kerki: U.S.S.R. 31 K6
Kerkira: & *i.*, Greece 23 C5
Kermadec Trench: Pacific Ocean 42 H10
Kermadec Is.: Pac. O. 42 H9
Kerman: Iran 32 G4
*Kermanshah: Iran 32 E4
Kern: *r.*, U.S.A. 52 B3
Kerrara: *i.*, Scot. 16 C3
Kerr Reservoir: U.S.A. 51 G2
Kerry: *Co.*, Irish Rep. 15 B4
Kerry Head: *c.*, Irish Republic 15 B4
Kerulen: *r.*, Mong. 36 E1
Kesan: Turkey 23 E4
Kesennuma: Japan 38 D2
Kesh: N. Ireland 15 D2
Keswick: England 14 C2
Keszthely: Hungary 22 C3
Ketchikan: U.S.A. 46 J5
Kettering: England 13 E2
Kewanee: U.S.A. 51 E1
Keweenaw Peninsula: U.S.A. 53 H1
Key, Lough: Irish Rep. 15 C2
Key Largo: *i.*, U.S.A. 51 F4
Keynsham: England 12 D3
Keystone Reservoir: U.S.A. 50 C2
Key West: U.S.A. 51 F5
Khabarovsk: U.S.S.R. 29 Q8
Khairpur: Pakistan 34 A3
Khalkís: Greece 23 D5
Khandwa: India 34 C4
Khaniá: Crete 23 D5
Khanka, Lake: China/U.S.S.R. 36 J2
Khan Tengri: *mtn.*, China 33 M2
Khanty-Mansiysk: U.S.S.R. 31 K1
Khanzi: Botswana 61 D12
Kharagpur: India 34 E4
Kharan Kalat: Pak. 34 A3
Khar'kov: U.S.S.R. 30 D3
KHARTOUM: Sudan 59 M5
Khasi Hills: India 35 F3
Khatanga: U.S.S.R. 29 N3
Kherson: U.S.S.R. 30 C4
Khingan Mts.: China 36 G1
Khiva: U.S.S.R. 31 J5
Khmel'nitskiy: U.S.S.R. 22 E3
Khobso Gol Nor: *l.*, Mongolia 36 C1
Khodzheyli: U.S.S.R. 31 H5
Kholmsk: U.S.S.R. 29 R8
Khorog: U.S.S.R. 31 L6
Khotin: U.S.S.R. 22 E3
Khrom-Tau: U.S.S.R. 31 H3
Khuzdar: Pakistan 34 A3
Khyber Pass: Afg./Pak. 34 B2
Kiamusze: China 36 J1
Kian: China 36 F5
Kianta Lake: Finland 18 E2
Kibali-Ituri Game Reserve: Zaire 60 E7
Kicking Horse Pass: Canada 46 M6
Kidderminster: Eng. 12 D2
Kidlington: England 13 E3
Kidsgrove: England 12 D1
Kidwelly: Wales 12 B3
Kiel Canal: Ger. F.R. 24 B1
Kielce: Poland 22 D2
Kielder Water: *res.*, England 14 D1
Kiev: & *res.*, U.S.S.R. 22 E2
Kigoma: Tanzania 61 E8
Kii-suido: *str.*, Japan 38 B3
Kikinda: Yugoslavia 22 D3
Kilbeggan: Irish Rep. 15 D3
Kilbrannan Sound: Scotland 17 C4
Kilcock: Irish Rep. 15 E3
Kilcormac: Irish Rep. 15 D3
Kilcullen: Irish Rep. 15 E3
Kildare: & *Co.*, Irish Republic 15 E3
Kilglass Lough: Irish Republic 15 C3
Kilimanjaro: *mtn.*, *now* Uhuru 61 G8
Kilkee: Irish Rep. 15 B4
Kilkeel: N. Ireland 15 F2
Kilkenny: & *Co.*, Irish Republic 15 D4
Kilkieran Bay: Irish Republic 15 B3
Kilkis: Greece 23 D4
Killala: & *bay*, Irish Republic 15 B2
Killaloe: Irish Rep. 15 C4
Killarney: Irish Rep. 15 B4
Killchianaig: Scot. 17 C3
Killiecrankie Pass: Scotland 16 E3
Killmallock: Irish Rep. 15 C4
Killorgin: Irish Rep. 15 B4
Killybegs: Irish Rep. 15 C2
Killyleagh: N. Irel. 15 F2
Kilmaluag: Scot. 16 B2
Kilmarnock: Scot. 17 D4
Kilpisjärvi: Finland 18 D2
Kilrea: N. Ireland 15 E2
Kilrush: Irish Rep. 15 B4
Kilsyth: Scotland 17 D4
Kilwinning: Scotland 17 D4
Kilworth Mts.: Irish Republic 15 C4
Kimball: U.S.A. 53 E2
Kimberley: S. Africa 61 D13
Kimitsu: Japan 38 f iv
Kinabalu, Mt.: Mal. 37 F9
Kinale, Lough: Irish Republic 15 D3
Kinbrace: Scotland 16 E1
Kinder Scout: *mtn.*, England 14 E3
Kindu: Zaire 61 E8
Kineshma: U.S.S.R. 30 E2
Kineton: England 13 E2
Kingisepp: U.S.S.R. 19 D4
King I.: Australia 40 G8
Kingman: Ariz., U.S.A. 52 C3
Kingman: Kans., U.S.A. 50 C2
Kings: *r.*, Irish Rep. 15 D4
Kingsbridge: England 12 C4
Kings Canyon Nat. Park: U.S.A. 52 B3
Kingsclere: England 13 E3
Kingscourt: Irish Rep. 15 E3
King's Lynn: Eng. 13 G2
Kingsport: U.S.A. 51 F2
Kingston: Canada 47 U8
KINGSTON: Jamaica 49 L6
Kingston: N.Z. 41 A4
Kingston-upon-Hull: England 14 F3
Kingstree: U.S.A. 51 G3
Kingsville: U.S.A. 50 C4
Kingswood: England 12 D3
Kington: England 12 C2
Kingussie: Scotland 16 D2
King William I.: Can. 47 Q3
Kinleith: N.Z. 41 C2
Kinlochewe: Scot. 16 C2
Kinlochleven: Scot. 16 D3
Kinnairds Head: Scot. 16 G2
Kinross: Scotland 17 E3
Kinsale: Irish Rep. 15 C5
Kinsale, Old Head of: Irish Republic 15 C5
Kinsarvik: Norway 19 A3
KINSHASA: Zaire 61 C8
Kinston: U.S.A. 51 G2
Kintore: Scotland 16 F2
Kintyre: *i.*, Scot. 17 C4
Kintyre, Mull of: *penin.*, Scotland 15 F1
Kippure: *mtn.*, Irish Republic 15 E3
Kirchheim: Ger. F.R. 25 B2
Kirgiz S.S.R.: U.S.S.R. 31 L5
KIRIBATI (Gilbert Islands): Pac. O. 42 G7
Kirin: China 36 H2
Kirkaldy: Scotland 17 E3
Kirkby: England 14 D3
Kirkby in Ashfield: Eng. 13 E1
Kirkby Lonsdale: Eng. 14 D2
Kirkbymoorside: Eng. 14 F2
Kirkby Stephen: Eng. 14 D2
Kirkcudbright: Scot. 17 D5
Kirkenes: Norway 18 F2
Kirkham: England 14 D3
Kirkintilloch: Scot. 17 D4
Kirkland Lake: *sett.*, Canada 47 T7
Kirklareli: Turkey 23 E4
Kirksville: U.S.A. 50 D1
Kirkuk: Iraq 30 E6
Kirkwall: Orkney Is. 16 e iv
Kirov: U.S.S.R. 30 F2
Kirovabad: U.S.S.R. 30 F5
Kirovograd: U.S.S.R. 30 C4
Kirovsk: R.S.F.S.R., U.S.S.R. 18 F2
Kirovsk: Turkomen S.S.R., U.S.S.R. 31 J6
Kirriemuir: Scotland 16 F3
Kirton in Lindsey: Eng. 14 F3
Kiruna: Sweden 18 D2
Kiryu: Japan 38 C2
Kisangani: Zaire 60 E7
Kisarazu: Japan 38 f iv
Kishinev: U.S.S.R. 22 E3
Kishiwada: Japan 38 b ii
Kishm: Afghanistan 31 L6
Kiskunfélegyháza: Hungary 22 C3
Kislovodsk: U.S.S.R. 30 E5
Kiso: *r.*, Japan 38 c i
Kisogawa: Japan 38 c i
Kissimmee: *r.*, U.S.A. 51 F4
Kisumu: Kenya 60 F8
Kitaibaraki: Japan 38 D2
Kitakyushu: Japan 38 B3
Kitaura: *l.*, Japan 38 g iii
Kitchener: Canada 47 T8
Kithira: *i.*, Greece 23 D5
Kíthnos: *i.*, Greece 23 D5
Kitimat: Canada 46 K6
Kitwe: Zambia 61 E10
Kitzbühel: Austria 25 C2
Kitzbühel Alps: *mtns.*, Austria 25 C2
Kiuchuan: China 36 B3
Kivak: U.S.S.R. 29 V5
Kiviyli: U.S.S.R. 19 E4
Kiwu, Lake: Zaire 61 E8
Kiyosumiyama: *mtns.*, Japan 38 g iv
Kjølan Mts.: Norway/Sweden 18 -
Kjustendil: Bulgaria 23 D4
Klagenfurt: Austria 25 C2
Klaipeda: U.S.S.R. 19 D4
Klamath: *r.*, U.S.A. 52 A2
Klamath Falls: *town*, U.S.A. 52 A2
Klar: *r.*, Nor./Swed. 19 B3
Klatovy: Czech. 24 C2
Kluane Nat. Park: Canada 46 H4
Knapdale: *penin.*, Scot. 17 C4
Knap Point: Scot. 17 C4
Knaresborough: Eng. 14 E2
Knighton: Wales 12 C2
Knockadoon Hd.: *c.*, Irish Republic 15 D5
Knockboy: *mtn.*, Irish Republic 15 B5
Knockmealdown Mts.: Irish Republic 15 D4
Knottingley: England 14 E3
Knoxville: U.S.A. 51 F2
Knutsford: England 12 D1
Kobe: Japan 38 b ii
Koblenz: Ger. F.R. 24 B1
Kobrin: U.S.S.R. 22 D2
Kochel: Ger. F.R. 25 C2
Kochi: Japan 38 B3
Kodaira: Japan 38 f iv
Kodiak I.: U.S.A. 46 E5
Kodok: Sudan 59 M6
Kofu: Japan 38 C2
Koga: Japan 38 f iii
Kohat: Pakistan 34 B2
Kohima: India 35 F3
Kokand: U.S.S.R. 31 L5
Kokchetav: U.S.S.R. 31 K3
Kokhtla Yarve: U.S.S.R. 19 E4
Kokkola: Finland 18 D3
Kokomo: U.S.A. 51 E1
Koko Nor: *l.*, *see* Tsing Hai 36 B3
Kola: *r.*, U.S.S.R. 18 G2
Kola Peninsula: U.S.S.R. 28 F4
Kolding: Denmark 19 A4
Kolhapur: India 34 B5
Köln *see* Cologne 24 B1
Kolomna: U.S.S.R. 30 D2
Kolomyya: U.S.S.R. 22 E3
Kolyma: *r. & plain*, U.S.S.R. 29 S4
Kolyuchin, Gulf of: U.S.S.R. 29 V4
Kolyvan': U.S.S.R. 31 N3
Komaki: Japan 38 c i
Komandor Islands: U.S.S.R. 29 T6
Komárno: Hungary 22 C3
Komba: Zaire 60 D7
Kominato: Japan 38 g iv
Kom Ombo: Egypt 59 M4
Komono: Japan 38 c i
Komotini: Greece 23 E4
Kompong Saom: Kampuchea 37 C8
Komrat: U.S.S.R. 22 E3
Komsomolsk-na-Amur: U.S.S.R. 29 Q7
Konan: Japan 38 c i
Kongola: Zaire 61 E9
Kongsberg: Norway 19 A4
Kongsvinger: Norway 19 B3
Konosha: U.S.S.R. 30 E1
Konosu: Japan 38 f iii
Konotop: U.S.S.R. 30 C3
Konstanz: Ger. F.R. 25 B2
Kontum: Vietnam 38 D4
Konya: Turkey 30 C6
Kootenai: *r.*, U.S.A. 46 M7
Kopar: Yugoslavia 25 C2
Kopavogur: Iceland 18 a ii
Köping: Sweden 19 C4
Koppang: Norway 18 B3
Koppeh Dagh: *mtns.*, Iran 31 H6
Korbach: Ger. F.R. 24 B1
Korcë: Albania 23 D4
Korčula: *i.*, Yugo. 23 C4
Kordofan: *Prov.*, Sudan 59 L6
Koriyama: Japan 38 D2
Korosten': U.S.S.R. 22 E2
Korshunova: U.S.S.R. 29 O6
Kortrijk: Belgium 20 C2
Kos: *i.*, Greece 23 E5
Košice: Czech. 22 D3
Kosciusko, Mt.: Austl. 41 H8
Kosh-Agach: U.S.S.R. 31 O4
Koshiki-retto: *arch.*, Japan 38 A3
Kosi: *r.*, India/Nepal 34 E3
Kosigaya: Japan 38 f iv
Kosovska Mitrovica: Yugoslavia 23 D4
Kostroma: U.S.S.R. 30 E2
Kostrzyn Odrz. (Küstrin): Poland 24 C1
Koszalin: Poland 22 C2
Kota: India 34 C3
Kota Bahru: Mal. 37 C9
Kota Kinabalu: Mal. 37 F9
Kotelnich: U.S.S.R. 30 F2
Köthen: Ger. D.R. 24 C1
Kotka: Finland 19 E3
Kotlas: U.S.S.R. 30 F1
Kotor: Yugoslavia 23 C4
Kotri: Pakistan 34 A3
Kotzebue: U.S.A. 46 C3
Kounradskiy: U.S.S.R. 31 M4
Kouvola: Finland 19 E3
Kovel': U.S.S.R. 22 D2
Kovrov: U.S.S.R. 30 E2
Koyaguchi: Japan 38 b ii
Kozáni: Greece 23 D4
Kozu-shima: *i.*, Japan 38 C3
Kra, Isthmus of: Thailand 37 B9
Kragerø: Norway 19 A4
Kragujevac: Yugo. 23 D4
Krakatau: *i.*, Indon. 37 D12
Kraljevo: Yugo. 23 D4
Kralupy: Czech. 24 C1
Kramfors: Sweden 18 C3
Kranjska Gora: Yugo. 25 C2
Krasnodar: U.S.S.R. 30 D4
Krasnovodsk: U.S.S.R. 30 G5
Krasnoyarsk: U.S.S.R. 31 P2
Krasnyy Kut: U.S.S.R. 30 F3
Krasnyy Luch: U.S.S.R. 30 D4
Kratie: Kampuchea 37 D8
Krefeld: Ger. F.R. 24 B1
Krelinga: U.S.S.R. 19 D4
Kremenchug: U.S.S.R. 30 C4
Kremenets: U.S.S.R. 22 E2
Krems: Austria 22 C3
Krishna: *r.*, India 34 C5
Krishnanagar: India 34 E4
Kristiansand: Nor. 19 A4
Kristianstad: Sweden 19 B4
Kristiansund: Nor. 18 A3
Kristinehamn: Swed. 19 B4
Krivoy Rog: U.S.S.R. 30 C4
Krk: *i.*, Yugoslavia 23 B3
Kronach: Ger. F.R. 24 C1
Kronotskiy Bay: U.S.S.R. 29 T7
Kronshtadt: U.S.S.R. 19 E3
Kruger Nat. Park: South Africa 61 F12
Kruševac: Yugoslavia 23 D4
Ksar-el-Kebir: Mor. 21 A5
Ksar el Boukhari: Algeria 21 C5
Kuala Lipis: Mal. 37 C10
KUALA LUMPUR: Malaysia 37 C10
Kuala Trengganu: Malaysia 37 C9
Kuantan: Malaysia 37 C10
Kuban': U.S.S.R. 30 D4
Kuching: Sarawak, Malaysia 37 E10
Kudat: Indonesia 37 F9
Kufra Oasis: Libya 59 K4
Kufstein: Austria 25 C2
Kuhmo: Finland 18 E3
Kuldïga: U.S.S.R. 19 D4
Kulmbach: Ger. F.R. 24 C1
Kulunda Steppe: U.S.S.R. 31 M3
Kulundinskoye, Lake: U.S.S.R. 31 M3
Kumagaya: Japan 38 f iii
Kumamoto: Japan 38 B3
Kumasi: Ghana 58 E7
Kumla: Sweden 19 C4
Kunar: *r.*, Afg./Pak. 34 B2
Kungälv: Sweden 19 B4
Kungrad: U.S.S.R. 31 H5
Kunlun Mts.: China 34 C1
Kunming: China 34 C5
Kuopio: Finland 18 E3
Kupang: Indonesia 37 G13
Kurashiki: Japan 38 B3
Kure: Japan 38 B3
Kurgan: U.S.S.R. 31 K2
Kuria Muria Is.: Oman 32 G7
Kurihashi: Japan 38 f iii
Kurikka: Finland 18 D3
Kuril Islands: U.S.S.R. 42 E2
Kuril Ridge: Sea of Okhotsk 42 E2
Kuril Trench: Pac. O. 42 E2
Kurnool: India 34 C5
Kurow: N.Z. 41 B3
Kursk: U.S.S.R. 30 D3
Kurskiy Zaliv: *lag.*, U.S.S.R. 19 D4
Kurume: Japan 38 B3
Kushida: Japan 38 c ii
Kushka: U.S.S.R. 31 J6
Kushva: U.S.S.R. 31 J2
Kustanay: U.S.S.R. 31 J3
Küstrin *see* Kostrzyn Odrz 24 C1
Kut: Iraq 32 E4
Kutahya: Turkey 30 C6
Kutaisi: U.S.S.R. 30 E5
Kutch, Gulf of: India 34 A4
Kutno: Poland 22 C2
Kuusamo: Finland 18 E2
Kuusankoski: Finland 19 E3
KUWAIT: 32 E5
KUWAIT: Kuwait 32 E5
Kuwana: Japan 38 c i
Kuybyshev: U.S.S.R. 30 G3
Kuybyshev: U.S.S.R. 31 M2
Kuzbass: *geog. reg.*, U.S.S.R. 31 O2
Kvaløy: *i.*, Norway 18 C2
Kvalsund: Norway 18 D1
Kwanghwa: China 36 E4
Kwantung Peninsula: China 36 G3
Kweilin: China 36 E5
Kweiyang (Kweichu): China 36 D5
Kyoga, Lake: Ug. 60 F7
Kyoga-saki: *cape*, Japan 38 C2
Kyonan: Japan 38 f iv
Kyongsong *see* SEOUL 36 H3
Kyoto: & *Pref.*, Japan 38 b i
Kyushu: *i.*, Japan 38 B3
Kyushu-Palau Ridge: Pacific Ocean 42 C5
Kyushu- Sanchi: *mtns.*, Japan 38 B3
Kyzyl: U.S.S.R. 29 M7
Kyzyl-Kum: *des.*, U.S.S.R. 31 J5
Kzyl-Orda: U.S.S.R. 31 K5

L

La Banda: Argentina 56 B2
Labe: *r.*, Czech. 24 C1
Laboulaye: Arg. 56 B3
Labrador: *geog. reg.*, Canada 47 X6
Labrador Basin N. Atl. Ocean 10 E2
Labrador City: Can. 47 W6
Labuan: *i.*, Mal. 37 F9
La Carlota: Argentina 56 B3
La Carolina: Arg. 56 B3
Laccadive Is. *see* Lakshadweep 33 K8
Laccadive Sea: Ind. O. 33 K8
la Chaux: France 25 B2
la Chaux de Fonds: Switzerland 25 B2
Lachlan: *r.*, Austl. 40 G/H7
Lacken Reservoir: Irish Republic 15 E3
La Coruña: Spain 21 A4
La Crosse: U.S.A. 53 G2
La Cumbre: Arg. 56 B3
Ladakh Range: China/India 34 C2
Ladoga, Lake: U.S.S.R. 30 C1
Ladybank: Scotland 16 E3
Ladysmith: S. Africa 61 E13
Lac: Pap.-N.G. 40 H2
Lærdalsøyri: Nor. 19 A3
Læsø: *i.*, Denmark 19 B4
Lafayette: Ind., U.S.A. 51 E1
Lafayette: La., U.S.A. 50 D3
Lagan: *r.*, N. Irel. 15 F2
Lågen: *r.*, Norway 18 A3
Laggan, Loch: Scot. 16 D3
Laghouet: Algeria 58 F2
Lagoa Vermelha: *town*, Brazil 56 D2
LAGOS: Nigeria 58 F7
La Grande: Canada 47 U6
La Grande: U.S.A. 52 B1
La Grange: U.S.A. 51 E3
La Guaira: Ven. 49 N7
La Guardia: Port. 21 A4
Laguna: Brazil 56 E2
Laguna Madre: *lag.*, U.S.A. 50 C4
Lahn: *r.*, Ger. F.R. 24 B1
Lahore: Pakistan 34 B2
Lahr: Ger. F.R. 25 B2
Lahti: Finland 19 E3
Lairg: Scotland 16 D1
Lajes: Brazil 56 D2
La Junta: U.S.A. 53 E3
Lake Chad Basin: Chad 58 J6
Lake Charles: *city*, U.S.A. 50 D3
Lake City: U.S.A. 51 F3
Lake District Nat. Park: England 14 C2
Lakeland: U.S.A. 51 F4
Lake Mead Nat. Recreation Area U.S.A. 52 C3
Lakhimpur: India 34 D3
Laksefjorden: *fd.*, Nor. 18 E1
Lakselv: Norway 18 E1
Lakshadweep (Laccadive Is.): *Union Territ.*, Ind. 33 K8
Lalibela: Ethiopia 59 N6
La Linea: Spain 21 A5
la Louvière: Belg. 24
La Maddelena: Sardinia 21
La Madrid: Arg. 56
Lamar: U.S.A. 53
Lambay I.: Irish Rep. 15
Lambeth: England 13
Lambourn: England 13
Lame: N. Ireland 15
Lame Deer: U.S.A. 52
Lamesa: U.S.A. 50
Lamía: Greece 23
Lammermuir Hills: Scotland 17
La Montana: *geog. reg.*, Peru 54
Lampedusa: *i.*, Italy 23
Lampeter: Wales 12
Lanak Pass: China/India 34
Lanark: Scotland 17
Lancashire: *Co.*, Eng. 14
Lancaster: England 14
Lancaster: Ohio, U.S.A. 51
Lancaster: Pa., U.S.A. 51
Lancaster Sound: Can. 47
Lanchow (Kaolan, Lanzhou): China 36
Lancing: England 13
Landau: Ger. F.R. 25
Landeek: Austria 25
Lander: U.S.A. 52
Landerneau: France 20
Landsberg: Ger. F.R. 25
Land's End: Eng. 12
Landshut: Ger. F.R. 25
Landskrona: Sweden 19
Langensalza: Ger. D.R. 24
Langeoog: *i.*, Ger. F.R. 24
Langholm: Scotland 17
Langjökull: *ice-cap*, Iceland 18
Langres, Plateau de: France 20
Lans, Mont de: Fr. 25
Lansing: U.S.A. 51
Lanus: Argentina 56
Lanzarote: *i.*, Canary Islands 58
Lanzhou *see* Lanchow 36
Laoag: Philippines 37
Lao Cai: Vietnam 37
Laois: *Co.*, Irish Rep. 15
Laon: France 20
LAOS: 37
La Paloma: Uruguay 56
La Paz: Argentina 56
LA PAZ: Bolivia 54
La Paz: Mexico 48
La Pelada: Arg. 56
La Plata: Arg. 56
Lappeenranta: Fin. 18
Laptev Sea: U.S.S.R. 29
Laptev Strait: U.S.S.R. 29
Lapua: Finland 18
La Puerta: Arg. 56
La Punta: Arg. 56
L'Aquila: Italy 23
Larache: Morocco 21
Laramie: U.S.A. 53
Laranjeiras do Sul: Brazil 56
Laranjinha: *r.*, Brazil 56
Larche: France 25
Laredo: U.S.A. 50
Largs: Scotland 17
La Rioja: *Prov.*, Arg. 56
Lárisa: Greece 23
Lark: *r.*, England 13
la Rochelle: France 20
la Roche-sur-Yon: Fr. 20
La Romana: Dom. Rep. 49
Larsen Ice Shelf: Antarctica 55
Larvik: Norway 19
Las Cruces: U.S.A. 52
La Serena: Chile 55
Lashic: Burma 33
Las Lajitas: Arg. 56
Las Lomitas: Arg. 56
Las Palmas: Canary Is. 58
Las Peñas: Arg. 56
La Spezia: Italy 25
Las Piendras: Uruguay 56
Lassen Peak: *mtn.*, U.S.A. 52
Las Termas: Arg. 56
Lastoursville: Gabon 61
Las Varillas: Arg. 56
Las Vegas: Nev., U.S.A. 52
Las Vegas: N. Mex., U.S.A. 53
Latakia: Syria 30
Latina: Italy 23
La Torna: Arg. 56
la Tour-du-Pin: Fr. 25
Latvian Soviet Socialist Republic: U.S.S.R. 19
Lauder: Scotland 17
Launceston: Austl. 41
Launceston: England 12
Laurel: Miss., U.S.A. 51
Laurel: Mont., U.S.A. 52
Laurencekirk: Scot. 16
Lausanne: Switzerland 25
Laut: *i.*, Indonesia 37
Lavaisse: Arg. 56
Laval: France 20
Lavalle: Catamarea, Argentina 56
Lavalle: Corrientes, Argentina 56
Lavenham: England 13
Laverton: Australia 40
Lawrence: U.S.A. 50
Lawton: U.S.A. 50
Laxford, Loch: Scot. 16
Lea: *r.*, England 13
Leach: *r.*, England 13
Lead: U.S.A. 53
Leadon: *r.*, England 12

* *See page 80*

dro N. Alem:
entina 56 C2
e, Lough: Irish
ublic 15 B4
nerhead: England 13 F3
ANON: 30 D7
non: Oreg., U.S.A. 52 C2
non: Tenn., U.S.A. 51 E2
rk: Poland 22 C2
e: Italy 23 C4
o: Italy 25 B2
: r., Ger. F.R. 25 C2
iguanas, Isla de
Argentina 56 C3
lade: England 13 E3
tal: valley, Aus. 25 C2
eusot: France 25 A2
ury: England 12 D2
r., Irish Rep. 15 B5
s: England 14 E3
s: U.S.A. 53 F1
: England 12 D1
Ger. F.R. 24 B1
warden: Neth. 24 B1
win, Cape: Austl. 40 A7
vard Is.: West
es 49 O6
spi: Phil. 37 G8
orn (Livorno):
y 25 C3
iano: Italy 25 B2
ica: Poland 22 C2
India 34 C2
avre. France 20 C2
te: Ger. F.R. 24 B1
ester: England 13 E2
estershire: Co.,
land 13 F2
en: Neth. 24 A1
h: England 14 D3
h Creek: Austl. 40 F7
nton Buzzard:
land 13 F3
ster, Mt.: Irish
oublic 15 E4
zig: Ger. D.R. 24 C1
a: Portugal 21 A5
on: England 13 H2
: Scotland 17 E4
im: Co., Irish
oublic 15 C2
ip: Irish Rep. 15 E3
r., Neth. 24 B1
an, Lac see
neva, Lake of 25 B2
Mans: France 20 C3
e: Brazil 56 a i
go: Ger. F.R. 24 B1
menjoen Nat.
k: Finland 18 E2
a: r., U.S.S.R. 29 P5
e, Lough: Irish
oublic 15 D3
nabad: U.S.S.R. 31 L5
nakan: U.S.S.R. 30 E5
ngrad: U.S.S.R. 19 F4
nogorsk: U.S.S.R. 31 N3
n Peak: mtn.,
S.S.R. 31 L6
nsk-Kuznetskiy:
S.S.R. 31 O3
s: France 20 C2
f: Libya 59 J2
ben: Austria 22 C3
minster: England 12 D2
n: Mexico 48 F5
n: Spain 21 A4
n: r., U.S.A. 50 C3
nora: Austl. 40 C6
el: U.S.S.R. 22 E2
ontine Alps: mtns.,
y/Switz. 25 B2
uy: France 21 C3
da: Spain 21 C4
na, Valle de: Arg. 56 A2
wick: Shet. Is. 16 b i
Baux: France 25 A3
bos: i., Greece 23 E5
Cayes: Haiti 49 M6
Ecréhou: is.,
annel Islands 12 a ii
kovac: Yugo. 23 D4
Landes: reg., Fr. 21 B4
ie: Scotland 17 E3
OTHO: 61 E13
Sables-d'Olonne:
nce 21 B3
Saintes: is.,
sser Antilles 49 O6
ser Antilles: is.,
est Indies 49 O6
zno: Poland 22 C2
chworth: England 13 F3
hbridge: Canada 46 N7
cia: Columbia 54 D4
erkenny: Irish Rep. 15 D2
ven: Belgium 24 A1
ádheia: Greece 23 D5
ange: Norway 18 B3
eque, Cape: Austl. 40 C4
en: Scotland 17 F3
en, Loch: Scot. 17 E3
e, r., Scot. 16 D3
erkusen: Ger. F.R. 24 B1
kás: i., Greece 23 D5
ves: England 13 G4
vis: i., Scot. 16 B1
vis Pass: N.Z. 41 B3
wiston: U.S.A. 52 B1
wistown: U.S.A. 52 D1
ngton: U.S.A. 51 F2
bourn: England 14 E2
dsdorp: S. Africa 61 E12
land: England 14 D3
te: i., Phil. 37 G8
sa: China 35 F3
oyang: China 36 G2
rd: r., Canada 46 L4
erec: Czech. 22 C2
by: U.S.A. 52 B1
eral: U.S.A. 50 B2
LIBERIA: 58 D7
LIBREVILLE: Gabon 60 A7
LIBYA: 58/9 J3
Libyan Desert: Africa 59 K3
Libyan Plateau: Egypt 59 L2
Lichfield: England 13 E2
Lichinga: Mozambique 61 G10
Licking: r., U.S.A. 51 F2
Lida: U.S.S.R. 22 E2
Liddel Water: r.,
Scotland 17 F4
Lidköping: Sweden 19 B4
Lido: Italy 25 C2
LIECHTENSTEIN: 25 B2
Liège: Belgium 24 B1
Lienz: Austria 25 C2
Liepāja: U.S.S.R. 19 D4
Lier: Belgium 24 A1
Liestal: Switzerland 25 B2
Leitrim: Co., Irish Rep. 15 C2
Liffey: r., Irish
Republic 15 E3
Lifford: Irish Rep. 15 D2
Ligny: hist., Belg. 24 A1
Liguria: reg., Italy 25 B3
Ligurian Alps: mtns.,
Italy 25 B3
Ligurian Apennines:
mtns., Italy 25 B3
Lijo: r., Finland 18 E2
Likasi: Zaire 61 E10
Lilla Bælt: str.,
Denmark 19 A4
Lille: France 20 C2
Lillehammer: Norway 19 B3
Lillestrøm: Norway 19 B4
Lilongwe: Malawi 61 F10
LIMA: Peru 54 C6
Lima: U.S.A. 51 F1
Limavady: N. Irel. 15 E1
Limburg: Ger. F.R. 24 B1
Limburg: reg., Neth. 24 B1
Limeira: Brazil 56 a i
Limerick: & Co., Irish
Republic 15 C4
Limfjorden: fd.,
Denmark 19 A4
Límnos: i., Greece 23 D5
Limogenes: France 20 C3
Limon: U.S.A. 53 E3
Limpopo: r., Africa 61 F12
Linares: Mexico 50 C5
Linares: Spain 21 B5
Lincoln: Argentina 56 B3
Lincoln: England 13 F1
Lincoln: U.S.A. 50 C1
Lincolnshire: Co.,
England 13 F1
Lincoln Wolds: hills,
England 14 F3
Lindau: Ger. F.R. 25 B2
Lindos: Rhodes 23 E5
Line Is.: Pacific O. 42/3 K7
Ling: r., Scotland 16 C2
Lingen: Ger. F.R. 24 B1
Lingga: i., Indon. 37 C11
Linguère: Senegal 58 B5
Lini: China 36 F3
Linköping: Sweden 19 C4
Linlithgow: Scot. 17 E4
Linnhe, Loch: Scot. 16 C3
Linslade: England 13 F3
Linton: U.S.A. 53 E1
Linz: Austria 25 C2
Lion, Golfe du: Fr. 21 C4
Lion Nat. Park:
U.S.A. 52 C3
Lipari Is.: Italy 23 B5
Lipetsk: U.S.S.R. 30 D3
Liphook: England 13 F3
Lippstadt: Ger. F.R. 24 B1
Lisbellaw: N. Irel. 15 D2
LISBON: Portugal 21 A5
Lisburn: N. Irel. 15 E2
Lisburne, Cape: U.S.A. 46 B3
Liscannor Bay: Irish
Republic 15 B4
Lisdoonvarna: Irish
Republic 15 B3
Lisianski: i.,
Hawaiian Islands 42 H4
Lisieux: France 20 C3
Liskeard: England 12 B4
Lismore: Australia 41 J6
Lismore: Irish Rep. 15 D4
Lismore I.: Scot. 16 C3
Lisnaskea: N. Irel. 15 D2
Listowel: Irish Rep. 15 B4
Lithgow: Australia 41 J7
Lithuanian S.S.R.:
U.S.S.R. 19 D4
Little Bahama Bank:
The Bahamas 51 G4
Little Bitter Lake:
Egypt 59 Ins.
Little Colorado: r.,
U.S.A. 52 D4
Little Dart: r., Eng. 12 C4
Little Falls: town,
Minn., U.S.A. 53 G1
Littlefield: U.S.A. 50 B3
Littlehampton: Eng. 13 F4
Little Kanawha: r.,
U.S.A. 51 F2
Little Minch: channel,
Scotland 16 B2
Little Ouse: r., Eng. 13 G2
Littleport: England 13 G2
Little Rock: U.S.A. 50 D3
Little St. Bernard
Pass: Italy/France 25 B2
Little Sioux: r., U.S.A. 50 C1
Little Snake: r., U.S.A. 52 D2
Liuchow: China 36 D6
Livermore, Mt.: U.S.A. 50 B3
Liverpool: England 14 D3
Liverpool Bay: Eng. 14 C3
Livingston: Scotland 17 E4
Livingston: Mont.,
U.S.A. 52 C1
Livingston: Tenn.,
U.S.A. 51 E2
Livingstone Falls: Zaire 61 B9
Livingstone: Malawi 61 F10
Livo: r., Finland 18 E2
Livorno see Leghorn 25 C5
Lizard: England 12 A5
Lizard Pt.: England 12 A5
Ljubljana: Yugoslavia 22 B3
Ljungan: r., Sweden 18 C3
Ljungby: Sweden 19 B4
Ljusdal: Sweden 18 C3
Ljusnan: r., Sweden 18 C3
Llandeilo: Wales 12 B3
Llandovery: Wales 12 C3
Llandrindod Wells:
Wales 12 C2
Llandudno: Wales 12 C1
Llanelli: Wales 12 B3
Llanfairfechan: Wales 12 C1
Llanfyllin: Wales 12 C2
Llangefni: Wales 12 B1
Llangollen: Wales 12 C2
Llanidloes: Wales 12 C2
Llano: U.S.A. 50 C3
Llano Estacado: plat.,
U.S.A. 53 E4
Llanos de Guarayos:
plain, Bolivia 54 F7
Llanos de la Rioja:
plain, Argentina 56 A2
Llanos, Sierra de los:
ra., Argentina 56 A3
Llanos de Guarayo:
plain, Bolivia 54 F7
Llanrwst: Wales 12 C1
Llantrisant: Wales 12 C3
Llanwern: Wales 12 D3
Llanwrtyd Wells:
Wales 12 C2
Lleyn Peninsula:
Wales 12 B2
Lloret de Mar: Spain 21 C4
Lloydminster: Can. 46 O6
Llyn Clywedog
Reservoir: Wales 12 C2
Loanhead: Scotland 17 E4
Lobito: Angola 61 B10
Lobos: Argentina 56 C4
Locarno: Switz. 25 B2
Lochaline: Scot. 16 C3
Lochalsh, Kyle of:
penin., Scotland 16 C2
Lochboisdale: Scot. 16 A2
Lochcarron: Scot. 16 C2
Lochgelly: Scot. 17 E3
Lochgilphead: Scot. 17 C3
Lochinver: Scot. 16 C1
Lochmaben: Scot. 17 E4
Lochmaddy: Scot. 16 A2
Lochnager: mtn.,
Scotland 16 E3
Lochy, Loch: Scot. 16 D3
Lockerbie: Scot. 17 E4
Lodi: Italy 25 B2
Lodi: U.S.A. 52 A3
Łódź: Poland 22 C2
Lofoten Islands:
Norway 18 B2
Loftus: England 14 F2
Lofty Range: Austl. 40 F7
Logan: W. Va., U.S.A. 51 F2
Logan: Utah, U.S.A. 52 C2
Logan, Mt.: Can. 46 H4
Logan, Mull of:
cape, Scotland 17 C5
Logansport: U.S.A. 51 E1
Logroño: Spain 21 B4
Loir: r., France 20 B3
Loire: r., France 21 B3
Loja: Ecuador 54 C4
Loja: Spain 21 B5
Lokan Reservoir:
Finland 18 E2
Lokchong: China 36 E5
Lokka: Finland 18 E2
Løkken: Norway 18 A3
Lolland: i., Denmark 19 B5
Lomas de Vallejos:
Argentina 56 C2
Lomas de Zamora:
Argentina 56 C3
Lombardy: reg., Italy 25 B2
Lombardy, Plain of:
Italy 25 B2
Lomblen: i., Indon. 37 G12
Lombok: i. & str.,
Indonesia 37 F12
Lomé: Togo 58 F7
Lommel: Belgium 24 B1
Lomond, Loch: Scot. 17 D3
London: Canada 47 T8
LONDON: & Met. Co.,
United Kingdom 13 F3
Londonderry: & Co.,
N. Ireland 15 D2
Londrina: Brazil 56 D1
Long, Loch: Scot. 17 D3
Long Bay: U.S.A. 51 G3
Long Beach: city,
U.S.A. 52 B4
Longbenton: England 14 E1
Long Crendon: Eng. 13 E3
Long Eaton: Eng. 13 E2
Longford: & C., Irish
Republic 15 D3
Long Island: Bahamas 49 L5
Long Island: U.S.A. 51 H1
Longmont: U.S.A. 53 D2
Long Mountain: Wales 12 C2
Long Mynd: hill,
England 12 D2
Longreach:
Australia 40 G5
Longridge: England 14 D3
Long Sutton: Eng. 13 G2
Longton: England 12 D2
Longuyon: France 24 B2
Longview: Tex., U.S.A. 50 D3
Longview: Wash.,
U.S.A. 52 A1
Longwy: France 24 B2
Lons le Saunier: Fr. 25 B2
Looe: England 12 B4
Lookout, Cape:
U.S.A. 51 G3
Loop Head: cape,
Irish Republic 15 B4
Lopez, Cape: Gabon 61 A8
Lorain: U.S.A. 51 F1
Lorca: Spain 21 B5
Lord Howe Rise:
Pacific Ocean 42 F9
Lorena: Brazil 56 a i
Lorient: France 20 B3
Lorn: Firth of:
est., Scotland 16 C3
Lorrach: Ger. F.R. 25 B2
Lorraine: Old prov.,
France 24-5 B2
Los Alamos: U.S.A. 52 D3
Los Andes: Chile 55 D10
Los Angeles: U.S.A. 52 B4
Los Gigantes: mtn.,
Argentina 56 B3
Lossiemouth: Scot. 16 E2
Los Telares: Arg. 56 B2
Lostwithiel: England 12 B4
Lot: r., France 21 C4
Lota: r., Finland/
U.S.S.R. 18 E2
Lothian: Reg., Scot. 17 E/F4
Louboma: Congo 61 B8
Loue: r., France 25 B2
Loughborough: Eng. 13 E2
Lough Conn: Irish Rep. 15 D3
Loughrea: Irish Rep. 15 C3
Loughton: Eng. 13 G3
Louisburgh: Irish Rep. 15 B3
Louisiade:
Papua-New Guinea 41 J3
Louisiana: State,
U.S.A. 50 D3
Louisville: U.S.A. 51 E2
Loup: r., Nebr.,
U.S.A. 53 F2
Loup City: U.S.A. 53 F2
Lourdes: France 21 B4
Louth: England 14 G3
Louth: Co., Irish Rep. 15 E3
Louviers: Fr. 20 C3
Lower California:
State, Mexico 48 D4
Lower Lough Erne:
Northern Ireland 15 D2
Lower Red Lake: U.S.A. 53 F1
Lower Tunguska: r.,
U.S.S.R. 29 L5
Lowestoft: England 13 H2
Lowther Hills: Scot. 17 E4
Loyang: China 36 E4
Lu: r., see Salween 36 B7
Lualaba: r., Zaire 61 E9
Luanda: Angola 61 B9
Luang Prabang: Laos 37 C7
Luangwa Nat. Park:
Zambia 61 F10
Lubango: Angola 61 B10
Lubbock: U.S.A. 50 B3
Lübeck: & bay,
German F.R. 24 C1
Lubéron, Montagne du:
France 25 B3
Lublin: Poland 22 D2
Lubumbashi: Zaire 61 E10
Lucan: Irish Rep. 15 E3
Lucas: r., Argentina 56 C3
Lucca: Italy 25 C3
Luce Bay: Scotland 17 D5
Lucerne see Luzern 25 B2
Lucin: U.S.A. 52 C2
Luckenwalde: Ger. D.R. 24 C1
Lucknow: India 34 D3
Lüdenscheid: Ger. F.R. 24 B1
Lüderitz: Namibia 61 C13
Ludhiana: India 34 C2
Ludlow: England 12 D2
Ludlow: U.S.A. 52 B4
Ludvika: Sweden 19 C3
Ludwigsburg: Ger. F.R. 24 B2
Ludwigshafen:
German F.R. 24 B2
Ludwigslust: Ger. D.R. 24 C1
Lufkin: U.S.A. 50 D3
Luga: & r., U.S.S.R. 19 F4
Lugano: Switz. 25 B2
Lugg: r., U.K. 12 C2
Lugo: Spain 21 A4
Lugoj: Romania 22 D3
Lugnaquillia: mtn.,
Irish Republic 15 E4
Luichart, Loch: Scot. 16 D2
Luichow Peninsula:
China 36 D6
Luing: i., Scot. 17 C3
Lujan: Argentina 56 C3
Lule: r., Sweden 18 D2
Luleå: Sweden 18 D2
Lüleburgaz: Turkey 23 E4
Lumberton: U.S.A. 51 G3
Lumsden: N.Z. 41 A4
Luna, Lago de: Arg. 56 C2
Lund: Sweden 19 B4
Lundy I.: England 12 B3
Lune: r., England 14 D2
Lüneburg: & Heath,
German F.R. 24 C1
Lunéville: France 25 B2
Lungkiang see
Tsitsihar 36 E11
Lupeni: Romania 23 D3
Lure: France 25 B2
Lurgan: N. Ireland 15 E2
LUSAKA: Zambia 61 E11
Lusambo: Zaire 61 D8
Lushai Hills: India 35 F4
Lüta: China 36 G3
Luton: England 13 F3
Lutsk: U.S.S.R. 22 E2
Lutterworth: England 13 E2
LUXEMBOURG: 24 B2
LUXEMBOURG:
Luxembourg 24 B2
Luxor: Egypt 59 M3
Luzern (Lucerne)
city & l., Switz. 25 B2
Luzon: i., Phil. 37 G7
L'vov: U.S.S.R. 22 D3
Lyakhoy Islands:
U.S.S.R. 29 R3
Lybster: Scotland 16 E1
Lycksele: Sweden 18 C3
Lycksele Lappmark:
geog. reg., Sweden 18 C2
Lydd: England 13 G4
Lydenburg: S. Africa 61 E13
Lydney: England 12 D3
Lyeksa Lake: U.S.S.R. 18 F3
Lyme Bay: England 12 D4
Lyme Regis: England 12 C4
Lymington: England 13 E4
Lymm: England 14 D3
Lynchburg: U.S.A. 51 G2
Lyndhurst: England 13 E4
Lynher: r., England 12 B4
Lynmouth: England 12 C3
Lynn Lake: sett., Can. 46 P5
Lynton: England 12 C3
Lyon: r., Scotland 16 D3
Lyon, Loch: Scot. 16 D3
Lyons (Lyon): Fr. 25 A2
Lys'va: U.S.S.R. 31 H2
Lytham St. Anne's
England 14 C3
Lyttelton: N.Z. 41 B3

M

Ma'ān: Jordan 32 C4
Maanselkä: hills,
Finland 18 E2
Maarianhamina: Fin. 19 D3
Maas (Meuse): r.,
Netherlands 24 B1
Maastricht: Neth. 24 B1
Mablethorpe: Eng. 13 G1
McAlester: U.S.A. 50 C3
McAllen: U.S.A. 50 C4
Macao: Port, overseas
prov., China 36 E6
Macapa: Brazil 54 H3
McArthur's Head:
cape, Scotland 17 C4
Masefield: Eng. 12 D1
M'Clintock Channel:
Canada 46 P1
M'Clure Strait: Can. 46 L1
McComb: U.S.A. 50 D3
McCook: U.S.A. 53 E2
Macdonnell Ranges:
Australia 40 E5
Macduff: Scotland 16 F2
Maceió: Brazil 54 L5
Macerata: Italy 23 B4
McGehee: U.S.A. 50 D3
Macgillycuddy's Reeks:
mtns., Irish Rep. 15 B4
McGrath: U.S.A. 46 D4
Machars, The: dist.,
Scotland 17 D5
Machida: Japan 38 f iv
Machrihanish: & bay,
Scotland 17 C4
Machu Picchu: Peru 54 D6
Machynlleth: Wales 12 C2
McIntosh: U.S.A. 53 E1
Mackay: Australia 41 H5
Mackay, Lake: Austl. 40 D5
Mackenzie: r., Can. 46 J3
Mackenzie: Guyana 49 P8
Mackenzie Bay: Can. 46 H3
Mackenzie Highway:
Can. 46 M5
McKinley, Mt.: U.S.A. 46 E4
McKinney: U.S.A. 50 C3
Macnean Lower,
Lough: N. Ireland 15 D2
Macnean Upper,
Lough: Irish Rep. 15 C2
Mâcon: France 25 A2
Macon: U.S.A. 51 F3
Macquarie I.: Southern
Ocean 42 E12
McRae: U.S.A. 51 F3
Macroom: Irish Rep. 15 C5
MADAGASCAR: 61 –
Madagascar Basin:
Indian Ocean 35 d vii
Madagascar Ridge:
Indian Ocean 35 c viii
Madan: Pap.-N.G. 40 H2
Maddalena Pass:
Italy/France 25 B3
Madeira: i., Atlantic. O. 58 B2
Madeira: r., Brazil 54 F5
Madeleine, Îles-de-la-:
is., Canada 47 X7
Madera: U.S.A. 52 A3
Madesimo: Italy 25 B2
Madhya Pradesh:
State, India 34 C4
Madison: Fla., U.S.A. 51 F3
Madison: Ind., U.S.A. 51 E2
Madison: S. Dak.,
U.S.A. 51 E1
Madison: Wis., U.S.A. 53 F2
Madisonville: U.S.A. 51 E2
Madiun: Indonesia 37 E12
Madras: India 34 D6
MADRID: Spain 21 B4
Madura: i., Indon. 37 E12
Maebashi: Japan 38 C2
Maesteg: Wales 12 C3
Mafeking: S. Africa 61 E13
Mafra: Brazil 56 E2
Magadan: U.S.S.R. 29 S6
Magallanes see Punta
Arenas 55 D14
Magdalena: Arg. 56 C4
Magdalena: r., Col. 54 D2
Magdeburg: Ger. D.R. 24 C1
Magee I.: N. Ireland 15 F2
Magellan, Strait of:
Chile 55 E14
Magenta: Italy 25 B2
Maggiore, Lake: Italy 25 B2
Maghera: N. Ireland 15 E2
Magherafelt: N. Irel. 15 E2
Magnitogorsk: U.S.S.R. 31 H3
Magnolia: U.S.A. 50 D3
Magwe: Burma 33 O6
Mahajunga:
Madagascar 61 J11
Mahanadi: r., India 34 D4
Maharashtra: State,
India 34 C5
Mahia Peninsula: N.Z. 41 C2
Mahón: Menorca 21 C5
Maidenhead: Eng. 13 F3
Maidstone: England 13 G3
Maiduguri: Nigeria 58 H6
Maigue: r., Irish
Republic 15 C4
Maimana: Afghanistan 31 J6
Main: r., Ger. F.R. 24 B2
Main: r., N. Irel. 15 E2
Mai-Ndombe Lake:
Zaire 61 C8
Maine: r., Irish
Republic 15 B4
Mainland: i., Ork. Is. 16 d iv
Mainland: i., Shet. Is. 16 b i
Maiskhal: Bangl. 35 F4
Maitland: Australia 41 J7
Maizuru: Japan 38 C2
Majorca: i., see
Mallorca 21 C5
Makabe: Japan 38 g iii
Makarikari Salt Pan:
Botswana 61 E12
Makassar, Strait of:
Indonesia 37 F11
Makat: U.S.S.R. 30 G4
Makeni: Sierra Leone 58 C7
Makeyevka: U.S.S.R. 30 D4
Makhachkala: U.S.S.R. 30 F5
Makó: Hungary 22 D3
Makran: geog. reg.,
Iran/Pakistan 32 H5
Makurazaki: Japan 38 B3
Makushino: U.S.S.R. 31 K2
Malabar Coast: India 34 B6
Malacca: Malaysia 37 C10
Malacca, Strait of:
Indonesia/Malaysia 37 C10
Málaga: Spain 21 B5
Malahide: Irish Rep. 15 E3
Malakal: Sudan 59 M7
Malakand: Pakistan 34 B2
Malang: Indonesia 37 E12
Malanje: Angola 61 C9
Malar, Lake: Sweden 19 C4
Malatya: Turkey 30 D6
MALAWI: 61 F10
Malawi (Nyasa),
Lake: E. Africa 61 F10
MALAYSIA: 37 –
Mal Bay: Irish Rep. 15 B4
Malbork: Poland 22 C2
Malden I.: Pacific O. 43 K7
MALDIVES
(Maldive Is.): 33 K9
Maldonado: Uruguay 56 C3
Maléa, Cape: Greece 23 D5
Malheur: r. & Lake,
U.S.A. 52 B2
MALI: 58 E5
Malindi: Kenya 61 H8
Malin Head: cape,
Irish Republic 15 D1
Mallaig: Scotland 16 C3
Mallorca (Majorca):
i., Balearic Islands 21 C5
Mallow: Irish Rep. 15 C4
Malmberget: Sweden 18 D2
Malmédy: Belgium 24 B1
Malmesbury: England 12 D3
Malmesbury: S. Africa 61 C14
Malmö: Sweden 19 B4
Maloja Pass: Switz. 25 B2
Malonga: Zaire 61 D10
Måløy: Norway 18 A3
Malpelo Island: Colom. 54 B3
MALTA: 23 B5
Malta: U.S.A. 52 D1
Maltby: England 14 E3
Maltion Nature Park:
Finland 18 E2
Malton: England 14 F2
Maluku: is., see
Moluccas 37 H10
Malvan: India 34 B5
Malvern Hills: Eng. 12 D2
Mamaia: Romania 23 E4
Mamba: Japan 38 e iii
Mamry, Lake: Poland 22 D2
Man, Isle of: U.K. 14 B2
Manaar: Sri Lanka 34 a ii
Manaar, Gulf of:
India/Sri Lanka 34 C7
Manacle Point: Eng. 12 A4
Manado: Indonesia 37 G10
MANAGUA: Nicaragua 49 J7
MANAMA: Bahrain 32 F5
Mana Pass: China 34 C2
Manapouri, Lake: N.Z. 41 A4
Manaus: Brazil 54 F4
Manazuru: Japan 38 f iv
Manchester: England 14 D3
Manchester: U.S.A. 47 M1
Manchuna: reg., China 36 H2
Mandal: Norway 19 A4
Mandalay: Burma 33 P6
Mandan: U.S.A. 53 E1
Mandasor: India 34 C4
Manfredonia: Italy 23 C4
Mangalia: Romania 23 E4
Mangalore: India 34 B6
Mangotsfield: Eng. 12 D3
Mangueira, Lagoa:
Brazil 56 D3
Mangum: U.S.A. 50 C3
Mangyshlak Peninsula:
U.S.S.R. 30 G5

* See page 80

veden 18 D2
erto: r., Arg. 56 B1
nlhausen: Ger. D.R. 24 C1
kachevo: U.S.S.R. 22 D3
kalla_:
men P.D.R. 32 E8
kden (Shenyang):
ina 36 G2
ko: Japan 38 b ii
heim: Ger. F.R. 24 B1
house: France 25 B2
l: *i.*, & *sound*,
otland 16 C3
laghareirk Mts.:
sh Republic 15 B4
laghcarn: *mtn.*,
rthern Ireland 15 D2
laghmore: *mtn.*,
rthern Ireland 15 E2
laittivu: Sri Lanka 34 b ii
ler Mts.: Indon. 37 E10
let, The: *penin.*,
sh Republic 15 A2
l Head: *cape*,
kney Islands 16 e iii
lingar: Irish Rep. 15 D3
tan: Pakistan 34 B2
mbles, The: Wales 12 B3
mbles Head: *cape*,
ales 12 C3
na: *i.*, Indon. 37 G12
nchen *see* Munich 25 C2
ncie: U.S.A. 51 E1
ndo: *r.*, Spain 21 B5
ngbere: Zaire 60 E7
nich (München):
rman F.R. 25 C2
nster: Ger. F.R. 24 B1
onio: Finland 18 D2
onio: *r.*, Finland/
veden 18 D2
: *r.*, Austria 25 C2
chison: *r.*, Austl. 40 B6
cia: Spain 21 B5
esul: *r.*, Rom. 22 D3
freesboro: U.S.A. 51 E2
mansk: U.S.S.R. 18 F2
om: U.S.S.R. 30 E2
oran: Japan 38 D1
oto-zaki: *cape*,
pan 38 B3
ray: *r.*, Austl. 40 G7
ray Bridge: Austl. 40 F8
rumbidgee: *r.*,
stralia 40 G7
upara: N.Z. 41 C2
s: Turkey 30 E6
sashino: Japan 38 f iv
SCAT: Oman 32 G6
scatine: U.S.A. 51 D1
skogee: U.S.A. 50 C2
sselburgh: Scot. 17 E4
ssoorie: India 34 C2
stafakemalpasa:
rkey 23 E5
stang Island:
S.A. 50 C4
tankiang: China 36 H2
tsu: Japan 38 D1
tsu-wan: *bay*,
pan 38 D1
tton I.: Irish
public 15 B4
yun-Kum: *des.*,
S.S.R. 31 L5
zaffarpur: India 34 E3
anza: Tanzania 61 E8
eru, Lake: Zaire 61 E9
akka River Nat.
rk: U.S.A. 51 F4
cenae: Greece 23 D5
tkyina: Burma 33 P5
nensingh: Bangl. 35 F4
nydd Bach: *mtn.*,
ales 12 B2
nydd Du: *hills*,
ales 12 C3
nydd Eppynt: *hills*,
ales 12 C2
dalsjökull: *ice-cap*,
land 18 b ii
sore: India 34 C6

s: Irish Republic 15 E3
hingwea: Tan. 61 G10
ogdoches: U.S.A. 50 D3
unday: & *r.*, Par. 56 D2
or: Morocco 21 B5
stved: Denmark 19 B4
jd: *des.*, Saudi
abia 32 D5
ahama: Japan 38 c i
a Hills: India/
rma 35 F3
aland: *State*,
lia 35 F3
ano: Japan 38 C2
aoka: Kyoto, Japan 38 b ii
aoka: Niigata,
pan 38 C2
apattinam: India 34 C6
ara: *r.*, Japan 38 c i
asaki: Japan 38 A3
ashima: Japan 38 c ii
ato: Japan 38 B3
les Mts.: Irish
public 15 C4
oya: Japan 38 c i
pur: India 34 C4
ykanizsa: Hung. 22 C3
a: Ryukyu Is. 36 H5
anni Nat. Park:
nada 46 N4
uel Mapá: Arg. 56 A3
sworth: Eng. 12 D3
n: Canada 47 X5
ni Tal: India 34 C3
n: & *r.*, Scot. 16 E2

NAIROBI: Kenya 61 G8
Najd: *geog. reg.*, Saudi Arabia 32 D5
Naka: Japan 38 a i
Nakaminato: Japan 38 D2
Nakatsu: japan 38 B3
Nakhichevan: U.S.S.R. 30 F6
Nakhodka: U.S.S.R. 36 J2
Nakhon Ratchasima: Thailand 37 C7
Naknek: U.S.A. 46 D5
Nakuru: Kenya 61 G8
Nal: *r.*, Pakistan 34 A3
Namangan: U.S.S.R. 31 L5
Namib Desert: Namibia 61 B12
NAMIBIA (South-West Africa): 61 –
Nampula: Moz. 61 G11
Namsos: Norway 18 B3
Namur: Belgium 24 A1
Nanao: Japan 38 C2
Nanchang: China 36 F5
Nancheng: China 36 D4
Nan Clár: *l.*, Scot. 16 D1
Nancy: France 25 B2
Nanda Devi: *mtn.* India 34 C2
Nandan: Japan 38 a ii
Nanga Parbat: *mtn.*, India 34 B1
Nangchen Japo: China 36 A4
Nanjing *see* Nanking 36 F4
Nanking (Nanjing): China 36 F4
Nan Ling: *mtns.*, China 36 E5
Nanning (Yengning): China 36 D6
Nânsei Is.: *see* Ryukyu Islands 36 H5
Nan Shan: *ra.*, China 36 B3
Nanso: Japan 38 g iv
Nantes: & *r.*, France 20 B3
Nanto: Japan 38 c ii
Nantwich: England 12 D1
Nant-y-môch Reservoir: Wales 12 C2
Nanumea: *i.*, Tuvalu 42 G7
Nanyuki: Kenya 60 G7
Nao, Cabo de: Spain 21 C5
Naoetsu: Japan 38 C2
Napa: U.S.A. 52 A3
Napier: N.Z. 41 C2
Naples: Italy 23 B4
Nar: *r.*, England 13 G2
Nara: & *Pref.*, Japan 38 b ii
Narbada: *r.*, India 34 C4
Narberth: Wales 12 B3
Narbonne: France 21 C4
Narew: *r.*, Poland 22 D2
Narita: Japan 38 g iv
Naruto: Chiba, Japan 38 g iv
Naruto: Shikoku, Japan 38 B3
Narvik: Norway 18 C2
Nar'yan-Mar: U.S.S.R. 28 H4
Nasca Ridge: Pac. O. 43 R9
Naseby: England 13 E2
Nashville: U.S.A. 51 E2
Nasik: India 34 B5
Näsi Lake: Finland 18 D3
Näsiriyah: Iraq 32 E4
NASSAU: The Bahamas 51 G4
Nasser, Lake: Egypt 59 M4
Nässjö: Sweden 19 B4
Natal: Brazil 54 L5
Natal: *Prov.*, S. Afr. 61 F13
Natchez: U.S.A. 50 D3
Natchitoches: U.S.A. 50 D3
Natuna Is. (Bunguran): Indon. 37 D10
Naturaliste, Cape: Australia 40 B7
NAURU: 42 F7
Navan: Irish Rep. 15 E3
Navarin, Cape: U.S.S.R. 29 U5
Navasota: *r.*, U.S.A. 50 C3
Naver: *r.*, Scotland 16 D1
Naver, Loch: Scot. 16 D1
Návpaktos: Greece 23 D5
Návplion: Greece 23 D5
Náxos: *i.*, Greece 23 E5
Nayoro: Japan 38 D1
Nazca: Peru 54 D7
Naze, The: *pt.*, Eng. 13 H3
Nazili: Turkey 23 E5
N'DJAMENA: Chad 58 J6
Ndola: Zambia 61 E10
Neagh, Lough: N. Irel. 15 E2
Neápolis: Greece 23 D5
Neath: Wales 12 C3
Nebit-Dag: U.S.S.R. 30 G6
Nebraska: *State*, U.S.A. 53 E2
Nebraska City: U.S.A. 50 C1
Neches: *r.*, U.S.A. 50 C3
Neckar: *r.*, Ger. F.R. 24 B2
Needham Market: Eng. 13 H2
Needles: U.S.A. 52 C4
Needles, The: *cape*, England 13 E4
Nefyn: Wales 12 B2
Negra, Laguna: Uru. 56 D3
Negomba: Sri Lanka 34 a ii
Negro: *r.*, Arg. 55 F12
Negro: *r.*, Brazil 56 E2
Negro: *r.*, Brazil 54 F4
Negro: *r.*, Paraguay 56 C1
Negro: *r.*, Uruguay 56 C3
Negros: *i.*, Phil. 37 G9
Nehbandar: Iran 32 H4
Neimenggu: *Aut. Reg.*, *see* Inner Mongolia 36 F2
Neisse (Nysa): *r.*, Ger. D.R./Poland 24 C1
Neiva: Colombia 54 C3
Nellore: India 34 C6

Nelson: England 14 D3
Nelson: N.Z. 41 B3
Nelson: *r.*, Canada 47 R5
Nema: Mauritania 58 D5
Neman: U.S.S.R. 19 D4
Neman: *r.*, U.S.S.R. 22 E2
Nemuro: Japan 36 L2
Nenagh: Irish Rep. 15 C4
Nenana: U.S.A. 46 F4
Nene: *r.*, England 13 F2
Neosho: *r.*, U.S.A. 50 C2
NEPAL: 34 D3
Nephin: *mtn.*, Irish Republic 15 B2
Nephin Beg Range: *mtns.*, Irish Rep. 15 B2
Nerchinsk: U.S.S.R. 29 O7
Neretva: *r.*, Yugo. 23 C4
Neskaupstadhur: Ice. 18 c i
Ness, Loch: Scot. 16 D2
Neston: England 12 C1
NETHERLANDS: 24 B1
Neubrandenburg: German D.R. 24 C1
Neuchâtel: & *l.*, Switzerland 25 B2
Neufchâteau: Belg. 24 B2
Neufchâteau: France 25 B2
Neumünster: Ger. F.R. 24 B1
Neunkirchen: Ger. F.R. 24 B2
Neuquén: Argentina 55 E11
Neuruppin: Ger. D.R. 24 C1
Neuse: *r.*, U.S.A. 51 G2
Neusiedler, Lake: Austria 22 C3
Neuss: German F.R. 24 B1
Neustadt: Ger. F.R. 24 B2
Neustrelitz: Ger. D.R. 24 C1
Nevada: *State*, U.S.A. 52 B3
Nevada, Sierra: *mtns.*, Spain 21 B5
Nevada, Sierra: *ra.*, U.S.A. 52 B3
Nevada City: U.S.A. 52 A3
Never: U.S.S.R. 29 P7
Nevers: France 20 C3
Nevis: *i.*, Leeward Islands 49 O6
Nevis, Loch: Scot. 16 C3
New Alresford: Eng. 13 E3
New Amsterdam: *i.*, Indian Ocean 35 f viii
Newark: N.J., U.S.A. 51 H1
Newark: Ohio, U.S.A. 51 F1
Newark-on-Trent: Eng. 13 F1
New Bern: U.S.A. 51 G2
Newbiggin-by-the-Sea: England 14 E1
New Braunfels: U.S.A. 50 C4
New Britain: *i.*, Papua-New Guinea 40 J2
New Brunswick: *Prov.*, Canada 47 W7
Newburgh: Scotland 16 E3
Newburgh: U.S.A. 51 H1
Newburn: England 14 E2
Newbury: England 13 E3
New Caledonia: *i.*, Pacific Ocean 42 F9
New Caledonian Basin: Pacific Ocean 42 F9
Newcastle: Austl. 41 J7
Newcastle: N. Irel. 15 F2
New Castle: Pa., U.S.A. 51 F1
Newcastle: Wyo., U.S.A. 53 E2
Newcastle Emlyn: Wales 12 B2
Newcastle-under-Lyme: England 12 D1
Newcastle-upon-Tyne: England 14 E2
Newcastle West: Irish Republic 15 B4
NEW DELHI: & *State*, India 34 C3
New England: *reg.*, U.S.A. 47 M1
Newenham, Cape: U.S.A. 46 C5
Newent: England 12 D3
New Forest: *reg.*, England 13 E4
Newfoundland: *Prov.*, Canada 47 Y6
Newfoundland Basin: N. Atlantic Ocean 10 F3
New Galloway: Scot. 17 D4
New Glasgow: Can. 47 X7
New Guinea: *i.*, Indon./Pap.-N.G. 40 –
Newhaven: England 13 G4
New Haven: U.S.A. 51 H1
New Hebrides *now* VANUATU 42 F8
New Hebrides Trench: Pac. O. 42 F8
New Iberia: U.S.A. 50 D3
New Ireland: *i.*, Papua-New Guinea 40 J1
New Jersey: *State*, U.S.A. 51 H1
Newmarket: England 13 G2
New Mexico: *State*, U.S.A. 52/3 D4
New Mills: England 14 E3
Newnan: U.S.A. 51 F3
Newnham: England 12 D3
New Orleans: U.S.A. 50 D4
New Plymouth: N.Z. 41 B2
Newport: I. of Wight, England 13 E4
Newport: Salop, Eng. 12 D2
Newport: Wales 12 D3
Newport News: U.S.A. 51 G2
Newport-on-Tay: Scotland 16 F3
Newport Pagnell: England 13 F2
New Providence The Bahamas 51 G4

Newquay: England 12 A4
New Quay: Wales 12 B2
New Romney: Eng. 13 G4
New Ross: Irish Rep. 15 E4
Newry: N. Ireland 15 E2
New South Wales: *State*, Australia 40-1 H7
Newton: Iowa, U.S.A. 50 D1
Newton: Kans., U.S.A. 50 C2
Newton Abbot: Eng. 12 C4
Newton le Willows: England 14 D3
Newton Stewart: Scotland 17 D5
Newtown: Wales 12 C2
Newtownabbey: N. Irel. 15 F2
Newtownards: N. Irel. 15 F2
Newtown Hamilton: N. Ireland 15 E2
Newtownstewart: N. Ireland 15 D2
New Ulm: U.S.A. 53 G2
New York: *State*, U.S.A. 51 G1
NEW ZEALAND: 41 –
Neyagawa: Japan 38 b ii
Neyland: Wales 12 B3
Nez de Jobourg: *pt.*, France 12 b i
Ngami, Lake: Bots. 61 D12
N'Gaoundéré: Cam. 58 H7
Ngauruhoe: *mtn.*, New Zealand 41 C2
Ngorongoro Conservation Area: Tanzania 61 F8
Nguru: Nigeria 58 H6
Niagara Falls: U.S.A. 49 L1
NIAMEY: Niger 58 F6
Nias: *i.*, Indon. 37 B10
NICARAGUA: 49 –
Nicaragua, Lake: Nic. 49 J7
Nice: France 25 B3
Niceville: U.S.A. 51 E3
Nicobar Is.: Indian O. 35 h iv
Nidd: *r.*, England 14 E2
Niedere Tauern: *mtns.*, Austria 25 C2
Nienburg: Ger. F.R. 24 B1
NIGER: 58 H5
Niger: *r.*, W. Africa 58 G7
NIGERIA: 58 –
Nihoa: *i.*, Hawaiian Islands 42 J4
Niigata: Japan 38 C2
Niihama: Japan 38 B3
Niihau: *i.*, Hawaiian Islands 42 J4
Nii-shima: *i.*, Japan 38 C3
Nijmegen: Neth. 24 B1
Nikolayev: U.S.S.R. 30 C4
Nikolayevsk: U.S.S.R. 29 R7
Nikko-kokuritsu-kōen: *nat. park*, Japan 38 C2
Nikopol': U.S.S.R. 30 C4
Nikšic: Yugoslavia 23 C4
Nil Biru: *Prov.*, Sudan 59 M6
Nile: *r.*, Africa 59 M4
Niles: U.S.A. 51 E1
Nilgiri Hills: India 34 C6
Nîmes: France 21 C4
Nimrud: Iraq 30 E6
Nimule: Sudan 59 M8
Nineveh: Iraq 30 E6
Ninghsia *see* Yinchuan 36 D3
Ningpo: China 36 G5
Niobara: *r.*, U.S.A. 53 F2
Niort: France 20 B3
Nipigon, Lake: Can. 46 57
Niš: Yugoslavia 23 D4
Nishinomiya: Japan 38 b ii
Nishiwaki: Japan 38 a ii
Niteroi: Brazil 56 b i
Nith: *r.*, Scotland 17 D4
Nithdale: *val.*, Scotland 17 E4
Nitra: Czechoslovakia 22 C3
Nivelles: Belgium 24 A1
Nizhniy-Tagil: U.S.S.R. 31 J2
Nobeoka: Japan 38 B3
Noboribetsu: Japan 38 D1
Noda: Japan 38 f iv
Nodaway: *r.*, U.S.A. 50 C1
Nogaysk: U.S.S.R. 30 D4
Nogoyá: & *r.*, Arg. 56 C3
Noirmount Pt.: Jersey 12 a ii
Nojima-zaki: *cape*, Japan 38 f v
Nokia: Finland 18 D3
Nome: U.S.A. 46 B4
Nonacho Lake: Can. 46 O4
Noordoostpolder: *polder*, Netherlands 24 B1
Noranda: Canada 47 U7
Norden: Ger. F.R. 24 B1
Nordenham: Ger. F.R. 24 B1
Norderney: *i.*, Ger. F.R. 24 B1
Nordfjordeid: Nor. 18 A3
Nordhausen: Ger. D.R. 24 C1
Nordhorn: Ger. F.R. 24 B1
Nördlingen: Ger. F.R. 25 C2
Nordvik: U.S.S.R. 29 O3
Nore: *r.*, Kilkenny, Irish Republic 15 D4
Nore: *r.*, Laois, Irish Republic 15 D4
Norfolk: *Co.*, Eng. 13 G2
Norfolk: Nebr., U.S.A. 53 F2
Norfolk: Va., U.S.A. 51 G2
Norfolk Broads: *reg.*, England 13 H2
Norfolk Island: Pac. O. 42 F9
Noril'sk: U.S.S.R. 29 L4
Norman: *r.*, Austl. 40 G4
Normandie, Collines de: *hills*, Fr. 20 B3
Normanton: Austl. 40 G4
Norman Wells: Can. 46 K3
Nørresundby: Den. 19 A4
Norrköping: Sweden 19 C4
Norrtälje: Sweden 19 C4

Norseman: Austl. 40 C7
Norte, Sierra del: *ra.*, Argentina 56 B3
Northallerton: England 14 E2
Northam: Australia 40 B7
North American Basin: N. Atlantic Ocean 10 E4
Northampton: Eng. 13 F2
Northamptonshire: *Co.*, England 13 F2
North Battleford: Can. 46 O6
North Bay: *town*, Canada 47 U7
North Bend: U.S.A. 52 A2
North Berwick: Scot. 17 F3
North Canadian: *r.*, U.S.A. 53 E3
North Cape: N.Z. 41 B1
North Cape: Norway 18 E1
North Carolina: *State*, U.S.A. 51 F2
North Cascades Nat. Park: U.S.A. 52 A1
North Channel: British Isles 15 F1
North Dakota: *State*, U.S.A. 53 E1
North Dorset Downs: England 12 D4
North Downs: *hills*, England 13 G3
North Dvina: *r.*, U.S.S.R. 30 F1
Northeast Providence Channel: The Bahamas 51 G4
North Eifel Nature Park: Ger. F.R. 24 B1
Northern Ireland: *admin. reg.*, U.K. 15 E2
Northern Territory: *Territ.*, Australia 40 –
Northern Sporades: *is.*, Greece 23 D5
North Esk: *r.*, Scot. 16 F3
North Fiji Basin: Pacific Ocean 42 G8
Northfleet: England 13 G3
North Foreland: *pt.*, England 13 H3
North Hinksey: England 13 E3
North Island: N.Z. 41 –
NORTH KOREA: 36 H3
Northland: *dist.*, N.Z. 41 B2
North Little Rock: U.S.A. 50 B3
North Pacific Ocean: 42-3 –
North Platte: & *r.*, U.S.A. 53 E2
North Ronaldsay: *i.*, Orkney Islands 16 e iii
North Sea: Europe 14 G2
North Sos'va: *r.*, U.S.S.R. 28 J5
North Sound: Irish Republic 15 B3
North Sound, The: *bay*, Orkney Islands 16 e iii
North Tyne: *r.*, England 14 D1
North Uist: *i.*, Scot. 16 A2
Northumberland: *Co.*, England 14 D1
Northumberland Nat. Park: England 14 D1
North Walsham: Eng. 13 H2
Northwest Highlands: *mtns.*, Scotland 16 –
Northwest Pac. Basin: Pacific Ocean 42 E3
Northwest Providence Channel: The Bahamas 51 G4
Northwest Territories: *Territ.*, Canada 46-7 –
Northwich: England 12 D1
North York Moors Nat. Park: England 14 F2
North Yorkshire: *Co.*, England 14 E2
Norton: U.S.A. 51 F2
Norton Sound: U.S.A. 46 C4
NORWAY: 18/19 –
Norwich: England 13 H2
Noshiro: Japan 38 C1
Noss Hd.: Scotland 16 E1
Nossi Bé: *i.*, Malagasy Republic 61 I10
Nossob: *r.*, Bots./Namibia 61 D13
Notec: *r.*, Poland 22 C2
Notogawa: Japan 38 c i
Noto-Hanto: *penin.*, Japan 38 C2
Nottingham: England 13 E2
Nottinghamshire: *Co.*, England 13 E1
Nouadhibou: Mauritania 58 B4
NOUAKCHOTT: Mauritania 58 B5
NOUMÉA: New Caledonia 40 M5
Nova Iguaçu: Brazil 56 b i
Novara: Italy 25 B2
Nova Scotia: *Prov.*, Canada 47 X7
Nova Scotia Basin: N. Atlantic Ocean 10 E4
Novaya Zemlya: *is.*, U.S.S.R. 28 H3
Novgorod: U.S.S.R. 30 C2
Novi Ligure: Italy 25 B3
Novi Pazar: Yugo. 23 D4
Novocherkassk: U.S.S.R. 30 E4
Novograd Volynskiy: U.S.S.R. 22 E2
Novo Hamburgo: Brazil 56 D2
Novo-kuznetsk: U.S.S.R. 31 O3
Novomoskovsk: U.S.S.R. 30 D3
Novonazyvayevka: U.S.S.R. 31 L2
Novopolotsk: U.S.S.R. 22 E1
Novosibirsk: U.S.S.R. 31 N3
Novosibirskiye Ostrova: *is.*, U.S.S.R. 29 R2
Novorossiysk: U.S.S.R. 30 D5
Novouzensk: U.S.S.R. 30 F3
Nowa Sól: Poland 22 C2
Novyy Port: U.S.S.R. 28 K4
Nowy Sącz: Poland 22 D3
Nubian Desert: Sudan 59 M4
Nueces: *r.*, U.S.A. 50 C4
Nueva Galia: Arg. 56 A4
Nueva Palmira: Uru. 56 C3
Nueva Población: Argentina 56 B1
Nuevo Laredo: Mex. 50 C4
Nuits-St. Georges: France 25 A2
Nullarbor Plain: Austl. 40 D7
Numazu: Japan 38 e iv
Nuneaton: England 13 E2
Nunivak: *i.*, Bering Sea 46 B4
Nunkiang: China 36 H1
Nuoro: Sardinia 21 a i
Nuremberg (Nürnberg): German F.R. 24 C2
Nurmes: Finland 18 E3
Nürnberg *see* Nuremberg 24 C2
Nushki: Pakistan 34 A3
Nuwara Eliya: Sri Lanka 34 b ii
Nyahururu: Kenya 60 G7
Nyala: Sudan 59 K6
Nyasa (Malawi), Lake: E. Africa 61 F10
Nybro: Sweden 19 C4
Nyenchen Tanglha: *ra.*, China 34-5 E2
Nyíregyháza: Hungary 22 D3
Nykøbing: Denmark 19 B5
Nykøbing: Denmark 19 A4
Nyköping: Sweden 19 C4
Nynäshamn: Sweden 19 C4
Nyon: Switz. 25 B2
Nysa: Poland 22 C2
Nysa: *r.*, *see* Neisse 24 C1

O

Oa: *penin.*, Scotland 17 B4
Oa, Mull of: *channel*, Scotland 17 B4
Oadby: England 13 E2
Oahe Reservoir: U.S.A. 53 E1
Oahu: *i.*, Hawaiian Islands 43 K4
Oakdale: U.S.A. 52 A3
Oakengates: England 12 D2
Oakes: U.S.A. 53 F1
Oakham: England 13 F2
Oakland: U.S.A. 52 A3
Oak Ridge: U.S.A. 51 F2
Oamaru: N.Z. 41 B4
Oamishirasato: Japan 38 g iv
Oaxaca: Mex. 48 G6
Ob': *r.*, U.S.S.R. 28 J4
Ob', Gulf of: U.S.S.R. 28/9 K4
Oban: Scotland 16 C3
Obata: japan 38 c ii
Obbia: Somali Rep. 59 P7
Oberammergau: German F.R. 25 C2
Oberhausen: Ger. F.R. 24 B1
Obidos: Brazil 54 G4
Obi Is.: Indonesia 37 H11
Obu: Japan 38 c i
Ocala: U.S.A. 51 F4
Ocean Island: Pac. O. 42 F7
Oceanside: U.S.A. 52 B4
Ochil Hills: Scotland 16 E3
Ocmulgee: *r.*, U.S.A. 51 F3
Oconee: *r.*, U.S.A. 51 F3
Oda: Japan 38 B2
Odate: Japan 38 D1
Odawara: Japan 38 f iv
Odda: Norway 19 A3
Ödemis: Turkey 23 E5
Odense: Denmark 19 B4
Odenwald: *mtns.*, German F.R. 24 B2
Oder (Odra): *r.*, Ger. D.R./Poland 24 C1
Odessa: U.S.A. 50 B3
Odessa: U.S.S.R. 30 C4
Odra: *r.*, *see* Oder 24 C1
Oeno Island: Pac. O. 43 N9
Offaly: *Co.*, Irish Rep. 15 D3
Offenburg: Ger. F.R. 25 B2
Ofunato: Japan 38 D2
Oga: Japan 38 C2
Ogaden: *reg.*, Ethiopia 59 O7
Oga-Hanto: *penin.*, Japan 38 C2
Ogaki: Japan 38 c i
Ogallala: U.S.A. 53 E2
Ogano: Japan 38 e iii
Ogawa: Saitama, Japan 38 f iii
Ogawa: Baraki, Japan 38 g iii
Ogden: U.S.A. 52 C2
Oglio: *r.*, Italy 25 C2
Ohai: N.Z. 41 A4
Ohakune: N.Z. 41 C2
Ohara: Japan 38 g iv
Ohata: Japan 38 D1
Ohio: *State*, U.S.A. 51 F1
Ohio: *r.*, U.S.A. 51 E2
Ohito: Japan 38 e iv
Ohře (Eger): *r.*, Czechoslovakia 24 C1

Page ref.
Ohrid, Lake: Albania/Yugoslavia 23 D4
Oi: r., Japan 38 b i
Oich, Loch: Scotland 16 D2
Oise: r., France 20 C3
Oiso: Japan 38 f iv
Oita: Japan 38 B3
Ojika-Hanto: penin., Japan 38 D2
Ojos del Salado: mtn., Argentina 54 E9
Oka: r., U.S.S.R. 30 E2
Okanogan: r., Canada/U.S.A. 52 B1
Okaya: Japan 38 C2
Okayama: Japan 38 B3
Okazaki: Japan 38 d ii
Okeechobee, Lake: U.S.A. 51 F4
Okehampton: England 12 B4
Okha: India 34 A4
Okhotsk: U.S.S.R. 29 R6
Okhotsk, Sea of: U.S.S.R. 29 –
Oki-gunto: i., Japan 38 B2
Okinawa: i., Ryukyu Islands 36 H5
Oklahoma: State, U.S.A. 50 C2
Oklahoma City: U.S.A. 50 C2
Oklawaha: r., U.S.A. 51 F4
Okmulgee: U.S.A. 50 C2
Okovango Basin: marsh, Botswana 61 D11
Okt'abr'sk: U.S.S.R. 31 H4
Okushiri-shima, i., Japan 38 C1
Okutama: Japan 38 f iv
Öland: i., Sweden 19 C4
Olbia: Sardinia 21 a i
Oldenburg: Ger. F.R. 24 B1
Oldenzaal: Neth. 24 B1
Old Fletton: England 13 F2
Oldham: England 14 D3
Oldmeldrum: Scot. 16 F2
Old Nene: r., Eng. 13 F2
Old Sarum: hist., England 13 E3
Olduvai Gorge: Tanzania 61 G8
Olean: U.S.A. 51 G1
Olekminsk: U.S.S.R. 29 P5
Olenegorsk: U.S.S.R. 18 F2
Olenek: r., U.S.S.R. 29 P3
Oléron, Île d': Fr. 20 B3
Olhão: Portugal 21 A5
Olimar Grande: r., Uruguay 56 D3
Olimpo: Brazil 56 D3
Oliva: Argentina 56 B3
Olney: England 13 F2
Olomouc: Czech. 22 C3
Olpe: German F.R. 24 B1
Olsztyn: Poland 22 D2
Olten: Switzerland 25 B2
Oltul: r., Romania 23 D4
Olympia: Greece 23 D5
Olympia: U.S.A. 52 A1
Olympic Nat. Park: U.S.A. 52 A1
Olympus: mtn. Greece 23 D5
Omagh: N. Ireland 15 D2
OMAN: 32 G6
Oman, Gulf of: Arabian Sea 32 G6
Omdurman: Sudan 59 M5
Ome: Japan 38 f iv
Omigawa: Japan 38 g iv
Omi-hachiman: Japan 38 c i
Omiya: Japan 38 f iv
Omsk: U.S.S.R. 31 L2
Omuta: Japan 38 B3
Omutinskoye: U.S.S.R. 31 K2
Onega, Lake: U.S.S.R. 30 D1
O'Neill: U.S.A. 53 F2
Onekotan: i., U.S.S.R. 29 S8
Oniishi: Japan 38 f iii
Ono: Japan 38 a ii
Onslow Bay: U.S.A. 51 G3
Onstwedde: Neth. 24 B1
Ontario: Prov., Canada 47 S6
Ontario, Lake: Canada/U.S.A. 49 L1
Oodnadatta: Austl. 40 F6
Ooldea: Australia 40 E7
Oostelijk Flevoland: polder, Neth. 24 B1
Oosterhesselen: Neth. 24 B1
Oosterhout: Neth. 24 A1
*Ootacamund: India 34 C6
Opanake: Sri Lanka 34 b ii
Opatija: Yugoslavia 23 B3
Opava: Czech. 22 C3
Opelika: U.S.A. 51 E3
Opelousas: U.S.A. 50 D3
Opochka: U.S.S.R. 19 E4
Opole: Poland 22 C2
Oporto: Portugal 21 A4
Opotiki: N.Z. 41 C2
Opunake: N.Z. 41 B2
Oradea: Romania 22 D3
Oraison: France 25 B3
Orange: Australia 41 H7
Orange: France 25 A3
Orange: r., Namibia/S. Africa 61 C13
Orange: U.S.A. 50 D3
Orangeburg: U.S.A. 51 F3
Orange Free State: Prov., S. Africa 61 E13
Oranienburg: Ger. D.R. 24 C1
Orbigo: r., Spain 21 C4
Orbost: Australia 41 H8
Orchy r., Scotland 16 D3
Ord: r., Australia 40 D4
Ordos Plateau: China 36 D3
Ordzhonikidze: U.S.S.R. 30 E5
Örebro: Sweden 19 C4
Oregon: State, U.S.A. 52 A2
Oregon City: U.S.A. 52 A1
Orekhovo-Zuyevo: U.S.S.R. 30 D2
Orel': U.S.S.R. 30 D3
Orem: U.S.A. 52 C2
Orenburg: U.S.S.R. 30 H3
Orense: Spain 21 A4
Orford: England 13 H2
Orford Ness: penin., England 13 H2
Organ Pipe Cactus Nat. Park: U.S.A. 52 C4
Orgeyev: U.S.S.R. 22 E3
Orihuela: Spain 21 B5
Ori. Lake: Finland 18 E3
Orinoco: r., Ven. 54 F2
Orissa: State, India 34 D4
Oristano: Sardinia 21 a ii
Orizaba: & mtn., Mex. 48 G6
Orkanger: Norway 18 A3
Orkney Is.: Scotland 11 C1
Orlando: U.S.A. 51 F4
Orleães: Brazil 56 E2
Orléans: France 20 C3
Ormskirk: England 14 D3
Ornain: r., France 25 B2
Örnsköldsvik: Sweden 18 C3
Oronsay: i., Scotland 17 B3
Oroshaza: Hungary 22 D3
Orrin: r., Scotland 16 D2
Orsha: U.S.S.R. 22 F2
Orsk: U.S.S.R. 31 H3
Ortigueira: Spain 21 A4
Ortler: mtn., Italy 25 C2
Oruro: Bolivia 54 E7
Orvieto: Italy 23 B4
Orwell: r., England 13 G2
Osage: r., U.S.A. 50 D2
Osaka: & Pref., Japan 38 b ii
Osaka-wan: bay, Japan 38 b ii
Osh: U.S.S.R. 31 L5
O-shima: i., Japan 38 C3
Oshkosh: U.S.A. 53 H2
Oshogbo: Nigeria 58 F7
Osijek: Yugoslavia 23 C3
Oskaloosa: U.S.A. 50 D1
Oskarshamn: Sweden 19 B4
OSLO: Norway 19 B4
Oslofjorden: fd., Nor. 19 B4
Osmanabad: India 34 C5
Osnabruck: Ger. F.R. 24 B1
Osório: Brazil 56 D2
Ossa, Mount: Australia 40 H9
Ostend: Belgium 20 C2
Österdal: r., Sweden 19 B3
Östersund: Sweden 18 B3
Ostiglia: Italy 25 C2
Ostrava: Czech. 22 C3
Ostrov: U.S.S.R. 19 E4
Ostrovnoye: U.S.S.R. 29 T4
Ostrowiec Swietokrzyski: Pol. 22 D2
Ostrow Weilkopolski: Poland 22 C2
Osumi Is.: Japan 36 J4
Oswestry: England 12 C2
Otacílio Costa: Brazil 56 D2
Otago: dist., N.Z. 41 A4
Otago Peninsula: N.Z. 41 B4
Otaki: Japan 38 g iv
Otaru: Japan 38 D1
Otley: England 14 E3
Otra: r., Norway 19 A4
Otranto, Str. of: Mediterranean Sea 23 C5
Otsu: Japan 38 b i
Otsuki: Japan 38 e iv
Otta: Norway 18 A3
OTTAWA: & r., Canada 47 U7
Ottawa: Ill., U.S.A. 51 E1
Ottawa: Kans., U.S.A. 50 C2
Ottery: r., Eng. 12 B4
Ottery St. Mary: England 12 C4
Ottingen: Ger. F.R. 24 C2
Ottumwa: U.S.A. 50 D1
Ötztal Alps: mtns., Austria 25 C2
Ouachita: r., U.S.A. 50 D3
Ouachita Mts.: U.S.A. 50 D3
*OUAGADOUGOU: Upper Volta 58 E6
Ouargla: Algeria 58 G2
Oubangui: r., Africa 59 K8
Oudenaarde: Belgium 24 A1
Oudtshoorn: S. Africa 61 D14
Ouezzane: Morocco 58 D2
Oughter, Lough: Irish Republic 15 D2
Ouilmes: Argentina 56 A2
Oujda: Morocco 58 E2
Oulangan Nat. Park: Finland 18 E2
Oulu: & r., Finland 18 E2
Oulu Lake: Finland 18 E3
Ounas: r., Finland 18 E2
Oundle: England 13 F2
Ourthe: r., Belgium 24 B1
Ou-Sammyaku: mtns., Japan 38 D2
Ouse: r., E. Sussex, England 13 G4
Ouse: r., N. Yorks., England 14 F3
Outer Hebrides: is., Scotland 16 A2
Outer Skerries: is., Shetland Islands 16 c i
Outokumpu: Finland 18 E3
Ovalle: Chile 55 D10
Oversee: Ger. F.R. 20 D2
Overton: Wales 12 D2
Overtorneå: Sweden 18 D2
Oviedo: Spain 21 A4
Ovindoli: Italy 23 B4
Owando: Congo 61 C8
Owel, L.: Irish Rep. 15 D3
Owen, Mt.: N.Z. 41 B3
Owen Falls: Uganda 60 F7
Owensboro: U.S.A. 51 F2
Owens Lake: U.S.A. 52 D3
Owen Stanley Range: Papua-New Guinea 40 H2
Owyhee Reservoir: & r., U.S.A. 52 B2
Oxelösund: Sweden 19 C4
Oxford: England 13 E3
Oxfordshire: Co., England 13 E3
Oxnard: U.S.A. 52 B4
Oxus: r., see Amu Dar'ya 31 J6
Oykel: r., Scotland 16 D2
Oyodo: Japan 38 b ii
Oyonnax: France 25 B2
Oyster Haven: Irish Republic 15 C5
Ozark Plateau: U.S.A. 50 D2
Ozarks, Lake of the: U.S.A. 50 D2
Özd: Hungary 22 D3
Ozu: Japan 38 B3

P

Paan see Batang 36 B5
Pabbay: i., Scotland 16 A2
Pachacamac: Peru 54 C6
Pachung: China 38 A3
Pacific Grove: U.S.A. 52 C3
Pacific Ocean: 44/5 –
Padang: Indonesia 37 C11
*Paderborn: Ger. F.R. 24 B1
Padova see Padua 25 C2
Padre Island: U.S.A. 50 C4
Padstow: England 12 B4
Padua (Padova): Italy 25 C2
Paducah: U.S.A. 51 E2
Paeroa: N.Z. 41 C2
Pagoda Point: Burma 33 O7
Paide: U.S.S.R. 19 E4
Paignton: England 12 C4
Päijänne: l., Finland 18 E3
Painswick: England 12 D3
Paintsville: U.S.A. 51 F2
Paisley: Scotland 17 D4
Pakanbaru: Indon. 37 C10
PAKISTAN: 34 –
Pakokku: Burma 33 P6
Pakwach: Uganda 60 F7
Palatka: U.S.A. 51 F4
Palau Is.: Caroline Is. 37 J9
Palawan: i., Phil. 37 F9
Palembang: Indon. 37 C11
Palencia: Spain 21 B4
Palermo: Sicily 23 B5
Palestine: U.S.A. 50 C3
Palghat: India 34 C6
Palime: Togo 58 F7
Palisade: U.S.A. 52 B2
Palk Strait: India/Sri Lanka 34 a ii
Pallas-Ouinastunturin Nat. Park: Finland 18 E2
Palliser, Cape: N.Z. 41 C3
Palma de Mallorca: Mallorca 21 C5
Palmares do Sul: Brazil 56 D3
Palmas, Cape: Liberia 58 D8
Palmeira: Brazil 56 D2
Palmerland: penin., Antarctica 55 E17
Palmerston North: New Zealand 41 C3
Palmyra: Syria 30 D7
Palmyra Island: Pacific Ocean 43 J6
Palos, Cabo de: Spain 21 B5
Palpalá: Argentina 56 A1
Pamiers: France 21 C4
Pamirs: mtns., Asia 31 L6
Pamlico Sound: U.S.A. 51 G2
Pampa: geog. reg., Argentina 55 F11
Pampa: U.S.A. 50 B2
Pampa de las Salinas: salt lake, Argentina 56 A3
Pampa de los Guanacos: sett., Arg. 56 B2
Pampa Húmeda: geog. reg., Argentina 56 B4
Pampa Seca: geog. reg., Argentina 56 A4
Pamplona: Spain 21 B4
PANAMA: 49 –
PANAMA: Panama 49 L8
Panama, Gulf of: Panama 54 C2
Panama Canal: Panama 49 Ins.
Panama City: U.S.A. 51 E3
Panay: i., Philippines 37 G8
Pančevo: Yugoslavia 23 D4
Pando: Uruguay 56 C3
Panevežys: U.S.S.R. 19 D4
Pangbourne: England 13 E3
Pangnirtung: Canada 47 W3
Pangong Range: China 34 D2
Panjim: India 34 B5
Panshan: China 38 D1
Pant: r., England 13 G3
Pantar: i., Indonesia 37 G12
Pantelleria: i., Sicily 23 B5
Paoting (Chingyuan): China 36 F3
Paotow (Baotou): China 36 D2
Papakura: N.Z. 41 B2
Pap Stour: i., Shetland Islands 16 b i
Pap Westray: i., Orkney Islands 16 e iii
Papenburg: Ger. F.R. 24 B1
Paps, The: mtn., Irish Republic 15 B4
PAPUA-NEW GUINEA: 40 –
Papua: dist., Pap.-N.G. 40 G2
Papua, Gulf of: Papua-New Guinea 40 G2
Pará: r., Brazil 54 H4
Paracas: Peru 54 C6
Paracel (Xisha) Is.: China 37 E7
Paraguarí: Paraguay 56 C2
PARAGUAY: 54 G8
Paraiba do Sul: r., Brazil 56 b i
Paraibuna: & r., Brazil 56 a i
Paraitinga: r., Brazil 56 a i
Parakou: Benin 58 F7
*PARAMARIBO: Surinam 54 G2
Paramushir: i., U.S.S.R. 29 S7
Paraná: Argentina 56 B3
Paraná: State, Brazil 56 D1
Paraná, Lake: Arg. 56 C2
Paraná de las Palmas: r., Arg. 56 C3
Paranaguá: Brazil 56 E2
Paraná Guazú: r., Argentina 56 C3
Paraná Ibicuy: r., Argentina 56 C3
Paranapanema: r., Brazil 56 a i
Parbati: r., India 34 C4
Parbhani: India 34 C5
Parchim: Ger. D.R. 24 C1
Pardo: r., Parana, Brazil 56 E2
Pardo: r., Rio Grande do Sul, Brazil 56 D2
Pardubice: Czech. 22 C3
Parepare: Indonesia 37 F11
PARIS: France 20 C3
Paris: U.S.A. 50 C3
Parkersburg: U.S.A. 51 F2
Park Range: mtns., U.S.A. 52 D2
Park Rapids: town, U.S.A. 53 F1
Parma: Italy 25 C3
Parma: U.S.A. 51 F1
Parnaíba: Brazil 54 K4
Parnassos: mtn., Greece 24 D5
Pärnu: U.S.S.R. 19 D4
Parry Is.: Canada 46 O1
Parsons: U.S.A. 50 C2
Partenen: Austria 25 C2
Partenkirchen: German F.R. 25 C2
Partizansk: U.S.S.R. 29 Q9
Partry Mts.: Irish Republic 15 B3
Pasadena: U.S.A. 52 B4
Pasaje: r., Argentina 56 B2
Pascagoula: & r., U.S.A. 51 E3
Pasco: U.S.A. 52 B1
Pasni: Pakistan 34 c iv
Paso de los Libres: Argentina 56 C2
Paso de los Toros: Uruguay 56 C3
Paso de Patria: Par. 56 C2
Passage de la Déroute: Channel Is./France 12 a ii
Passage West: town, Irish Republic 15 C5
Passau: Austria 22 B3
Passau: Ger. F.R. 25 C2
Passero, Cape: Sicily 23 C5
Passo Fundo: & r., Brazil 56 D2
Pasto: Colombia 54 C3
Patagonia: geog. reg., Argentina 55 D13
Patchway: England 12 D3
Paterson: U.S.A. 51 H1
Pathankot: India 34 C2
Pathfinder Reservoir: U.S.A. 52 D2
Patiala: India 34 C2
Pátmos: i., Greece 23 E5
Patna: India 34 E3
Patos, Lagoa dos: Brazil 56 D3
Pátrai: Greece 23 D5
Pau: France 21 B4
Paulista: Brazil 56 a i
Paulistana: Brazil 54 K5
Paulo Alfonso Falls: Brazil 54 L5
Pavia: Italy 25 B2
Pavlodar: U.S.S.R. 31 M3
Payette: & r., U.S.A. 52 B2
Paysandú: Uruguay 56 C3
Peace: r., Canada 46 N5
Peacehaven: England 13 F4
Peace River: town, Canada 46 M5
Peak District Nat. Park: England 13 E1
Peake Deep: N. Atl. O. 10 H3
Peale, Mt.: U.S.A. 52 D3
Pearl: r., U.S.A. 50 D3
Pearsall: U.S.A. 50 C4
Peary Channel: Canada 47 Q1
Pease: r., U.S.A. 50 C3
Peć: Yugoslavia 23 D4
Pecas, Ilha das: i., Brazil 56 E2
Pechenga: U.S.S.R. 18 F2
Pechora: r., U.S.S.R. 28 H4
Pecos: & r., U.S.A. 50 B3
Pécs: Hungary 22 C3
Pedras Atlas: Brazil 56 D3
Pedro Miguel Locks: Panama 49 Ins.
Pedro, Point: Sri Lanka 34 b ii
Pedro R. Fernández Argentina 56 C2
Peebles: Scotland 17 E4
Pee Dee: r., U.S.A. 51 G3
Peel: I. of Man 14 B2
Peel Fell: mtn., Scot. 17 F4
Pegasus Bay: N.Z. 41 B3
Pegu: Burma 33 P7
Peian: China 36 H1
Peine: Ger. F.R. 24 C1
Peipus, Lake U.S.S.R. 19 E4
Peíxe, Lagoa do: Brazil 56 D3
Peíxe, Rio do: r., Brazil 56 D2
PEKING (Beijing): China 36 F3
Pelee Island: Canada 51 F1
Pelican Point: Namibia 61 B12
Peljekaise Nat. Park: Sweden 18 C2
Peloponnese: penin., Greece 23 D5
Pelotas: Brazil 56 D3
Pelotas: r., Brazil 56 D2
Pelusium, Bay of: Egypt 59 Ins.
Pelvoux, Mont: France 25 B3
Pemba: Mozambique 61 H10
Pemba: i., Tanzania 61 G9
Pembroke: Wales 12 B3
Pembroke Dock: Wales 12 B3
Pembrokeshire Coast Nat. Park: Wales 12 A3
Peña Colorado: mtn., Argentina 56 B1
Peñarroya: Spain 21 A5
Penarth: Wales 12 C3
Penasco: r., U.S.A. 53 E4
Pencarreg, Mynydd: mtn., Wales 12 B2
Pendembu: Sierra Leone 58 C7
Pendleton: U.S.A. 52 B1
Pend Oreille Lake: U.S.A. 52 B1
Penganga: r., India 34 C4
Penicuik: Scotland 17 E4
Peninsular Malaya: admin., Malaysia 37 C10
Penmaenmawr: Wales 12 C1
Pennar: r., India 34 C6
Pennine Alps: mtns., Switzerland 25 B2
Pennines, The: mtns., England 14 E2-3
Pennsylvania: State, U.S.A. 51 G1
Penrith: England 14 D2
Penryn: England 12 A4
Pensacola: U.S.A. 51 E3
Penticton: Canada 46 M7
Pentire Pt.: England 12 B4
Pentland Firth: str., Scotland 11 C1
Pentland Hills: Scot. 17 E4
Pen-y-Ghent: mtn., England 14 D2
Penza: U.S.S.R. 30 F3
Penzance: England 12 A4
Peoria: U.S.A. 51 E1
Perche, Collines du: hills, Fr. 20 C3
Pergamino: Argentina 56 B3
Périgueux: France 21 C3
Perm: U.S.S.R. 30 H2
Pernik: Bulgaria 23 D4
Perpignan: France 21 C4
Perry: r., England 12 D2
Pershore: England 12 D2
Persian Gulf see Gulf, The 32 F5
Perth: Australia 40 B7
Perth: Scotland 16 E3
PERU: 54 –
Peru Basin: Pacific O. 43 Q8
Peru-Chile Trench: Pacific Ocean 43 S9
Perugia: Italy 23 B4
Perugorría: Argentina 56 C2
Pesaro: Italy 25 C3
Pescadores: is., Taiwan 36 F6
Pescara: Italy 23 B4
Peschiera: Italy 25 C2
Peshawar: Pakistan 34 B2
Petange: Luxembourg 24 B2
Peterborough: Canada 47 U8
Peterborough: Eng. 13 F2
Peterhead: Scotland 16 G2
Peter I.: Southern O. 55 A17
Peterlee: England 14 E2
Petersburg: U.S.A. 51 G1
Petersfield: England 13 F3
Petone: N.Z. 41 B3
Petrified Forest Nat. Park: U.S.A. 52 D3
Petrila: Romania 23 D3
Petropavlovsk: U.S.S.R. 31 K3
Petropavlovsk-Kamchatskiy: U.S.S.R. 29 S7
Petrópolis: Brazil 56 b i
Petroseni: Romania 23 D3
Petrozavodsk: U.S.S.R. 30 C1
Petukhovo: U.S.S.R. 31 K2
Pevensey: England 13 G4
Pewsey, Vale of: Eng. 13 E3
Peyrano: Argentina 56 B3
Pfälzer Bergland: plat., German F.R. 24 B2
Pfälzer Wald: mtns., German F.R. 24
Pforzheim: Ger. F.R. 24
Phanom Dongrak: mtns., Thailand 37
Phan Rang: Vietnam 37
Phelps: U.S.A. 54
PHILIPPINES, THE: 37
Philippine Sea: Pac. O. 42
Philippine Trench: Pacific Ocean 42
Phillipsburg: U.S.A. 50
PHNOM PENH: Kampuchea 37
Phoenix: U.S.A. 52
Phoenix Is.: Pac. O. 42
Phuket Island: Thailand 37
Piacenza: Italy 25
Piatra-Neamt: Rom. 23
Piave: r., Italy 25
Pichanal: Argentina 56
Pickering: England 14
Pickering, Vale of: England 14
Picton: N.Z. 41
Piedmont: reg., Italy 25
Piedra Sola: Uruguay 56
Piedras Negras: Mexico 50
Pieksämäki: Finland 18
Pielinen: l., Finland 18
Pierre: U.S.A. 53
Pietarsaari: Finland 18
Pietermaritzburg: South Africa 61
Pietersburg: S. Africa 61
Pigeon: r., Canada/U.S.A. 53
Piggott: U.S.A. 50
Pihlaja Lake: Finland 18
Pihtipudas: Finland 18
Pikeville: U.S.A. 51
Pila: Italy 25
Pila: Poland 22
Pilaga: r., Argentina 56
Pilar: Paraguay 56
Pilcomayo, Parque Nacional: Argentina 56
Pinang: Malaysia 37
Pinang Taiping: i., Malaysia 37
Pinar del Rio: Cuba 49
Pindamonhangaba: Brazil 56
Pindus Mts.: Greece 23
Pine Bluff: sett., U.S.A. 50
Pine Islands: U.S.A. 51
Pine Island Sound: U.S.A. 51
Pine Pass: Canada 46
Pine Point: sett., Canada 46
Pinerolo: Italy 25
Pinhal: Brazil 56
Pinkiang see Harbin 36
Pinsk: U.S.S.R. 22
Pinto: Argentina 56
Pioche: U.S.A. 52
Piombino: Italy 23
Piquiri: r., Brazil 56
Piracícaba: & r., Brazil 56
Piraí do Sul: Brazil 56
Piraieus: Greece 23
Piraju: Brazil 56
Pirané: Argentina 56
Pirapó: r., Paraguay 56
Pirarajá: Uruguay 56
Piratini: r., Brazil 56
Piratini: r., Brazil 56
Pirgos: Greece 23
Pirmasens: Ger. F.R. 24
Pirna: Ger. D.R. 24
Pisa: Italy 25
Pisek: Czech. 22
Pistoia: Italy 25
Pit: r., U.S.A. 52
Pitcairn Island: Pac. O. 43
Pite: r., Sweden 18
Piteå: Sweden 18
Pitești: Romania 23
Pitlochry: Scotland 16
Pittsburg: Kans., U.S.A. 50
Pittsburg: Tex., U.S.A. 50
Pittsburgh: U.S.A. 51
Placentia Bay: Can. 47
Plácido Rosas: Uru. 56
Plainview: U.S.A. 50
Plata, Río de la: est., Arg./Uruguay 56
Platte: r., U.S.A. 53
Plattling: Ger. F.R. 25
Plauen: Ger. D.R. 24
Pleasanton: U.S.A. 50
Plenty, Bay of: N.Z. 41
Plentywood: U.S.A. 53
Pleven: Bulgaria 23
Plock: Poland 22
Ploești: Romania 23
Plombières: France 25
Plön: German F.R. 24
Plovdiv: Bulgaria 23
Plunge: U.S.S.R. 19
Plym: r., England 12
Plymouth: England 12
Plympton: England 12
Plynlimon: mtn., Wales 12
Plyussa: r., U.S.S.R. 19
Plura: Peru 54
Plzen: Czech. 22
Po: r., Italy 25
Poblado Celeste: Uru. 56
Pocatello: U.S.A. 52
Pocklington: England 14
Poçoes: Brazil 54
Pocomoke City: U.S.A. 51
Po Hai (Gulf of Chih li): China 36
P'ohang: S. Korea 38

* See page 80

See page 80

rman F.R. 25 B2
wandorf: Ger. F.R. 24 C2
wärbisch Hall: rman F.R. 24 B2
weinfurt: Ger. F.R. 24 C1
wenningen: rman F.R. 25 B2
werin: Ger. D.R. 24 C1
wyz: Switzerland 25 B2
ly, Isles of: U.K. 12 c iii
resby Sound: eenland 47 FF2
tia Sea: S. Atl. O. 10 F13
tland: *Kingdom*, K. 16/17
tt I.: Southern O 42 G13
ttsbluff: U.S.A. 53 E2
une: Scotland 16 C1
abster: Scotland 16 E1
anton: U.S.A. 51 G1
dian, Loch: Scot. 16 B3
nthorpe: England 14 F3
ford: England 13 G4
ford: U.S.A. 51 G2
forth, Loch: Scot. 16 B2
ham: England 14 E2
Islands: U.S.A. 51 F3
scale: England 14 C2
ton: England 12 C4
ttle: U.S.A. 52 A1
ha Oasis: Libya 58 H3
hura Desert: Peru 54 B5
o: *r.*, Argentina 56 B1
alia: U.S.A. 50 D2
lan: France 24 A2
bergh: England 14 D2
fel: Austria 25 C2
ovia: *r.*, Hond./ caragua 49 K7
ovia: Spain 21 B4
re: *r.*, Spain 21 C4
unda Punte: Arg. 56 C2
undo: *r.*, Arg. 56 B3
ura: *r.*, Spain 21 B5
dan: Japan 38 a ii
: *i.*, Scotland 16 C3
näjoki: Finland 18 D3
ne: *r.*, France 20 C3
ne, Baie de la: ance 20 B3
ondi-Takoradi: hana 58 E7
by: England 14 E3
enga: *r.*, Mong. 36 C1
estat: France 25 B2
ety-Tengiz, Lake: S.S.R. 31 L3
kirk: Scotland 17 F4
ma: U.S.A. 51 E3
sey: England 13 F4
sey Bill: *hd.*, Eng. 13 F4
va: Argentina 56 B2
vas: *geog. reg.*, azil 54 F5
marang: Indon. 37 E12
minoe Reservoir: S.A. 52 D2
miozernoye: S.S.R. 31 J3
mipalatinsk: S.S.R. 31 N3
nmān: *r.*, Iran 30 G6
ndai: Honshu, pan 38 D2
ndai: Kyushu, pan 38 B3
NEGAL: 58 B6
negal: *r.*, Maur./ enegal 58 C5
nja: *i.*, Norway 18 C2
nnan: Japan 38 b ii
nnar Dam: Sudan 59 M6
ns: France 20 C3
OUL (Kyongsong): Korea 36 H3
pt Île: *town*, anada 47 W6
quoia Nat. Park: S.A. 52 B3
rang: Indonesia 37 D12
remban: Malaysia 37 C10
rengeti Nat. Park: anzania 61 F8
ria: Brunei 37 E10
rian: Sarawak, Mal. 37 E10
rio: *r.*, Italy 25 B2
rov: U.S.S.R. 31 J2
rowe: Botswana 61 E12
rra da Apucarana: ., Brazil 56 D1
rra de Fartura: *ra.*, razil 56 D2
rra da Mantiqueira: ., Brazil 56 a i
rra da Pitanga: *ra.*, razil 56 D1
rra de Maracaju: ., Brazil 56 C1
rra do Canguçu: *ra.*, razil 56 D3
rra do Lagarto: *ra.*, razil 56 D1
rra do Mar: *ra.*, o de Janeiro, razil 56 b i
rra do Mar.: *ra.*, anta Catarina, Braz. 56 E2
rra do aranapiacaba: ., Brazil 56 E1
rra dos Parecis: ., Brazil 54 F6
rra dos Dourados: ., Brazil 56 D1
rra Geral: *ra.*, Braz. 56 D2
rrai: Greece 23 D4
rra Vermelha: ., Brazil 56 D1
rrezuela: Argentina 56 A3
rro das Encantades: ., Brazil 56 D3

Serro do Espinilho: *ra.*, Brazil 56 C2
Serro do Navio: Braz. 54 H3
Sestriere: Italy 25 B2
Sète: France 21 C4
Sétif: Algeria 21 D5
Seto-naikai (Inland Sea): Japan 38 B3
Seto-naikai-kokuritsu-koen: *nat. park*, Japan 38 a ii
Settle: England 14 D2
Setúbal: Portugal 21 A5
Sevan, Lake: U.S.S.R. 30 F5
Sevastopol': U.S.S.R. 30 C5
Seven Heads: *hd.*, Irish Republic 15 C5
Sevenoaks: England 13 G3
Severn: *r.*, England 12 D3
Severnaya Zemlya: *is.*, U.S.S.R. 29 M2
Severomorsk: U.S.S.R. 18 F2
Severoural'sk: U.S.S.R. 31 J1
Seville: Spain 21 A5
Seward: U.S.A. 46 F4
Seward Peninsula: U.S.A. 46 C3
SEYCHELLES: 35 d v
Seychelles-Mauritius Plateau: Ind. Ocean 35 e vi
Sevdhisfjördhur: Ice. 18 c i
Seymour: Tex., U.S.A. 50 C3
Sfax: Tunisia 58 H2
Sgurr Mor: *mtn.*, Scotland 16 D2
Sgurr na Ciche: *mtn.*, Scotland 16 C3
Sha Alam: Malaysia 35 C6
Shaftesbury: England 12 D3
Shah Faisalabad: Pak. 34 B2
Shahjahanpur: India 34 C3
*Shāhrūd: Iran 30 H6
Shakhty: U.S.S.R. 30 E4
Shalym: U.S.S.R. 31 D3
Shamrock: U.S.A. 50 B2
Shandong *see* Shantung 36 G3
Shanghai: China 36 G4
Shanklin: England 13 E4
Shannon: *r.*, Irish Republic 15 C4
Shannon, Mouth of the: Irish Republic 15 B4
Shannon Airport: Irish Republic 15 B4
Shansi (Shānxī): *Prov.*, China 36 E3
Shan States: Burma 33 P6
Shantung Penin.: China 36 G3
Shānxī; *Prov. see* Shansi 36 E3
Shaokuan: China 36 E6
Shap: England 14 D2
Shapinsay: *I.*, Orkney Islands 16 e iii
Sharjah: U.A.E. 32 G5
Sharon: U.S.A. 51 F1
Sharpnose Pts.: *hd.*, England 12 B4
Shasi: China 36 E4
Shasta, Mount: U.S.A. 52 A2
Shasta Lake: U.S.A. 52 A2
Shatsky Rise: Pac. O. 42 F3
Shatt al Arab: *r.*, Iraq/Iran 32 E4
Shattuck: U.S.A. 50 C2
Shawnee: Okla., U.S.A. 50 C2
Sheboygan: U.S.A. 53 H2
Sheeffry Hills: Irish Republic 15 B3
Sheelin, Lough: Irish Republic 15 D3
Sheep Haven: *bay*, Irish Republic 15 D1
Sheerness: England 13 G3
Sheffield: England 13 E1
Sheffield: U.S.A. 51 E3
Shefford: England 13 F2
Shelby: U.S.A. 52 C1
Shelbyville: U.S.A. 51 E2
Shelekov Bay: U.S.S.R. 29 S5
Shenandoah: *r.*, U.S.A. 51 G2
Shenandoah Nat. Park: U.S.A. 51 G2
Shendi: Sudan 59 M5
Shenyang *see* Mukden 36 G2
Shepetovka: U.S.S.R. 22 E2
Sheppey, Isle of: England 13 G3
Shepshed: England 13 E2
Shepton Mallet: England 12 D3
Sherbrooke: Canada 47 V7
Sherborne: England 12 D4
Sheridan: U.S.A. 52 D2
Sheringham: England 13 H2
Sherkin I.: Irish Rep. 15 B5
Sherlovaya Gora: U.S.S.R. 29 O7
Sherman: U.S.A. 50 C3
's-Hertogenbosch: Netherlands 24 B1
Shetland Islands: Scot. 16 ins.
Shevchenko: U.S.S.R. 30 G5
Shewbo: Burma 33 P6
Shiant Is.: Scotland 16 B2
Shiant Sound: Scot. 16 B2
Shibeli: *r.*, Som. Rep. 59 O8
Shibetsu: Japan 38 D1
Shiel, Loch: Scotland 16 C3
Shiel: *r.*, Scotland 16 C2
Shieldaig: Scotland 16 C2
Shifnal: England 12 D2
Shiga: *& Pref.*, Japan 38 b i
Shigaraki: Japan 38 c ii

Shigatse: China 34 E3
Shihchan: China 29 P7
Shihkiachwang: China 36 E3
Shikoku: *i.*, Japan 38 B3
Shikotsu-toya-kokuritsu-koen: *nat. park*, Japan 38 D1
Shillong: India 35 F3
Shima: Japan 38 c ii
Shima-Hanto: *penin.*, Japan 38 c ii
Shimizu: Japan 38 C2
Shimoga: India 34 C6
Shimonita: Japan 38 e iii
Shimonoseki: Japan 38 B3
Shimotsuma: Japan 38 f iii
Shin, Loch: Scotland 16 D1
Shingu: Japan 38 C3
Shinjo: Japan 38 D2
Shiogama: Japan 38 D2
Shiono-zaki: *cape*, Japan 38 C3
Shipki Pass: China/ India 34 C2
Shipley: England 14 C3
Shipston on Stour: England 13 E2
Shirakawa: Japan 38 D2
Shiraoi: Japan 38 D1
Shīrāz: Iran 32 F5
Shizunai: Japan 38 D1
Shizuoka: Japan 38 C3
Shkodër: Albania 23 C4
Shoebury Ness: *penin.*, England 13 G3
Sholapur: India 34 C5
Shoreham-by-Sea: England 13 F4
Shreveport: U.S.A. 50 D3
Shrewsbury: England 12 D2
Shuzenji: Japan 38 e v
Shwangliao: China 36 G2
Si: *r.*, China 36 E6
Sialkot: Pakistan 34 B2
Siam *now* THAILAND: 37 —
Siam, Gulf of: Mal./ Thailand 37 C8/9
Sian (Xi'an): China 36 D4
Siangtan: China 36 E5
Siauliai: U.S.S.R. 19 D4
Sibenik: Yugoslavia 23 C4
Sibi: Pakistan 34 A3
Sibiu: Romania 22 D3
Sibley: U.S.A. 53 F2
Sibolga: Indonesia 37 B10
Sibu: Sarawak, Mal. 37 E10
Sichuan: *Prov.*, *see* Szechwan 36 C4
Sicilian Channel: Sicily 23 B5
Sicily: *i.*, Italy 23 B5
Sidi-bel-Abbès: Alg. 21 B5
Sidlaw Hills: Scotland 16 E3
Sidmouth: England 12 C4
Sidney: N. Dak., U.S.A. 53 E1
Sidney: Nebr., U.S.A. 53 E2
Sidney Lanier, Lake: U.S.A. 51 F3
Sidra: *& gulf*, Libya 59 J2
Siedlce: Poland 22 D2
Sieg: *r.*, Ger. F.R. 24 B1
Siegburg: Ger. F.R. 24 B1
Siegen: Ger. F.R. 24 B1
Siena: Italy 23 B4
SIERRA LEONE: 58 C7
Siete Puntas: *r.*, Par. 56 C1
Sighet Marmatier: Romania 22 D3
Sigiriya: Sri Lanka 34 b ii
Siglufjördhur: Iceland 18 b i
Sigüenza: Spain 21 B4
Siirt: Turkey 30 E6
Sikhote Alin' Range: U.S.S.R. 29 Q8
Sikkim: *State*, India 34 E3
Silchar: India 35 F4
Silistra: Bulgaria 22 E4
Siljan: *lake*, Sweden 19 B3
Silkeston: U.S.A. 51 E2
Sillamäe: U.S.S.R. 19 E4
Silloth: England 14 C2
Silsden: England 14 E3
Silver City: U.S.A. 52 D4
Silvermine Mts.: Irish Republic 15 C4
Silverstone: England 13 E2
Silverton: Colo., U.S.A. 52 D3
Silverton: Ore., U.S.A. 52 A1
Simanggang: Sarawak, Malaysia 37 E10
Simferopol': U.S.S.R. 30 C4
Simla: India 34 C2
Simplon Pass: Switz. 25 B2
Simpson Desert: Australia 40 F5
Sinai: *mt.*, Egypt 32 B5
Sinaia: Romania 23 E3
Sinclair's Bay: Scot. 16 E1
Sind: *Prov.*, Pakistan 34 A3
SINGAPORE: 37 C10
Singaradja: Indonesia 37 F12
Singen: Ger. F.R. 25 B2
Singkep: *i.*, Indonesia 37 C11
Singora (Songkhla): Thai 37 C9
Sining: China 36 C3
Sinkiang-Ughur Aut Reg.: China 33 M2
Sinop: Turkey 30 D5
Sinuiju: N. Korea 36 G3
Sion: Switzerland 25 B2
Sion Mills: N. Ireland 15 D2
Sioux City: U.S.A. 50 C1
Sioux Falls: *city*, U.S.A. 53 F2
Siqueira Campos: Brazil 56 E1
Sira: *r.*, Norway 19 A4
Sirahama: Japan 38 f v
Siretul: *r.*, Romania 22 E3
Sirte: Libya 58 J2

Sisak: Yugoslavia 23 C3
Sisseton: U.S.A. 53 F1.
Sistan: *geog. reg.*, Iran 32 H4
Sistema Ibérico: *mtns.*, Spain 21 B4
Sisteron: France 25 B3
Sitapur: India 34 D3
Sitges: Spain 21 C4
Sittingbourne: Eng. 13 G3
Sivas: Turkey 30 D6
Siverskiy: U.S.S.R. 19 F4
Siwa: Egypt 59 L3
Skagerrak: *str.*, Denmark/Norway 19 A4
Skagway: U.S.A. 46 H5
Skanderborg: Denmark 19 A4
Skåne: *geog. reg.*, Sweden 19 C4
Skeena: *r.*, Canada 46 K6
Skegness: England 13 G1
Skellefte: *r.*, Sweden 18 C2
Skellefteå: Sweden 18 D3
Skelmersdale: Eng. 14 D3
Skerries: Irish Rep. 15 E3
Ski: Norway 19 B4
Skibbereen: Irish Republic 15 B5
Skiddaw: *mtn.*, Eng. 14 C2
Skien: Norway 19 A4
Skipton: England 14 D3
Skiros: *i.*, Greece 23 D5
Skive: Denmark 19 A4
Skokholm I.: Wales 12 A3
Skomer I.: Wales 12 A3
Skopje: Yugoslavia 23 D4
Skövde: Sweden 19 B4
Skye: *i.*, Scotland 16 B2
Slagelse: Denmark 19 B4
Slaney: *r.*, Irish Rep. 15 E4
Slantsy: U.S.S.R. 19 E4
Slavonski Brod: Yugoslavia 22 C3
Sleaford: England 13 F2
Slea Hd.: Irish Rep. 15 A4
Sleat, Pt. of: Scot. 16 C2
Sleat, Sound of: Scotland 16 C2
Sleetmute: U.S.A. 46 D4
Slieve Anierin: *mtn.*, Irish Republic 15 D2
Slieve Aughty Mts.: Irish Republic 15 C3
Slieve Beagh: N. Irel. 15 D2
Slieve Bloom: *mtns.*, Irish Republic 15 D3
Slieve Car: *mtn.*, Irish Republic 15 B2
Slieve Donard: *mtn.*, N. Ireland 15 F1
Slieve Elva: *mtn.*, Irish Republic 15 B3
Slievefelim Mts.: Irish Republic 15 C4
Slieve Gallion: *mtn.*, N. Ireland 15 E2
Slieve Gamph: *mtn.*, Irish Republic 15 C2
Slieve Gullion: *mtn.*, N. Ireland 15 E2
Slieve Mish Mts.: Irish Republic 15 B4
Slievenamon: *mtn.*, Irish Republic 15 D4
Slieve Rushen: *mtn.*, N. Ireland 15 D2
Slieve Snaght: *mtn.*, Irish Republic 15 D1
Sligo: *& Co.*, Irish Rep. 15 C2
Sligo Bay: Irish Republic 15 C2
Slioch: *mtn.*, Scot. 16 C2
Sliven: Bulgaria 22 E4
Slough: England 13 F3
Slupsk: Poland 22 C2
Slutsk: U.S.S.R. 22 E2
Slyne Head: Irish Republic 15 A3
Smerderevo: Yugoslavia 23 D4
Smith: Canada 46 N5
Smoky Hill: *r.*, U.S.A. 53 E3
Smøla: *i.*, Norway 18 A3
Smolensk: U.S.S.R. 30 C3
Snaefell: *mtn.*, Ice. 18 b ii
Snaefell: *mtn.*, Isle of Man 14 B2
Snag: Canada 46 H4
Snake: *r.*, U.S.A. 52 B1
Sniadwy, Lake: Pol. 22 D2
Snizort, Loch: Scot. 16 B2
Snowdon: *mtn.*, Wales 12 B1
Snowdonia Nat. Park: Wales 12 C2
Snyder: U.S.A. 50 B3
Soar: *r.*, England 13 E2
Soay Sound: Scotland 16 B2
Sobat: *r.*, Sudan/ Ethiopia 59 M7
Sobue: Japan 38 c i
Soche (Yarkand): China 33 L3
Sochi: U.S.S.R. 30 D5
Society Is.: Pac. O. 43 K8
Socotra: *i.*, Arabian Sea 32 F8
Socorro: U.S.A. 52 D4
Soda Mts.: Libya 58 H3
Sodankylä: Finland 18 E2
Söderhamn: Sweden 19 C3
Södertälje: 19 C4
Soest: Ger. F.R. 24 B1
Soest: Netherlands 24 B1
Sofala (Beira): Moz. 61 F11
SOFIYA: Bulgaria 23 D4
Sognafjorden: *fd.*, Norway 19 A3
Sogndal: Norway 18 A3
Soham: England 13 G2
Söke: Turkey 23 E5
Sokol: U.S.S.R. 30 E2

Sokoto: Nigeria 58 G6
Soledade: Brazil 56 D2
Solent, The: *channel*, England 13 E4
Soligorsk: U.S.S.R. 22 E2
Solihull: England 13 E2
Solikamsk: U.S.S.R. 30 H2
Sol'-Iletsk: U.S.S.R. 30 H3
Solimoès: *r.*, *see* Amazon 54 E4
Solingen: Ger. F.R. 24 B1
Sollefteå: Sweden 18 C3
Solomon: *r.*, U.S.A. 50 C2
SOLOMON ISLANDS: 42 E7
Solomon Rise: Pac. O. 42 E6
Solothurn: Switzerland 25 B2
Solway Firth: *est.*, England 14 C2
Somali Basin: Indian Ocean 35 d iv
SOMALI REPUBLIC: 59 P8
Sombor: Yugoslavia 22 C3
Sombrero: *i. & passage*, W. Indies 49 O6
Sombrio: Brazil 56 E2
Sombrio, Lagoa do: Brazil 56 E2
Somerset: U.S.A. 51 F2
Somerset: *Co.*, Eng. 12 C3
Somerset I.: Canada 47 R2
Somerton: England 12 D3
Someşcul: *r.*, Rom. 22 D3
Somme: *r.*, France 20 C3
Son: *r.*, India 34 D4
Sønderborg: Denmark 19 A5
Søndre Strømfjord: Greenland 47 Z3
Sondrio: Italy 25 B2
Songea: Tanzania 61 G10
Songkhla: Thailand 37 C9
Sonobe: Japan 38 b i
Sonoita: Mexico 52 C4
Soochow: China 36 G4
Soonwald: *mtns.*, German F.R. 24 B2
Sopot: Poland 22 C2
Sopron: Hungary 22 C3
Soria: Spain 21 B4
Soriano: Uruguay 56 C3
Sorocaba: Brazil 56 a i
Soroki: U.S.S.R. 22 E3
Sørøya: *i.*, Norway 18 D1
Sorrento: Italy 23 B4
Sorsele: Sweden 18 C2
Sortvala: U.S.S.R. 18 F3
Sos'va: U.S.S.R. 31 J2
Souk Ahras: Algeria 21 D5
Sounds, The: N.Z. 41 B3
Souris: *r.*, Canada/ U.S.A. 53 E1
Sousse: Tunisia 58 H1
Southam: England 13 E2
Southampton: Eng. 13 E4
Southampton I.: Can. 47 T4
South Atlantic Ocean 10 —
South Australia: *state*, Australia 40 E/F6
South Australian Basin: Pac. O. 42 B10
South Bend: U.S.A. 51 E1
South Benfleet: Eng. 13 G3
Southborough: Eng. 13 G3
South Boston: U.S.A. 51 G2
South Carolina: *State*, U.S.A. 51 F3
South Cave: Eng. 14 F3
South China Sea: S.E. Asia 37 E8
South Dakota: *State*, U.S.A. 53 E2
South Dorset Downs: *hills*, England 12 D4
South Downs: *hills*, England 13 F4
Southeast Indian Basin: Ind. O. 35 j viii
Southeast Indian Ridge: Ind. O. 35 h ix
Southeast Pacific Basin: Pac. O. 43 Q12
Southend-on-Sea: England 13 G3
Southern Alps: N.Z. 41 B3
Southern Cross: Austl. 40 C7
Southern Ocean: 10 L13
Southern Sierra Madre: *ra.*, Mex. 48 G6
Southern Uplands: Scotland 17 E4
South Fiji Basin: Pacific Ocean 42 G9
South Foreland: *hd.*, England 13 H3
South Georgia: *i.*, Atlantic Ocean 55 L14
S. Glamorgan: *co.* Wales 12 C3
South Indian Basin: Southern Ocean 35 d x
South Island: N.Z. 41 —
SOUTH KOREA: 36 H3
Southland: *Dist.*, N.Z. 41 A4
South Molton: Eng. 12 C3
South Orkney Is.: Southern Ocean 55 J16
South Pacific Ocean: 42-3 -
South Platte: *r.*, U.S.A. 53 E2
Southport: England 14 C3
South Ronaldsay: *i.*, Orkney Islands 16 e iv
South Sandwich Is.: Southern Ocean 55 N15
South Sandwich Trench: S. Atl. O. 10 H13
South Shetland Is.: Southern Ocean 55 G16
South Shields: Eng. 14 E2
South Sioux City: U.S.A. 50 C1
South Sound: Irish Republic 15 B3

South Tyne: *r.*, England 14 D2
South Uist: *i.*, Scot. 16 A2
Southwark: England 13 F3
Southwell: England 13 F1
South-West Africa *now* NAMIBIA 61 —
Southwest Cape: N.Z. 41 A4
Southwest Indian Ridge: Ind. O. 35 c viii
Southwest Pacific Basin: Pac. O. 43 K10
Southwold: England 13 H2
South Yorkshire: *Co.*, England 14 E3
Sovetsk: U.S.S.R. 19 D4
Soviet Harbour: U.S.S.R. 29 Q8
Sowerby Bridge: Eng. 14 E3
SPAIN: 21 B4
Spalding: England 13 F2
Spandau: Ger. F.R. 24 C1
Spanish Head: I. of Man 14 B2
Spanish Town: Jamaica 49 L6
Sparks: U.S.A. 52 B3
Spartanburg: U.S.A. 51 F3
Spárti: Greece 23 D5
Spartivento, Cape: Italy 23 C5
Spartivento, C.: Sard. 21 a ii
Spasskoye: U.S.S.R. 31 K3
Speedwell, Cape: U.S.S.R. 28 H2
Spencer: U.S.A. 50 C1
Spencer Gulf: Austl. 40 F8
Spennymoor: England 14 E2
Spenser Mountains: New Zealand 41 B3
Sperrin Mts.: N. Irel. 15 D2
Spessart: *r.*, German F.R. 24 B2
Spey: *r.*, Scotland 16 E2
Speyer: German F.R. 24 B2
Spiekeroog: *i.*, German F.R. 24 B1
Spilsby: England 13 G1
Spitsbergen (Svalbard): *is.*, Arctic Ocean 28 D2
Spittal: Austria 25 C2
Split: Yugoslavia 23 C4
Split Lake: *sett. & l.*, Canada 47 Q5
Splügen Pass: Italy/ Switzerland 25 B2
Spokane: U.S.A. 53 B1
Spoleto: Italy 23 B4
Spree: *r.*, Ger. D.R. 24 C1
Springbok: S. Africa 61 C13
Springdale: U.S.A. 50 D2
Springer: U.S.A. 53 E3
Springfield: Colo., U.S.A. 53 E3
Springfield: Ill., U.S.A. 51 E2
Springfield: Mo., U.S.A. 50 D2
Springfield: Ohio, U.S.A. 51 F2
Springfield: Oreg., U.S.A. 52 A2
Spurn Head: England 14 G3
SRI LANKA: 34 —
Sretensk: U.S.S.R. 29 O7
Stack, Loch: Scotland 16 D1
Stacks Mts.: Irish Rep. 15 B4
Stade: German F.R. 24 B1
Stafford: England 12 D2
Staffordshire: *Co.*, England 12 D2
Staines: England 13 F3
Stalbridge: England 12 D4
Stallworthy, Cape: Canada 47 R0
Stamford: England 13 F2
Stamford Bridge: Eng. 14 F2
Stanhope: England 14 D2
Stanke Dimitrov: Bulgaria 23 D4
Stanley: England 14 E2
STANLEY: Falkland Islands 56 G14
Stansted: England 13 G3
Starachowice: Poland 22 D2
Stara Zagora: Bulgaria 23 E4
Stargard Szczeciński: Poland 22 C2
Starnberg: Ger. F.R. 25 C2
Starogard Gdański: Pol. 22 C2
Start Bay: England 12 C4
Start Point: England 12 C4
Start Point: Orkney Islands, Scotland 11 C1
Stassfurt: Ger. D.R. 24 C1
State College: U.S.A. 51 G1
Statesboro: U.S.A. 51 F3
Statesville: U.S.A. 51 F2
Staunton: U.S.A. 51 G2
Stavanger: Norway 19 A4
Staveley: England 13 E1
Stavelot: Belgium 24 B1
Stavropol': U.S.S.R. 30 E4
Stebbins: U.S.A. 46 C4
Steigerwald: *hills*, German F.R. 24 C2
Steinkjer: Norway 18 B3
Stelvio Nat. Park: Italy 25 C2
Stelvio Pass: Italy 25 C2
Stendal: Ger. D.R. 24 C1
Steppes: *geog reg.*, U.S.S.R. 31 -
Sterling: U.S.A. 53 C2
Sterlitamak: U.S.S.R. 30 H3
Steubenville: U.S.A. 51 F1
Stevenage: England 13 F3
Stevens Point: *town*, U.S.A. 53 H2
Stevenston: Scotland 17 D4
Stewart Island: N.Z. 41 A4

*See page 80

* See page 80

: Poland 22 C2
.: Irish Republic 15 C1
Sound: Irish Rep. 15 C1
wan: *bay*, Japan 38 B3
do: Argentina 56 B2
s: England 12 C4
alejos: Argentina 56 B2
i: Japan 38 B2
a: Senegal 58 B6
jourt: Algeria 58 G2
France 25 B2
use: France 21 C4
joo: Burma 33 P7
ai: France 20 C2
France 20 C3
r., England 13 E2
da-hachimantai-
ritsu-kōen: *nat.*
Japan 38 D1
nda: U.S.A. 51 G1
ester: England 13 E2
Law: England 14 E2
sville: Australia 41 H4
n: Wales 12 B2
na: Japan 38 C2
na-wan: *bay*,
n 38 C2
r., Japan 38 d ii
nashi: Japan 38 d ii
kawa: Japan 38 d ii
naka: Japan 38 b ii
a: Japan 38 d i
r: Tunisia 58 G2
on: Turkey 30 D5
Canada 46 M7
e: *& b.*, Irish Rep. 15 B4
ore: Irish Republic 15 D4
s: Sweden 19 B4
nt: Scotland 17 F4
ueras: Uruguay 56 C3
-Canada Highway 47 S7
kei: *Bantustan*,
h Africa 61 E14
vaal: *Prov.*,
h Africa 61 E12
ylvanian Alps:
s., Romania 23 D3
ni: Sicily 23 B5
stein: Ger. F.R. 25 C2
sia Puntana: *des.*,
entina 56 A3
gar: Wales 12 C3
ron: Wales 12 C2
Loch: Scotland 16 D3
a y Tres: Uruguay 56 D3
borg: Sweden 19 B4
adog Bay: Wales 12 B2
in: Czechoslovakia 22 C3
r., England 14 F3
ino: *reg.*, Italy 25 C2
o: Italy 25 C2
on: Canada 47 U8
on: Mo., U.S.A. 56 D1
on: N.J., U.S.A. 51 H1
Árboles: Uruguay 56 C3
o: Scilly Is. 12 c iv
nish Is.: Scotland 16 B3
Passos: Brazil 56 D2
Rios: Brazil 56 b i
so: Italy 25 C2
se Head: England 12 A4
German F.R. 24 B2
e: Italy 25 C2
ala: Greece 23 D5
Irish Republic 15 E3
omalee: Sri Lanka 34 b ii
: England 13 F3
lad: U.S.A. 53 E3
lad: *i.*, South
ntic Ocean 10 G10
IDAD AND
AGO: 49 O7
y: *r.*, U.S.A. 50 C3
li: Lebanon 30 D7
OLI:
ya 58 H2
lis: Greece 23 D5
ra: *Union Terr.*,
a 35 F4
n da Cunha: *i.*,
th Atlantic Ocean 10 J11
ndrum: India 34 C7
va: Czechoslovakia 22 C3
Rivières: *city*,
ada 47 V7
sk: U.S.S.R. 31 J3
hättan: Sweden 19 B4
heimen: *mtns.*,
way 18 A3
sø: Norway 18 C2
søysund: Norway 18 C2
a: U.S.A. 52 B3
dheim: Norway 18 B3
dheimsfjorden: *fd.*,
way 18 B3
n: Scotland 17 D4
o Head: *cape*,
tland 16 F2
Lake: N.W.T.,
ada 46 L4
bridge: England 12 D3
Turkey 23 E5
U.S.A. 51 E3
es: France 24 A2
Is.: Caroline Is. 42 E6
lo: Honduras 49 J6
lo: Peru 54 C5
o: Canada 47 X7
o: England 12 A4
or Consequences:
A. 52 D4
am Swamp: China 36 A3
ai: Nigeria 57 B1
gpo (Brahmaputra):
China/India 35 F3
o Nat. Park: Kenya 61 G8
nograd: U.S.S.R. 31 L3
erlig: Mongolia 36 C1
lyansk Reservoir:
.S.R. 30 E4
an (Jinan): China 36 F3

Tsing Hai (Koko Nor):
l., China 36 B3
Tsingtao (Qingdao):
China 36 G3
Tsinling Shan
(Qinlingshan): *ra.*,
China 36 D4
Tsitsihar (Lungkiang):
China 36 G1
Tsu: Japan 38 c ii
Tsuchiura: Japan 38 g iii
Tsugaru-kaikyo: *str.*,
Japan 38 D1
Tsukumi: Japan 38 B3
Tsukuba: Japan 38 g iii
Tsumeb: Namibia 61 C11
Tsuna: Japan 38 a ii
Tsuni: China 36 D5
Tsuru: Japan 38 e iv
Tsuruga: Japan 38 C2
Tsuruoka: Japan 38 C2
Tsushima: Japan 38 c i
Tsushima: *i.*, Japan 38 A3
Tsushima-kaikyo: *str.*,
Japan 38 A3
Tsuyama: Japan 38 B2
Tuam: Irish Republic 15 C3
Tuamotu Archipelago:
Pacific Ocean 43 L8
Tuatapere: N.Z. 41 A4
Tuapse: U.S.S.R. 30 D5
Tuath, Loch: Scotland 16 B3
Tubarão: Brazil 56 E2
Tubbercurry: Irish Rep. 15 C2
Tübingen: German F.R. 25 B2
Tubuai Is.: Pacific O. 43 K9
Tucson: U.S.A. 52 C4
Tucuman: *Prov.*, Arg. 56 A2
Tucumcari: U.S.A. 53 E3
Tucupita: Venezuela 49 O8
Tudela: Spain 21 B4
Tufts Abyssal Plain:
Pacific Ocean 43 L2
Tugssâq: Greenland 47 Z2
Tuktoyaktuk: Canada 46 J3
Tukums: U.S.S.R. 19 D4
Tula: U.S.S.R. 30 D3
Tulare: U.S.A. 52 B3
Tulcea: Romania 23 E3
Tulia: U.S.A. 50 B3
Tullahoma: U.S.A. 51 E2
Tullamore: Irish Rep. 15 D3
Tullow: Irish Republic 15 E4
Tuloma: *r.*, U.S.S.R. 18 F2
Tulsa: U.S.A. 50 C2
Tumaco: Colombia 54 C3
Tumkur: India 34 C6
Tummel: *r.*, Scotland 16 E3
Tumu Măgurele: Rom. 23 D4
Tundža: *r.*, Bulgaria 23 E4
Tungabhadra: *r.*, India 34 C5
Tunghwa: China 36 H2
Tungshan *see* Süchow 36 F4
Tung Ting, Lake: China 36 E5
TUNIS: Tunisia 58 G1
TUNISIA: 58 G2
Tunstall: England 12 D1
Tupelo: U.S.A. 51 E3
Tura: *r.*, U.S.S.R. 31 J2
Turanian Plain:
U.S.S.R. 31 H5
Turbat: Pakistan 34 c iv
Turbo: Colombia 49 L8
Turda: Romania 22 D3
Turgay: *& r.*, U.S.S.R. 31 J4
Turgutlu: Turkey 23 E5
Turin (Torino): Italy 25 B2
Turkana, Lake: Kenya 59 N8
Turkestan: U.S.S.R. 31 K5
TURKEY: 23 E5
Turkmen S.S.R.:
U.S.S.R. 31 H6
Turks Islands: W. Indies 49 M5
Turku: Finland 19 D3
Turlock: U.S.A. 52 A3
Turnagain, Cape: N.Z. 41 C3
Turnhout: Belgium 24 A1
Turnu-Severin: Rom. 23 D4
Turriff: Scotland 16 F2
Turvo: *r.*, Brazil 56 D2
Tuscaloosa: U.S.A. 51 E3
Tuscany: *Reg.*, Italy 25 C3
Tutlingen: Ger. F.R. 25 B2
Tuyan: China 36 D5
Tyrol: *Prov.*, Austria 25 C2
Tyrone: *Co.*, N. Ireland 15 D2
Tyrrhenian Sea: Italy 23 B4
Tyumen': U.S.S.R. 31 K2
Tywi: *r.*, Wales 12 B3
TUVALU: 42 G7
Tuxpan: Mexico 48 G5
Tuz, Lake: Turkey 30 C6
Tuzla: Yugoslavia 23 C4
Tweed: *r.*, Scotland/
England 17 F4
25 de Mayo: Argentina 56 B4
Twin Bridges: U.S.A. 52 C1
Twin Falls: *town*,
U.S.A. 52 C2
Tygda: U.S.S.R. 29 P7
Tyler: U.S.A. 50 C3
Tyndrum: Scotland 16 D3
Tyne: *r.*, England 14 E2
Tyne: *r.*, Scotland 17 F4
Tyne and Wear: *Co.*,
England 14 E2
Tynemouth: England 14 E1
Tyrone: *Co.*, N. Ireland 15 B4

U

Ube: Japan 38 B3
Ubeda: Spain 21 B5
Uberaba: Brazil 54 J7
Uberlandia: Brazil 54 J7
Ubon Ratchathani:
Thailand 37 C7
Ubsa Nor: *l.*, Mongolia 36 A1
Ubundi: Zaire 61 D8
Ucayali: *r.*, Peru 54 D5
Uchiura-wan: *bay*,
Japan 38 D1
Uckfield: England 13 G4
Udaipur: India 34 B4
Uddevalla: Sweden 19 B4
Udd Lake: Sweden 18 C2
Udine: Italy 25 C2
Udon Thani: Thailand 37 C7
Ueda: Japan 38 C2
Ueno: Japan 38 c ii
Uenohara: Japan 38 f iv
Ufa: U.S.S.R. 30 H3
Ufa: *r.*, U.S.S.R. 31 H2
Uffculme: England 12 C4
UGANDA: 60 F7
Ugie: *r.*, Scotland 16 G2
Uhuru (Kilimanjaro):
mtn., Tanzania 61 G8
Uinta Mountains:
U.S.A. 52 C2
Uji: *& r.*, Japan 38 b ii
Ujjain: India 34 C4
Ujung Pandang: Indon. 37 F12
Ukhta: U.S.S.R. 30 G1
Ukiah: U.S.A. 52 C3
Ukmerge: U.S.S.R. 19 D4
Ukrainian S.S.R.:
U.S.S.R. 30 B4
ULAN BATOR:
Mongolia 36 D1
Ulangom: Mongolia 36 A1
Ulan-Ude: U.S.S.R. 29 N7
Uldza: Mongolia 36 E1
Uliastay (Jibhalanta):
Mongolia 36 B1
Ullapool: Scotland 16 C2
Ullswater: *l.*, England 14 D2
Ulm: German F.R. 25 C2
Ulsan: S. Korea 38 A2
Ulu-Tau: U.S.S.R. 31 K4
Ulva: *i.*, Scotland 16 B3
Ulverston: England 14 C2
Ul'yanovsk: U.S.S.R. 30 F3
Ulyungur Nor: *l.*,
Mongolia 31 O4
Ülzen: German F.R. 24 C1
Uman': U.S.S.R. 22 F3
Umarkot: Pakistan 34 A3
Ume: *r.*, Sweden 18 C3
Umeå: Sweden 18 D3
Umm Said: Qatar 32 F5
*Umtali: Zimbabwe 61 F11
Ungava, Baie d': Can. 47 W5
Ungava, Péninsule d':
Canada 47 U4
União da Vitória:
Brazil 56 D2
UNION OF SOVIET
SOCIALIST
REPUBLICS 28-9 —
Uniontown: U.S.A. 51 G2
UNITED ARAB
EMIRATES: 32 F6
UNITED KINGDOM: 20 C2
UNITED STATES OF
AMERICA 48-9 —
United States Range:
Canada 47 U0
Unst: *i.*, Shetland Is. 16 c i
Uozu: Japan 38 C2
Upper Lough Erne:
N. Ireland 15 D2
Upper Klamath Lake:
U.S.A. 52 A2
Upper Red Lake: U.S.A. 53 G1
*UPPER VOLTA: 58 E6
Uppingham: England 13 F2
Uppsala: Sweden 19 C4
Upton-on-Severn:
England 12 D2
Ur: Iraq 32 E4
Ural: *r.*, U.S.S.R. 30 G3
Ural Mountains:
U.S.S.R. 28 —
Ural'sk: U.S.S.R. 30 G3
Uranium City: Canada 46 O5
Urawa: Japan 38 f iv
Ure: *r.*, England 14 E2
Ureshino: Japan 38 c ii
Urfa: Turkey 30 C6
Urgench: U.S.S.R. 31 J5
Urie: *r.*, Scotland 16 F2
Urlingord: Irish Rep. 15 D4
Urmia, Lake: Iran 30 F6
Urom: Nigeria 57 B2
Urr Water: *r.*, Scotland 17 E4
Uruguai: *r.*, *see*
Uruguay 56 C3
Uruguaiana: Brazil 56 C2
URUGUAY: 56 —
Uruguay (Uruguai): *r.*,
S. America 56 C3
Usa: Japan 38 B3
Usa: *r.*, U.S.S.R. 28 J4
Usk: *& r.*, Wales 12 D3
Usol'ye: U.S.S.R. 29 N7
Uspallata Pass:
Argentina/Chile 55 D10
Uspenskiy: U.S.S.R. 31 L4
Ussuri: *r.*, China/
U.S.S.R. 29 Q8
Ussuriysk: U.S.S.R. 29 Q9
Ustí: Czechoslovakia 22 B2
Ustínad Labem: Czech 24 C1
Ust' Kamenogorsk:
U.S.S.R. 31 N3
Ust-Kut: U.S.S.R. 29 N6
Ust-Urt Plateau:
U.S.S.R. 30-1 H5
Ust' Uyskoye: U.S.S.R. 31 J3
Usuki: Japan 38 B3
Utah: *State*, U.S.A. 52 C3
Utah Lake: U.S.A. 52 C2
Utashinai: Japan 38 D1
Ute: *cr.*, U.S.A. 53 E3
Utica: U.S.A. 49 L1
Utiel: Spain 21 B5
Utrecht: Netherlands 24 B1
Utrera: Spain 21 A5
Utsjoki: Norway 18 E1
Utsunomiya: Japan 38 C2
Uttaradit: Thailand 37 C7
Uttar Pradesh: *State*,
India 34 C3
Uttoxeter: England 13 E2
Uvalde: U.S.A. 50 C4
Uwajima: Japan 38 B3
Uxmal: *ruins*, Mexico 48 J5
Uyuni: Bolivia 54 E8
Uzbek S.S.R.: U.S.S.R. 31 J5
Uzhgorod: U.S.S.R. 22 D3
Uzlovaya: U.S.S.R. 30 D3

V

Vaal: *r.*, S. Africa 61 E13
Vaala: Finland 18 E3
Vaasa: Finland 18 D3
Vác: Hungary 22 C3
Vacacaí: *r.*, Brazil 56 D2
Vacaria: Brazil 56 D2
Vadodara: India 34 B4
Vadsø: Norway 18 E1
VADUZ: Liechtenstein 25 B2
Váh: *r.*, Czech. 22 C3
Vakh: *r.*, U.S.S.R. 31 M1
Valda Hills: U.S.S.R. 30 C2
Valdapenãs: Spain 21 B5
Valdés Penin.: Arg. 55 F12
Valdez: U.S.A. 46 F4
Valdivia: Chile 55 D11
Val d'Or: *sett.*, Can. 47 U6
Valdosta: U.S.A. 51 F3
Valence: France 25 A3
Valencia: Spain 21 B5
Valencia: Venezuela 49 N7
Valencia, Golfo de:
Spain 21 B5
Valenciennes: France 20 C2
Valentia I.: Irish Rep. 15 A5
Valentina: U.S.A. 53 E2
VALETTA: Malta 23 B5
Valga: U.S.S.R. 19 E4
Valjevo: Yugoslavia 23 C4
Valkeakoski: Finland 19 D3
Valladolid: Spain 21 B4
Valle, Rio del: *r.*,
Argentina 56 B1
Vallejo: U.S.A. 52 A3
Valley: *sett.*, Wales 12 B1
Valley City: U.S.A. 53 F1
Valmiera: U.S.S.R. 19 E4
Valparaíso: Chile 55 D10
Vals, Cape: Indonesia 40 F2
Val Tellina: Italy 25 B2
Val Venosta: *valley*,
Italy 25 C2
Van: *& l.*, Turkey 30 E6
Vancouver: Canada 46 L7
Vancouver: U.S.A. 52 A1
Vancouver, Mt.:
Canada/U.S.A. 46 H4
Vancouver Is.: Canada 46 K7
Väner, Lake: Sweden 19 B4
Vänersborg: Sweden 19 B4
Vännäs: Sweden 18 C3
Vannes: France 20 B3
Vannøy: *i.*, Norway 18 C1
Vanua Levu: *i.*, Fiji 42 G8
VANUATU (New
Hebrides): 42 F8
Varanasi: India 34 D3
Varangerfjorden: *fd.*,
Norway 18 E1
Varanger Pen.: Norway 18 E1
Varaždin: Yugoslavia 22 C3
Varberg: Sweden 19 B4
Vardar: *r.*,
Yugoslavia/Greece 23 D4
Vardø: Norway 18 F1
Varel: German F.R. 24 B1
Varela: Argentina 56 A3
Varese: Italy 25 B2
Varkaus: Finland 18 E3
Varna: Bulgaria 23 E4
Värnamo: Sweden 19 B4
Varty Reservoir:
Irish Republic 15 E3
Várzea, Rio de: *r.*,
Brazil 56 D2
Västerås: Sweden 19 C4
Västerdal: *r.*, Sweden 19 B3
Västervik: Sweden 19 B3
Vasyugan: U.S.S.R. 31 M2
Vatersay: *i.*, Scotland 16 A3
Vaternish Pt.: *hd.*, Scot. 16 B2
Vatnajökull: *ice-cap*,
Iceland 18 b ii
Vatter, Lake: Sweden 19 B4
Vaupés: *r.*, Colombia 54 D3
Vavuniya: Sri Lanka 34 b ii
Växjö: Sweden 19 B4
Vaygach Island:
U.S.S.R. 28 H3
Vedia: Argentina 56 B3
Veendam: Netherlands 24 B1
Vega: *i.*, Norway 18 B2
Vejle: Denmark 19 A4
Velázquez: Uruguay 56 D3
Velikaya: *r.*, U.S.S.R. 19 E4
Velikiye Luki: U.S.S.R. 30 C2
Vellore: India 34 C6
Velp: Netherlands 24 B1
Venado Tuerto: Arg. 56 B3
Vendée, Collines de:
hills, France 20 B3
Vendôme: France 20 C3
Venetian Alps: *mtns.*,
Italy 25 C2
Veneto: *reg.*, Italy 25 C2
Venezia *see* Venice 25 C2
VENEZUELA: 54 —
Venezuela, Gulf of: Ven. 49 M7
Venice (Venezia): *& g.*,
Italy 25 C2
Venta: *r.*, U.S.S.R. 19 D4
Ventimiglia: Italy 26 B3
Ventnor: England 13 E4
Ventspils: U.S.S.R. 19 D4
Vera: Argentina 56 B2
Verá, Lago: Paraguay 56 C2
Veracruz: Mexico 48 G6
Vercelli: Italy 25 B2
Verde: *r.*, Paraguay 56 C1
Verde: *r.*, U.S.A. 52 C4
Verdigris: *r.*, U.S.A. 50 C2
Verdon: *r.*, France 25 B3
Verdun: France 24 B2
Verkhoyansk: U.S.S.R. 29 Q4
Verkhoyansk Range:
U.S.S.R. 29 P4
Vermilion Lake: U.S.A. 53 G1
Vermilion: *& r.*, U.S.A. 53 F1
Vernal: U.S.A. 52 D2
Vernon: U.S.A. 50 C3
Véroia: Greece 23 D4
Verona: Italy 25 C2
Verviers: Belgium 24 B1
Vestfjorden: *fd.*, Nor. 18 C2
Vestmannaeyjar: *i.*,
Iceland 18 a ii
Vesuvius: *volc.*, Italy 23 B4
Veszprem: Hungary 22 C3
Vetlanda: Sweden 19 C4
Vevey: Switzerland 25 B2
Viana do Castelo: Port 21 A4
Viareggio: Italy 25 C3
Viborg: Denmark 19 A4
Vicente Lopez: Arg. 56 C3
Vicenza: Italy 25 C2
Vichadero: Uruguay 56 D3
Vichy: France 20 C3
Vicksburg: U.S.A. 50 D3
Victoria: Argentina 56 B3
Victoria: Canada 46 L7
VICTORIA: Hong Kong 36 E6
Victoria: Malta 23 B5
Victoria: U.S.A. 50 C4
Victoria: *r.*, Australia 40 E4
Victoria: *state*, Austl. 40-1 G8
Victoria, L: Africa 61 F8
Zimbabwe 61 E1
Victoria I.: Canada 46 O2
Victoria West: S. Africa 61 D17
Vidin: Bulgaria 22 D4
Vidzeme: *hills*, U.S.S.R. 19 E4
Viejo: *r.*, Argentina 56 B2
VIENNA: Austria 22 C3
Vienne: *r.*, France 25 A2
VIENTIANE: Laos 37 C7
Vierzon: France 20 C3
Vieste: Italy 23 C4
VIETNAM: 37 —
Vigevano: Italy 25 B2
Vigo: Spain 21 A4
Vijayawada: India 34 D5
Vikna: *i.*, Norway 18 B3
Vila Nova de Gaia:
Portugal 21 A4
Vila Real: Portugal 21 A4
Vilhelmina: Sweden 18 C3
Viljandi: U.S.S.R. 19 E4
Villa Alberdi: Arg. 56 A2
Villa Angela: Argentina 56 B2
Villa Carlos Paz: Arg. 56 B3
Villach: Austria 25 C2
Villa Constitución: Arg. 56 B3
Villa del Rosario: Arg. 56 B3
Villa Dolores: Arg. 56 A3
Villa El Alto: Arg. 56 A2
Villa Federal: Arg. 56 C3
Villaguay: Argentina 56 C3
Villa Hayes: Paraguay 56 C2
Villa Hernandarias:
Argentina 56 C3
Villa Huidobro: Arg. 56 B3
Villalba: Spain 21 A4
Villa María: Argentina 56 B3
Villa Ojo de Agua: Arg. 56 B2
Villa Oliva: Paraguay 56 C2
Villa Ocampo: Arg. 56 C2
Villarrobledo: Spain 21 B5
Villarrica: Paraguay 56 C2
Villa San Martin: Arg. 56 B2
Villefranche: France 25 B3
Villefranche-sur-Saône:
France 25 A2
Villengeh: German F.R. 25 B2
Villeneuves-sur-Lot: Fr. 21 C4
Villeurbanne: France 25 A2
Vilnius: U.S.S.R. 19 E5
Vilyuy: *r.*, U.S.S.R. 29 P5
Viña del Mar: Chile 55 D10
Vinaroz: Spain 21 C4
Vincennes: U.S.A. 51 E2
Vinde: *r.*, Sweden 18 C2
Vindhya Range: India 34 C4
Vineland: U.S.A. 51 G2
Vinh: Vietnam 37 D7
Vinkovci: Yugoslavia 23 C3
Vinnitsa: U.S.S.R. 22 E3
Virgin: *r.*, U.S.A. 52 C3
Virgin Is.: Caribbean
Sea 49 O6
Virginia: Irish Rep. 15 D3
Virginia: U.S.A. 53 G1
Virginia: *State*, U.S.A. 51 G2
Vis: *i.*, Yugoslavia 23 C4
Visalia: U.S.A. 52 B3
Visby: Sweden 19 C4
Viscount Melville
Sound: Canada 46 N2
Viseu: Portugal 21 A4
Vishakhapatnam: India 34 D5
Vistula: *r.*, Poland 22 C2
Vitebsk: U.S.S.R. 22 F1
Viterbo: Italy 23 B4
Viti Levu: *i.*, Fiji 42 G8
Vitim: *& r.*, U.S.S.R. 29 O6
Vitória: Brazil 54 K8
Vitoria: Spain 21 B4
Vitry de François: Fr. 24 A1
Vittoria Veneto: Italy 25 C2
Vize I. *see* Wiese I. 29 K2
Vizianagaram: India 34 D5
Vladimir: U.S.S.R. 30 E2
Vladimir Volynskiy:
U.S.S.R. 22 D2
Vladivostok: U.S.S.R. 29 Q9
Vlorë: Albania 23 C4
Vltava (Moldau): *r.*,
Czechoslovakia 24 C2
Vogelsberg Nat. Park:
German F.R. 24 B1
Voghera: Italy 25 B3
Voiron: France 25 B2
Volcán: Argentina 56 A1
Volcanic Plateau: N.Z. 41 C2
Volga: *r. & hills*,
U.S.S.R. 30 F3
Volgograd: U.S.S.R. 30 E4
Vologda: U.S.S.R. 30 D2
Vólos: Greece 23 D5
Vol'sk: U.S.S.R. 30 F3
Volta: *l. & dam*, Ghana 58 E7
Volta Redonda: Brazil 56 b i
Vorarlberg: *Prov.*, Aust. 25 B2
Vordingborg: Denmark 19 B5
Vorkuta: U.S.S.R. 28 J4
Voronezh: U.S.S.R. 30 D3
Voroshilovgrad:
U.S.S.R. 30 D4
Võru: U.S.S.R. 19 E4
Vosges: *mtns.*, France 25 B2
Voss: Norway 19 A3
Voynitsa: U.S.S.R. 18 F2
Vraca: Bulgaria 23 D4
Vršac: Yugoslavia 23 D4
Vryburg: S. Africa 61 D13
Vukovar: Yugoslavia 23 C3
Vyaz'ma: U.S.S.R. 30 C2
Vyborg: U.S.S.R. 19 E3
Vyrnwy: *l. & r.*, Wales 12 C2
Vyshniy-Volochek
U.S.S.R. 30 C2

W

Waal: *r.*, Netherlands 24 B1
Wabana: Canada 47 Z7
Wabash: *r.*, U.S.A. 51 E2
Waccasassa Bay:
U.S.A. 51 F4
Waco: U.S.A. 50 C3
Wada: Japan 38 g iv
Wadden Zee: *bay*, Neth. 24 B1
Waddington, Mount:
Canada 46 K6
Wadebridge: England 12 B4
Wadena: U.S.A. 53 F1
Wadi Halfa: *town*,
Sudan 59 M4
Wad Medani: Sudan 59 M6
Waha: Libya 59 J3
Wahpeton: U.S.A. 53 F1
Waiau: *& r.*, N.Z. 41 B3
Waigeo: *r.*, Indonesia 37 J11
Waikaremoana, Lake:
New Zealand 41 C2
Waikato: *r. & dist.*, N.Z. 41 C2
Wainfleet All Saints:
England 13 G1
Waingapu: Indonesia 37 G12
Waipara: New Zealand 41 B3
Waipawa: New Zealand 41 C2
Wairakei: New Zealand 41 C2
Wairoa: New Zealand 41 C2
Waitaki: *r.*, N.Z. 41 B3
Waitangi: New Zealand 41 B2
Waitara: New Zealand 41 B2
Wajima: Japan 38 C2
Wakatipu, Lake: N.Z. 41 A4
Wakayama: Japan 38 b ii
Wakeeney: U.S.A. 50 C2
Wakefield: England 14 E2
Wake Island: Pacific
Ocean 42 F5
Wakkanai: Japan 36 L1
Walbrzych: Poland 22 C2
Walcheren: *i.*, Neth. 24 A1
Waldshut: German F.R. 25 B2
Walensee: *l.*, Switz. 25 B2
Wales: *principality*, U.K. 12 C2
Walker Lake: U.S.A. 52 B3
Wallachia: *geog. reg.*,
Romania 23 D4
Wallasey: England 14 C3
Walla Walla: U.S.A. 52 B1
Wallingford: England 13 E3
Wallsend: England 14 E2
Walney I.: England 14 C2
Walsall: England 13 E2
Walton-on-the-Naze:
England 13 H3
Walvis Bay: *town*,
Namibia 61 B12
Walvis Ridge: S. Atl. O. 10 L10
Wanaka, Lake: N.Z. 41 A3
Wanda: Argentina 56 D2
Wandsworth: England 13 F3
Wanganui: *& r.*, N.Z. 41 C2
Wangen: German F.R. 25 B2
Wangerooge: *i.*,
Ger. F.R. 24 B1
Wanhsien: China 36 D4
*Wankie: Zimbabwe 61 E11
Wansbeck: *r.*, England 14 E1
Wantage: England 13 E3
Warangal: India 34 C5
Warburg: German F.R. 24 B1
Ware: England 13 F3
Wareham: England 12 D4
Warminster: England 12 D3
Warren: Idaho, U.S.A. 52 B1
Warren: Minn., U.S.A. 53 F1
Warren: Ohio, U.S.A. 51 F1
Warren: Pa., U.S.A. 51 G1
Warrenpoint: N. Ireland 15 E2
Warrington: England 14 D3
Warrnambool: Australia 40 G8
Warroad: U.S.A. 53 F1
WARSAW: Poland 22 D2
Warta: *r.*, Poland 22 C2
Warwick: England 13 E2
Warwickshire: *Co.*,
England 13 E2
Washington: England 14 E2
Washington: Ind. U.S.A. 51 E2
Washington, N.C.,
U.S.A. 51 G2
Washington: *State*,
U.S.A. 52 A1

e page 80

APPENDIX TO THE INDEX:

An asterisk alongside an index entry indicates either that the name itself has been changed, or that the country in which it is located has changed its name

Name changes since 1981

ACKNOWLEDGEMENTS

This edition has been revised and updated by Oxford Cartographers